13.50

D0848426

Adolescence and Youth in Prospect

Adolescence and Youth in Prospect

Edited by John P. Hill, *Cornell University*
and Franz J. Mönks, *University of Nijmegen*

HUMANITIES PRESS: ATLANTIC HIGHLANDS, N.J.

Library of Congress Cataloging in Publication Data

Main entry under title:
Adolescence and youth in prospect.
Bibliography: p.
1. Youth–Europe–Addresses, essays, lectures.
2. Adolescence–Addresses, essays, lectures. 3. Forecasting–Addresses, essays, lectures. I. Hill, John P., 1936– II. Mönks, Franz J.
HQ799.E9A32 1977 301.43'15 77-3431
ISBN 0-391-00715-7

Published 1977 in The United States of America by Humanities Press, Inc., Atlantic Highlands, New Jersey 07716
Published 1977 in England by IPC Science and Technology Press Limited
Printed in England by Adlard & Son Ltd
The Bartholomew Press, Dorking, Surrey
Bound by The Newdigate Press Ltd, Dorking, Surrey

Contents

Preface   vii

Part I The International Colloquium on Adolescence in the Year 2000

1 Overview and outcomes   1
John P. Hill and Franz J. Mönks

2 Summary record and conclusions   13
*John P. Hill, Franz J. Mönks, William Wall, Willem Welling and
Robert Weeda*

3 Some perspectives on adolescence in modern societies   28
John P. Hill and Franz J. Mönks

Part II Background papers

4 Adolescents' ethics and morals in the year 2000   79
Fred Mahler

5 The social plasticity of youth   95
Hilde and Leopold Rosenmayr

6 Cultural settings and adolescence and youth
around the year 2000   114
Samuel N. Eisenstadt

v

7 Youth in the year 2000: the problem of values   125
Marc Faessler

8 Genetics and adolescent development:
perspectives for the future   137
Marco Milani-Comparetti

9 Biological aspects of development at adolescence   148
Marcel Hebbelinck

10 Family and adolescents in the near future   159
Jerzy Piotrowski

11 Adolescent peer relations: a look to the future   171
Willard W. Hartup

12 The adolescent and the school in Europe   186
Torsten Husén

13 The attitudes of adolescents to education and work   201
Jacques Delors

Appendices

1 Participants in the International Colloquium   213

2 Selected books on adolescence   216

Preface

This book reports the deliberations of an international colloquium on adolescence in the year 2000 and presents some of the background papers prepared for that colloquium. Organized by the Jeugdprofiel 2000 Foundation of Amsterdam (itself a project of the R. C. Maagdenhuis Foundation), the International Colloquium was the first step in an effort to identify what action should be taken in the relatively short term by European societies to facilitate normal adolescent development up to the year 2000. The origin of this project and further aspirations for the Colloquium are considered in greater detail in the first chapter of the present volume.

Here, we should like to extend our appreciation to those who have been especially helpful to us in realizing the second objective of Jeugdprofiel 2000, getting this book into print. First thanks are due to those who contributed the papers printed in Part II of the book and who responded graciously and constructively when we had occasion to make suggestions about revisions and who, when English was not their primary language, encouraged and trusted us to make changes to improve the readability of the text. Similarly, our work has been facilitated by support of many kinds from the officers of 'JP 2000': R. van Maanen, Chairman; R. A. Weeda, Project Director; J. Schrofer, Project Executive; and E. M. Soethout, Executive Director of the Maagdenhuis Foundation, have been the persons we have most often dealt with in connection with the book itself. We recognize that their efforts have in turn been supported by other officers and staff members to whom we are also grateful. William Wall and Willem Welling, who chaired the session of the Colloquium, were joined by Robert Weeda and us on a drafting committee which, during the Colloquium itself, put together the original draft of the summary record and conclusions of the Colloquium (which appears as

Chapter 2). The writing they helped us do between 4 pm and 4 am on Thursday and Friday, September 17 and 18, provides the structure for this volume and we have found it a fruitful base for departure in preparing the rest of it. And, finally, in finishing our work, we have had occasion to consult William Hartup, Torsten Husén, Leopold Rosenmayr, William Wall, and Willem Welling about some editorial matters and we appreciate their quick response and wise advice.

Both of us are developmental psychologists with strong interests in early adolescence. In the preparation of this volume, and particularly the first and third chapters (which were our own responsibility and do not carry the endorsement of the Foundation or the participants in the Colloquium), we have no doubt that our professional biases have intruded occasionally into the selection and treatment of the material included. But we trust that these intrusions are neither too frequent nor unidentifiable. We have tried to report the deliberations of the Colloquium fairly and in a balanced way in keeping with its multidisciplinary character. We have not shied away from including our own judgements and retrospective conclusions and have tried to label them as such.

It is our hope that the book will be of interest to those scientists, practitioners, and policy makers who work with and on behalf of adolescents and their families. If we have been successful, it should also serve as a useful tool for the third step in the Jeugdprofiel 2000 project, a large scale international symposium designed to sift through the issues and recommendations herein and to come up with an agenda for those actions which European societies, individually and in concert and in both the private and public sectors, should be taking to facilitate development in early adolescence. Our work on this book is dedicated to that objective and we are pleased to have had this opportunity to contribute to it through such a concrete effort.

John P. Hill

Franz J. Mönks

1 Overview and outcomes

John P. Hill and Franz J. Mönks

'We are born twice over', Rousseau asserted, 'born into existence and born into life. . . .' At puberty, the second birth after which 'no human passion is a stranger', rearing and educating, previously but child's play, now are of the greatest importance. In 1762 at the publication of his *Emile*, Rousseau could conclude that 'this period when education is usually finished is just the time to begin'. Two hundred years later, an industrial, and possibly post-industrial, revolution away, we have provided secondary education for most of our young people. This education is not exactly what Rousseau had in mind for his privileged and educated readers. He urged that they dispense with hirelings and accept their responsibilities as parents: 'The real nurse is the mother and the real teacher is the father.' Rousseau's admonitions and advice influenced a return to domestic education for some at the upper levels of society in his time, a 'natural' education based upon observational learning, empathic role taking, and practice of parental roles rather than the parroting of precepts. However, the next 200 years brought a division of labour in society so various and prepotent as to make domestic education obsolete as the sole means of rearing the young for adult roles at all levels of society. The massive differentiation of adult roles in the workplace meant that the objective of socialization could no longer be the total duplication of the values and skills of the previous generation.

Whatever the fate of his specific prescriptions, Rousseau's influence on our conception of adolescence is so great that he has been said to have invented it (Musgrove, 1964). Echoes of Rousseau's concept of adolescence are found in G. Stanley Hall's (1904) important and perhaps equally influential treatise on the subject published in America. That concept of adolescence—as a rebirth, as a period requiring re-education, and above all, as a transitional stage in the life cycle between childhood and adulthood with its own opportunities and dangers—has been translated since then into reality by means of child labour, compulsory education, and juvenile justice legislation in industrialized societies (Bakan, 1971; Musgrove, 1964). More recently, in light of growing affluence in rising economies, mass marketing and mass media strategies have contributed to the definition of adolescence by promoting goods and services originating in the special needs and interests of young people. The result has been an increasing segregation of young people from both older and still younger generations in institutions of their own and the prolongation of a transitional status between childhood and adulthood.

Now industrialized societies are engaged in a thus far modest but potentially far-reaching reassessment of both the concept and the reality of adolescence. This re-examination has been brought about in no small measure by an increased consciousness of adolescence and youth raised by the youth movements of the past decade. Both the youth movements and the increased consciousness of youth are related, in turn, to the vast proportional increase of 12- to 24-year-olds in the population during the past decade, to the arrival of nearly universal secondary education, to the rapid increase in opportunities for higher education, and to concurrent changes in the role of women in the home and in the marketplace. The strain between changes in the preparation for adult life and declining opportunities in the labour market for vast numbers of educated young men and women has contributed significantly to defining contemporary concerns about adolescence in terms of conflicts between the facilitation of individual development and the demands made upon young people by highly urbanized and specialized societies in the service of their maintenance and perpetuation.

That we can use the phrase 'preparation for adult life' so easily as we have above is testimony to the degree of acceptance in modern society of Rousseau's and later Hall's concept of adolescence. The second birth has become one not into life but into preparation for it. It is the meaningfulness of that preparation that is in question—and the means of it. At the core of the modern effort to reassess adolescence is Rousseau's dichotomy between learning from practice and learning from the precepts of third parties, the extent to which we permit entry into the institutions of society for young people for purposes of their socialization. However, now, 200 years and more after the conceptual 'invention' of adolescence, the reassessment of it is vastly complicated by the web of institutions of which the family is but part. Domestic education is not the answer now as it was not then. But what are the alternatives? And how shall we discover them, evaluate them, and implement them?

In this book we report the proceedings, conclusions, and recommendations of one attempt at a re-examination of adolescence, the International Colloquium on Adolescence in the Year 2000, held in Amsterdam from 15–19 September 1975 under the sponsorship of the Jeugdprofiel 2000 Foundation. The present chapter provides an introduction to the Colloquium, its purposes and its structure, and to the volume itself.

Jeugdprofiel 2000

On the occasion of its fourth centenary in 1970, the R. C. Maagdenhuis Foundation of the Netherlands announced an ambitious new project devoted to assessing 'the whole range of problems concerning young people today'. Beginning in about 1570 with the establishment of a girls' orphanage, Het Rooms Catholijk Maagdenhuis (The Roman Catholic House of Maidens), the Foundation at first provided institutional care for 'girls christened in the Catholic Faith, born or resident in Amsterdam, both of whose parents had died and who had not yet attained the age of 15'. By 1783, the girls were housed in a monumental new building on the Spui, the Maagdenhuis, instead of in the separate houses that had previously made up the orphanage. In 1898, a new house for former Maagdenhuis girls was established, the St Elizabeth Gesticht, and came over the years to care for sick and needy old people as well until it was closed down in 1969. The Maagdenhuis itself had been closed down 17 years earlier, having become too inefficient to operate any longer. (The building subsequently became part of the University of Amsterdam and gained greater fame than it ever had as an orphanage when it was occupied by students as part of a turbulent demonstration in 1968.)

The closing of these physical facilities was accompanied by a reformulation of the Foundation's policies. It was decided that the Foundation would use the interest from its capital, augmented by the sale of the Maagdenhuis property, for deserving causes connected with the care of young people, part of the revenues of the capital due to the sales of the St Elizabeth Gesticht in 1969 are used for causes connected with old people's care. The Foundation, for example, provide gifts and interest free and low interest loans to a variety of organizations in the welfare field in addition to maintaining service flats for physically independent old people, a home for the chronically ill, and housing for a small group of former Maagdenhuis orphans. Thus, on its 400th birthday, in announcing its latest project, Jeugdprofiel 2000, the Foundation was not only maintaining its long tradition of commitment to young people but broadening its scope substantially.

Jeugdprofiel 2000 Foundation was created by Maagdenhuis in 1974 to determine what action should be taken in the relatively short term in order to facilitate normal adolescent development in the relatively long term (up to the year 2000). Planning for three initial phases of activity was undertaken: first, an international colloquium; second, a report on the proceedings of that colloquium and third, a symposium of ambitious proportions based upon the first two efforts. The current chairman of the R. C. Maagdenhuis Foundation, R. van Maanen, posed the problem in the following way in his opening remarks to the International Colloquium:

> Since the middle of this century, we have been faced by problems of youth which are no longer of the accidental individual type that can be explained sufficiently by missing links in the vital forces of an individual.
>
> On top of these individual problems more general causes of unrest and imbalance seem to be working, aggravating the existing individual causes of imbalance, and adding new groups of . . . adolescents who live in disharmony with themselves and the world.
>
> In our opinion, this situation calls for a thorough analysis because, under these circumstances, any new activity in this field of welfare may already be preconditioned decisively and adversely by influences which, if not taken into account, will frustrate any new action.
>
> Now, from our model, it might be deduced that these . . . influences might be environmental and of a general nature. What are these influences? Are they going to last through the coming 25 years? How will they further affect the adolescent?

Purposes and structure of the Colloquium

As the first step in addressing these questions, the International Colloquium was planned to bring together a small group of speculative thinkers and empirical research workers for an exchange of ideas on the subject of adolescence in the year 2000. (Brief biographies of the participants are provided in Appendix 1.) From the beginning it was recognized that the subject was a complex one demanding address from those of many disciplines and from many points of view. Participants were selected by a planning committee to represent three interrelated domains of interest:

(a) changes in patterns of individual development, biological and psychological;
(b) changes in institutions and organizations as these affect adolescence, including the family, peer group, school, and work settings; and
(c) changes in social values, ideologies, and policies as these influence the settings in which adolescents develop and changes in adolescence itself.

This basis for the Colloquium had several intended and unintended consequences. It did result in multidisciplinary participation: biology, economics, education, philosophy, psychology, sociology, and theology as well as practical politics were represented. This multidisciplinary mix and multinational representation led to occasional (and in retrospect surprisingly few) communication problems in the course of the meeting. It highlighted both the similarity and the diversity of the adolescent experience within and between national cultures. The similarity of the problems faced by adolescents from society to society was more impressive than the diversity. Some examples are the absence of coherent social policy relating to early adolescence, the absence of a variety of kinds of articulation between school and work settings, the heterogeneous demands mass scholarization has placed upon the school system. Basic differences from society to society were not so impressive and most often were attributable either to greater and lesser degrees of pluralization in the societies in question or to differential rates of change in technology, industrialization, and scholarization with which the emergence of phenomena typical of adolescence appear to be associated all over the world.

The range of disciplines also called attention to the narrowness of intradermal and intraphysic views of adolescent growth and behaviour, on the one hand, and reminded us, on the other, that neither adolescent development nor its facilitation are to be understood solely in terms of immediate crises and confrontations between generations, however dramatic these might be. While puberty brings the most dramatic change in the conditions of life since birth, it does not seem to set into train an inevitable set of behavioural and social consequences which can be understood outside the contexts in which development occurs. In the best of times and in the worst of times, the effects of the larger society on the adolescent are mediated largely by the family, the peer group, and the school. 'Storm and stress', 'rebelliousness', and 'the generation gap' are not universal phenomena—in many respects they are not even very wide-spread—and so they do not provide a very sound basis for discussion of adolescent development. When they do occur, they can best be appreciated by taking into account those opportunities and constraints visited upon the family, the peer group, and the school by the larger society and, the effect, in turn, of change in these settings on individual development.

Although not selected on this basis, it turned out that the conference participants had a rather broad range of experience on many fronts related to adolescent development in addition to their (for the most part) scholarly roles. They had, in fact, exercised some degree of influence on public policy and science policy related to young people. Among the group were advisers to ministries, foundations, agencies and programmes; administrators of institutes, departments, and centres concerned with training practitioners as well as researchers and with applied, demonstration, and action research as well as discipline oriented investigation. The participants' contributions suggest that theoretical and practical understandings of adolescence are not so far apart as it is popular to imagine. Perhaps if both scientific and social programmes for adolescence had received more attention, sufficient specialization might have already occurred to assure divorcement. At present, both suffer from insufficient attention and the gaps *within* scientific and social efforts dealing with adolescence are more impressive than those *between* them.

Policy focus

Contributors of papers for the Colloquium were asked to write from a disciplinary perspective although the document announcing the objects and organization of the Colloquium suggested that more was expected as well:

> To sociologists, political scientists, economists, and to all those who in general think primarily in terms of 'a changing and changed *world*', we

issue the challenge to pose questions in which the prominent consideration is man. Psychologists, educationalists, anthropologists, and all those who think primarily in terms of 'changing and changed *people*', will be challenged to place their understanding of human values in the context of the possible forms of *society* in the year 2000.

As will be noted shortly in a preview of the papers, contributors responded to these challenges in a variety of ways. In the Colloquium itself discussion was organized around contexts for development (family, peer groups, school, work and leisure) with the expectation that, in each case, material oriented toward individual biological and behavioural development would emerge. This did occur to a certain extent in the discussions and provided the basis for an observation we shall expand upon in Chapter 3, namely, that contexts for adolescent development have received some scholarly and scientific attention as have aspects of that development but the two are rarely studied by the same investigator in the same design.

In keeping with the Foundation's aim to make the Colloquium 'a brainstorming exchange of ideas', the papers were prepared as background papers for the meeting and were not presented either formally or informally at the meeting. Most were prepared in sufficient time to enable participants to read them before the meeting. The papers were cited frequently in discussion as a result, and points made in them not only served as the substantive basis for the discussion but were often elaborated, clarified, and illuminated in the course of it. Given the aim of the Colloquium and the procedure adopted, neither the papers nor the discussion were intended to provide exhaustive and systematic assessments of research knowledge in the areas covered and this was not the result. Several papers and the discussion itself revealed important gaps in our present knowledge, however, and these will receive due consideration in Chapter 3. In the main, the discussions were policy oriented, the participants attempting to identify the issues to which those seeking to facilitate adolescent development in the next quarter century ought to direct their attention. It was emphasized that scientific and social policy were themselves among the conditions influencing that development. Indeed, considerable concern was expressed about the relative absence of forceful policies at all levels of government. And where such policies do exist, there was concern about their focus upon deviance and its remedy instead of upon the facilitation of development and the prevention of problematic behaviour.

The future orientation of the Colloquium

The adolescents of today will, by the year 2000, be parenting adolescents of their own. When cast in this generational perspective, the year 2000 becomes part of the near (and not the distant) future. It offers a more realistic than fantastic target date for forecasting and planning; indeed, the year 2000 is so near that there is little time to implement some kinds of interventions. Consider those, for example, which are held to depend upon changes in family life and parenting behaviour. Those who are now in early adolescence will begin their parenting careers in about 10–12 years and the early experiences they provide for their children will have a major impact upon the latter when they reach adolescence.

On the other hand, the year 2000 is also far enough away that orienting one's thought toward it can lead to a kind of psychological distance from the present—a distance which should elicit thought about the lasting rather than the ephemeral aspects of development and the conditions for it. An orientation to the *near* future, then, emphasizes the importance of present action and provides a time frame for anticipating (and later, evaluating) the consequences of that action.

The Colloquium discussions were not futurological in any systematic sense. At the first session, the participants agreed that they would not choose among the alternative, contradictory, and often speculative models now available. Thus the conclusions and recommendations of the Colloquium are not derivations from some agreed upon futurological model. They are statements about the issues which need to be confronted and reflections of what might be desirable in light of current knowledge. Within the overall programme of Jeugdprofiel 2000, presumably the international symposium will further and more systematically define some 'alternative futures' in the sense in which Mahler (Chapter 4) uses the term.

Defining adolescence and youth

In addition to understanding something about the orientations of the Colloquium to policy and the near future, it will be helpful to clarify the term 'adolescence' as it was used in the Colloquium and as it will be used in this volume. In our retrospective judgement, we can trace most of the communications problems the Colloquium did have (which we have said were few in number) to the participants' insufficient precision in using this term (and its competitor, 'youth') in both sending and receiving messages to others. In the interest of improving the readability and utility of this volume and of avoiding the same difficulties in the international symposium to follow, we recommended revisions that take a standard usage into account. (Authors also have been given the option to demur from the standard and state why.) The papers have been edited with these considerations in mind.

In the discussion to follow we will rely heavily on chronological age to carry the burden of certain distinctions we want to make. We do not intend to claim or even suggest that chronological age groupings provide an effective means of *understanding* the biological, psychological, or socio-logical phenomena which render the notion of developmental stages or phases a useful one. Chronological age certainly does not cause the phenomena. However, if it is always understood that there is wide variation at either end, one can set upper and lower chronological age limits as a kind of shorthand for the stage or phase one is talking about. Most of the phenomena the participants in the Colloquium were interested in take place for most (but clearly not all) individuals in the period which extends roughly from 12 to 24 years of age. (And these were the rough brackets placed on discussion at the first meeting of the Colloquium itself.) One can, in terms of contemporary usage and scientific interest, split this period roughly in half, owing largely to the fact that secondary education for most comes to an end about then. That societies and scientists within them have different names for these two periods and age groups is our problem.

Our understanding of traditional and contemporary usages to refer to persons in the two age groups in a variety of nations is reflected in Table 1.

If one takes into account the emergent Dutch usage of *Jeugd* in place of *puberteit*—a usage the project name, Jeugdprofiel 2000, was in part designed to promote—there is a remarkable consistency in the Continental usage. That English is the language of this volume makes the choice a difficult one.

Table 1

Country language	12 to 18 yrs	18 to 24 yrs
American	Adolescence	Young adulthood (trad.) Youth (contemp.)
Dutch	Puberteit (trad.) Jeugd (contemp.)	Adolescentie
English	Adolescence	Young adulthood
French	Jeunesse	Adolescence
German	Jugendalter	Adoleszenz

In both America and in England, the term 'youth' is sometimes used to cover *both* age periods. In the USA, the deplorable fact that the national census lumps both together in the age grouping, 14–24, strengthens this tendency to dedifferentiate. The downward diffusion of styles and consumption patterns from the older to the younger age group encouraged by modern marketing techniques also contributes to blurring the distinction (to say nothing, for the moment, about the diffusion of the same styles and consumption patterns upward into the adult group). On the other hand, the relatively recent arguments of Keniston (1975) in relation to a new stage which he chose to call 'youth' has led to an increasingly specialized and universal meaning for this term (at least in the social sciences) in relation to the second period of interest.

Keniston (1975) has treated youth as a psychological stage of development emerging between adolescence and adulthood. Previously regarded as late adolescents or young adults, this new group is instead composed of persons who have settled the problem of developing autonomy yet who differ

> ... sharply from 'young adults' of age twenty-four whose place in society is settled, who are married and perhaps parents, and who are fully committed to any occupation. What characterises a growing minority of post-adolescents today is that they have not settled the questions whose answers once defined adulthood: questions of relationship to existing society; questions of vocation, questions of social role and life style (Keniston, 1975, p. 7).

While 'youth' in the Keniston sense is hardly a universal stage, we believe that the phenomena to which he is pointing are important. What we have labelled in Table 1 as traditional and contemporary American usages also mirrors current international realities. An important minority of (largely) affluent young people occupy the status of 'youth' in Keniston's psychological stage terms while others are 'young adults'. This further complicates an already complicated problem of terminology which we have resolved by reviewing the Colloquium participants' papers and making a rather arbitrary decision. It seems to us that, for the most part, when this set of participants referred to people in the 18- to 24-year-old range they were in fact, referring to 'youth' in the Keniston sense. And where they were not, the context made this clear as well. And where there was some disagreement or ambiguity, either in differentiating between the two age groups or between the two kinds of sociopsychological status in the older age group, we asked contributors to provide some clarification. Rosenmayr and Rosenmayr (Chapter 5) have, for example, taken exception to our usage and that of Keniston. On the whole, then, in this volume we shall use the term 'adolescence' to refer to the earlier period and 'youth' to refer to the later period.

That the primary intent of the Jeugdprofiel 2000 project in an overall sense and in the Colloquium is increased social responsiveness to the younger age group, adolescents, is manifest in the choice of the project's name. We believe that this interest was not clear to all participants and the result is an emphasis in some contributions on youth and young adults. From our point of view, this is a useful departure from the plan. Since the defining characteristics of any stage of development are elaborations of the endpoints or residuals of the preceding stage it is important that we know them. And, finally, emerging as we are from a period of intensive and extensive worldwide consciousness of youth, youth revolt and youth movements, it is important that our societies come to understand the similarities and the differences involved between the two age and status groups. For example, the similar appearance of the 14-year-old and the 24-year-old these days may have totally different meanings. That certain appearance characteristics are a badge of belonging to a clique or crowd may be more important for the early adolescent than what they say to the 24-year-old about adopting the customs and conventions of traditional adult roles.

Plan of the book

The remainder of Part I of this book contains two chapters: Chapter 2 consists of the Summary record and conclusions of the Colloquium as prepared at the time of the Colloquium itself and subsequently edited both for style and substance on the basis of comments made during the last sessions of the Colloquium. Chapter 3 presents a highly selective integration of the proceedings in the form of a discussion of some current perspectives on adolescence and their consequences for policy and research now and in the near future.

Part II of this volume contains most of the background papers written for the Colloquium. The first four chapters (those by Mahler, the Rosenmayrs, Eisenstadt, and Faessler) deal broadly with recent and anticipated changes in broader social and cultural systems that impinge upon adolescent development. In the next two contributions (Milani-Comparetti and Hebbelinck) the focus shifts to the level of individual biological development during adolescence. Finally, the last four papers, Chapters 10 through 13, focus upon four of the enduring contexts for adolescent development: the family (Piotrowski); the peer group (Hartup); the school (Husén); and the work setting (Delors).

References

Bakan, D. 1971. Adolescence in America: From idea to social fact, *Daedalus*, vol. 100, no. 4, pp. 979–996.

Hall, G. S. 1904. *Adolescence: Its psychology and its relations to physiology, anthropology, sociology, sex, crime, religion, and education*, vols. I and II. New York: Appleton.

Keniston, K. 1975. Prologue: Youth as a stage of life. In R. J. Havighurst and P. H. Dreyer (Eds.), *Youth: the Seventy-Fourth Yearbook of the National Society for the Study of Education*, Part I. Chicago: National Society for the Study of Education, pp. 3–26.

Musgrove, F. 1964. *Youth and social order*. Bloomington: Indiana University Press.

2 Summary record and conclusions

John P. Hill, Franz J. Mönks, William Wall,
Willem Welling and Robert Weeda

The International Colloquium, organized by Jeugdprofiel 2000, met from 15–19 September 1975 in Amsterdam. Its focus was adolescence in the year 2000. Participants in the Colloquium came from Austria, Belgium, the Federal Republic of Germany, France, Israel, Italy, Poland, Sweden, Switzerland, the UK, the USA and The Netherlands.

Various disciplines in the human and social sciences were represented. The subject for discussion was treated in terms both of an analysis of the immediate past and present and of such trends as could be identified as shaping the society of the year 2000. It was recognized from the outset that models offered so far about the situation and prevailing conditions of society at that time were highly speculative. Therefore the ideas set out below more often reflect what is desirable and to be hoped for than specific predictions emerging from some futurological model.

The discussions were, for the most part, policy oriented. No formal synthesis of the state of scientific knowledge was intended or attempted yet the absence of information about many areas of importance to policy was apparent. Scientific knowledge of adolescence lags far behind that for other periods in the life cycle. Investment now in discipline and problem oriented research on adolescent development and upon those conditions which affect it positively seems essential to informed decisions in the future. Both science policy *and* social policy of the present and the near future are among those current conditions that will shape adolescence in the year 2000.

The present chapter is an attempt to record the essence of the dialogue which took place and the general conclusions reached. It is not the sole result of the discussions. The remainder of the present work includes a more elaborated synthesis of those discussions (Chapter 3) and a presentation of some of the individual papers written by participants for the purposes of the meeting.

Adolescence in perspective

Turbulence and an oppositional nature are not universally characteristic of the adolescent period. The youth movements of the 1960s attracted the active participation of minorities of young people. The extrapolation from the latter's behaviour and experience to that of adolescents as a whole provides a misleading basis for understanding adolescence and shaping social policy. The recurrence, frequency, and intensity of such movements around the year 2000 are impossible to predict given our present knowledge. Whatever the relative degree of tension, conflict and turbulence that characterizes societies between now and the year 2000, however, it cannot be assumed that dramatic turbulence in adolescence will automatically be an essential feature of it.

A number of scenarios dealing with the economic future of European societies has been advanced. Models for social planning based upon expectations of continuing economic growth are of doubtful validity. However, projections of economic development, labour differentiation and resource availability through the year 2000 are contradictory. Whatever the alternative scenario finally enacted, and whatever the particular problems it poses for adolescents, the solutions sought, attempted, or adopted will reflect tensions between authoritarian and participatory problem solving; between professional and voluntary contributions to the implementation of policy and programmes; between passive insistence on individual or group rights and active assumption of responsible roles; and between those who advocate open access to opportunities throughout the lifespan and those who do not.

Adolescence begins with the onset of puberty and a spurt in rate of physical growth at or near the beginning of the second decade of life and ends with the assumption of adult occupational and family roles within the third decade. There is considerable variability in the age at which the maturational processes which mark the period begin and end. Adolescence as we know it in modern societies is a creature of the industrial revolution and it continues to be shaped by the forces which defined that revolution: industrialization, specialization, urbanization, the rationalization and bureaucratization of human organizations and institutions, and continuing technological development.

Preparation for full adult roles in the societies shaped by these forces has been steadily prolonged so that the transitional period between childhood and adulthood has greatly increased over the past 100 years. In addition, the onset of physical and sexual maturation has occurred earlier and earlier for the past several decades, thereby prolonging the adolescent period even more.

The development of mass marketing strategies aimed at young people, the creation of separate systems of justice for juveniles, and the passage of child labour and compulsory education laws are reflections of and instruments in the creation of this lengthy transitional period. Perhaps its most striking manifestation is the arrival in Europe in the past 30 years of nearly universal secondary education. This has meant that the 13- and 14-year-olds who attained economic independence 30 years ago do not do so today. It has also meant an increasing segregation of adolescents from older generations in institutions which have had to be modified considerably to accommodate wider ranges of ability, experience, and motivation. In urban areas where schooling is arranged on the basis of neighbourhood, adolescents are segregated not only by generation but by social class. This segregation by age and social class restricts opportunities for learning about the life cycle and about the range of life careers in society.

The next 25 years will see the continuation of these trends, one important example being an increase in the proportion of young people who go on for post-secondary education and training, thus further postponing the assumption of fully adult responsibilities (and changing our conceptions of adulthood). The continued bureaucratization of institutions in society, the lack of attractiveness of existing youth organizations, a continued growth in size of organizations which serve adolescents and their families, and the trend toward centralized social planning at local and state levels seem likely to bring with them a greater homogenization of norms, ideologies, behaviour and experience.

At the same time this homogenization will serve as a base for increased diversity in the future and in itself instigate countertrends. The paradox of the future, then, is that of an increased pressure towards uniformity in many aspects of social life and the contrary tendency to value increased variability in some of its manifestations. The extent of homogeneity and variability and the spheres of social life in which it is manifested will vary within and across societies, of course, but barring cataclysm, no sudden transformations can be predicted on the basis of our present knowledge.

Whatever the value stance adopted, desired and undesired change will be slow in coming owing to the fundamentally conservative nature of the family and of other public and private institutions bent on survival. Instead of massive, overall changes, we may expect outcroppings of diversity, the net effect of which is a greater pluralization in society (as, for example, of lifestyles). Against a background of increasing homogenization, given modern communications systems, any instances of diversity may well seem indicative of more fundamental or widespread change than has actually occurred. Explosive upheavals may characterize the response to pluralization from time to time and these will often involve some adolescents just as they do some members of older generations. Improved means of inter- and intra-generational conflict resolution need to be developed to cope better with the tensions of pluralization.

This diversity within homogeneity will develop within the context not only of a general decline in population growth in Europe but of a substantial decrease in the proportion of the population in the adolescent age range. This may lead to an unwarranted neglect of the development of social policy and programmes related to adolescence where none now exist as well as to less effective implementation of programmes and policies where they do exist. Family size will also change in the future. Increases in the number of single-child and single-parent families suggest the serious reassessment of support systems now available to families.

Uncertainties about the economic future may also create a reversion to short term planning and a tendency to minimize risk taking in the development of programmes for adolescents. Given the slowness of change referred to above, action taken in the near future in relation to adolescence will have greater effect in the year 2000 than will any action contemplated then. Measures need to be taken now to preclude hasty, botched and ineffective action later.

The trend of the past century toward increasingly universalistic norms will continue. Equitable treatment of persons in all segments of society, regardless of age, sex, racial, ethnic or other background, will be pursued.

The consequences of the pressure for equal access to opportunities will be felt in gender, work, educational and other roles.

The development of global communications over the past few decades has meant increased exposure of adolescents to events and conditions of social life which, for the most part, had been previously apprehended only through familial or other adult mediation. It has provided a series of images of adolescence which are highly stereotyped and which stress deviance or overgeneralize from current events involving minorities, to the total adolescent population. The audience for these stereotypes includes parents, professionals, policy makers, and adolescents themselves. Channels of communication need to be developed in the decades ahead for the presentation of information about more typical adolescent development in a variety of sociocultural settings.

One of the central problems of adolescence is the development of identity, of a sense of who one is and what one will become in his or her own historical and sociocultural context. In the interest of developing this integration of personality, the following are affirmed: the right of individuals to differ; the recognition of diversity in the adolescent experience; the pluralism of personal values in society; the need to provide adolescents with opportunities to fill responsible roles, to make choices and to live with the consequences of their choices; and to explore, with appropriate support, guidance, and protection, those roles which seem uniquely matched to the individual's own background, interests, abilities, and aspirations.

Family

Increasing awareness of alternative family forms such as communes, cohabitation, and one-parent families has renewed speculation about 'the decline of the family'. The extent of actual change in the family circumstances in which adolescents are reared, of pluralism in family forms and the rate of that change has probably been much exaggerated in the mass media and in literature in the past five years. Whatever its forms, the family continues to be an important and conservative social institution.

Alternative family forms serve such traditional values as providing a base for socialization and personal development, emotional support and the like. There is considerable evidence that (at least in the traditional family context) emotional attachments of adolescents to their parents remain strong and this is unlikely to change. Parents by and large continue to be a major force in socialization in both their functions as models of adult behaviour and as sources of sanctions for behaviour of which they approve or disapprove. Occupational and educational aspirations are, for example, more strongly influenced by parental than by peer standards. Conflict between parent and peer pressures most often occurs in matters related to adolescent behaviour in the peer group and less often in relation to socialization for achievement. The so-called generation gap is much exaggerated and likely to lessen as adolescents and their elders have equal amounts of education. There is very little scientific evidence available on the developmental impacts during adolescence of growing up in other than a complete nuclear family.

Research to date suggests that there are no identifiable differences in social behaviour between children of mothers in employment and those who stay at home. Indeed there is some evidence to indicate that working mothers devote more time to children as a primary activity rather than as secondary to other activities (such as supervising children while cooking or cleaning). Virtually none of the available research has focused on influences on adolescents, however. Especially required here are studies about the impact of maternal employment upon the developing gender identity and achievement aspirations of both daughters and sons.

There is evidence that the proportion of divorces is higher in those societies where the proportion of employed women is high but the consequences of divorce for adolescent development have not been studied. In view of increasing rates of divorce in general, this is a deplorable omission.

The trend to equalizing gender roles encompasses both a greater overlap of behaviour in male and female roles and a greater diversity of acceptable patterns within each role. Aspects of child care and home making are increasingly performed by males and, as noted above, women are increasingly breadwinners. There is little evidence documenting the extent of such change and its distribution through society. We should expect less traditional gender role definition and behaviour in both sons and daughters of parents who value and model more equalitarian behaviour. Tension and conflict will result to the extent that such changes occur differentially at various levels in society. For example, it seems likely that the rate of change now is greater in middle-class families. Sons and daughters in those families may experience conflict with less traditionally reared peers and with adults who do not share their parents' values.

Related to increasing equality is the tendency to appreciate the family as a base for personal growth and development over and above its procreative functions, and instead of as a unit to be maintained in its own right. It is anticipated that this trend will continue, with consequential increases in the divorce rate and a growing schism between marriage and the family (for example, family law which emphasizes the interest of the individual in the family rather than the interest of the family as a whole).

The functions now served by institutions outside the family are dependent upon familial understanding of the institutions and support of them. The highest proportion of variance in school attainment, for example, continues to be attributable to the family. However, the family is not always equipped cognitively and emotionally to understand and use the institutions which are intended to serve it. The gap between making a service available and seeing to it that it is used by those for whom it was intended is, in general, a large one and perhaps more consequential for the adolescent than for the younger child since the choices made by and for the adolescent are more likely to be definitive for his future.

The trend among late adolescents to cohabit for a period of months or years is likely to continue. The dissolution of such relationships poses emotional, personal, and economic problems not unlike those characteristic of divorcing and divorced couples. Legislation and services need to be designed to take these problems into account.

Many parents are poorly prepared to deal with the changes—biological, psychological and social—which virtually recreate the person at and around puberty. Exaggerated and mythologized images of adolescents common in literature and in the mass media compound the problem. Educational programmes, particularly for first-time parents of adolescents, should be designed and widely implemented.

Education

The past decades have seen three developments:

(a) an almost universal participation of the 10/12–15/16-year-olds in secondary schools and a rapid increase of those over 16 in further and higher education;

(b) an increase in expenditures on education out of proportion to the increase in public resources generally; and

(c) a climate of organizational reform aimed at extension and equalization of opportunities and 'modernization' of curricula to take account of technological change.

The first of these trends has tended to maintain many more young people in a custodial institution, out of contact with the realities of adult life, and to stress a certain 'credentialism' which disadvantages many. The secondary school of today is faced with a serious problem of motivation among the low-performing students, many of whom come from deprived social backgrounds. The second trend of rising costs and investment in education, were it to continue, would absorb an impossibly high proportion of resources. The third has demonstrated the relative ineffectiveness of organizational change to bring about the desired innovations where these depend upon behavioural and attitudinal change.

The future faces us—in the light of falling age groups—with a relative reduction rather than an expansion in resources for formal education, and the tendency to seek further economy at the risk of quality. Nil growth must probably be accepted, but, within the limits of resources, redeployment priorities should be sought.

Criticisms of and demands made upon the school system are:

(a) it is excessively knowledge centred, with overemphasis on cognitive goals neglecting to foster and develop effective, aesthetic, ethical and other aspects of personality;

(b) it stresses competition along academic lines, reinforcing social inequalities, destroying confidence, and inviting opting out;

(c) it is unrelated to the outside world and maintains an artificial and counterproductive segregation of young and middle adolescents from the real world;

(d) by virtue of increasing size, bureaucratization and curricular specialization, it fragments adolescent experience, fosters alienation and presents bewildering choices without the means of choosing;

(e) the gulf between the school and life, and the mismatch between education and work, are paralleled by a constellation of factors (social

origins of teachers, content of text books etc.), which oppose school culture and home culture for many pupils;
(f) the increased hierarchization and bureaucratization concomitant with the increased size of the individual schools and the system at large.

The fundamental problems seem to concern:

(a) the nature of the styles of thinking required by an open pluralistic society in which responsible choice and the ability to adjust without undue stress are prime objectives;
(b) the relation of thinking styles (empirical, logical, aesthetic, moral, etc.) to knowledge and the cultural heritage;
(c) the 'pastoral' or 'guidance' role of the school, both so far as personal, moral, academic and vocational choices are concerned; and the maintenance of the identity of the individual in the face of the large, bureaucratic, fragmented structure;
(d) the relationship of the school to the parents and other influential adults; the general community; and the world of work;
(e) the building into the school curriculum of work experiences conducive to a smoother transition to adulthood.

Although formal schooling has been extended to all adolescents up to a certain age—a tower structure rather than a flat pyramid—and there are formal structures of further and higher education, the principal current development (and one which may become even more important in the next decade) is a basic change in the concept of education. From being a once for all process ending with the teens or, for the more favoured, with the early 20s, education is beginning to be conceived of as a lifelong process (*éducation permanente*).

Many countries, notably France, have, or are developing, legislation and institutional structures which have as their aims that:

(a) education should be a process associated with the whole of the lifespan and the individual should be able to move into and out of an educational system, as he or she needs to, without economic penalty;
(b) schooling with or without attendant qualifications, should not be the end of the process but a stage along the way;
(c) continuing or recurrent education should be associated with, and complementary to schools and not in conflict with them;

(d) recurrent or lifelong education should serve a wide range of functions for the individual from, for example, the chance to explore new realms of experience, to providing reassurance and intellectual support in the stress and anxiety of change, or providing the possibility of taking up a new career.

A third area of education, likely to develop and need fostering towards the year 2000, is more difficult to define, stimulate, and provide for. It concerns various *ad hoc*, spontaneous, or semi-organized groups of adolescents and adults, who engage together in various pursuits—temporarily or for a considerable period of time. These may be creative, artistic and so on; they may be social or service groups; they may simply be concerned with deeper exploration of relationships—or take a variety of other forms. They may be strictly adolescent—young or older—or they may mix the generations.

Two things seem to be crucial: the provision of facilities of various kinds—space, minimal equipment and resources and the like—to enable such spontaneous formations; and probably, some well trained professionals who can act as resource and facilitating staff.

Among the trends which are visible or which might be hoped for over the next three decades are:

(a) the need for schools to be seen as part of an extensive educational network of which informal groups and structures of continuing education form other parts;
(b) the need for the individual and the society (as represented by parents, employers and adolescents) to see education as a wide and continuing process. The idea of the 'educational drawing right' is relevant here;
(c) dissatisfaction with a competitive, knowledge centred educational model and the search for a more inclusive, person and development centred one, close to the actualities of life and the competences involved in being an adult in a modern society;
(d) a recognition that improvements in education, in access and the like, aimed at equality, in fact increase differences and the awareness of disadvantage. This raises the problem of education as an interventionist strategy;
(e) the conservatism of institutions and professions and their resistance to change. How can innovation be ensured?
(f) the peculiar role dissonances and conflict of the educator who is ex-

pected to be committed and fully at the disposal of those with whom he or she works, and the strong trend towards a negotiated and limited, paid for working responsibility.

Peer relations

Peer relations play an important role in adolescent development. Little is known about the direct effects of family life in adolescence, but peer relationships have been more intensively explored. Peers play an important role in determining the context of behaviour as well as in aspects of social and cognitive learning. Experiences with peers are vital in the development of standards and behaviour. Learning to master the expression of aggression is, for example, probably impossible in the family context alone since the unequal power of parents and children leads to resolution of issues on the basis of external power assertion rather than internal control.

Particularly important at present and for the future may be the way in which the peer group supports and indeed encourages changes which the family and adults, generally, may be unable or unwilling to bring about. Examples of this are: the incorporation of sexual behaviour in existing gender roles; the development of the capacity for intimacy in relationships with others; the experience of responsibility to and for others; the learning of cooperation on an equal footing; and other social skills and competences which require 'trying on' adult-like behaviour in adult-free contexts.

On the other hand, a complete division between the peer culture and adults seems undesirable; more vertical groupings of older and younger adolescents, adults and younger children should also be possible. Processes of bureaucratization in society, particularly in educational and leisure institutions, tend to inhibit this.

Segregation by social class in neighbourhoods, educational, and other institutions diminishes parent–peer conflicts since associations with peers are likely to take place within the same or similar value contexts. On the other hand, absence of association with adolescents and adults of other origins does not provide adequate socialization for citizenship roles in pluralistic societies. This strain in modern society requires more explicit attention—and a search for solutions—than it has heretofore received.

Such is the importance of the peer group to the attainment of maturity that attention should be given to ways in which peer relations can be fostered, supported, and used to provide the young with acceptable access to the resources of their society. Lack of integration into some peer relations network in early adolescence is one of the best predictors of late adolescent and young adult social deviance and psychopathology presently available. However, the planned use of peer groups by adults in the interest of implementing adult objectives or providing a 'good' peer experience for everyone carries with it the danger that the spontaneous and equalitarian virtues of peer groups will be transformed in such ways that its facilitation of development is impaired.

In some cases youth organizations provide the scene for strategies of adult intervention and communication. However, formal value oriented organizations of the traditional kind have never appealed to the entire age group and seem to have a diminishing appeal. This is especially true of those which have some kind of overt political, religious, or other affiliation. In their place, more diffused, less permanent, and more multiple networks, complexes and occasions for association or 'happenings' seem to be occurring. These are often oriented toward specific action, however diffuse, and allow an individual or a group to explore many more environments without more than temporary or partial commitment. Again, it is important that parents and the community provide the flexible resources to foster and encourage such exploration.

Occupational life and leisure

There is a basic contrast between instrumental and intrinsic satisfaction in work. Some expect a shift toward the first, the instrumental view; others—and they are in greater number—foresee an increased emphasis on the second, the intrinsic view. Among adolescents today both views are present and may succeed each other in the same individual. Moreover both are now legitimated by society. The discrepancy between these views ('the pay from work buys a lifestyle' *vs* 'I am what I do') is keenly felt by many adolescents today and may well increase by the year 2000.

On the other hand, social class differences seem likely to remain important:

(a) middle-class and upper middle-class adolescents and adults will continue to lay a strong emphasis on career and self-fulfilment in it; they will make use of work as a means to self-actualization;
(b) members of working-class groups will continue to consider work as primarily an instrumental activity.

The prolongation of education and the number of people participating in it have already led to a rise in occupational aspirations and expectations—a rise which cannot always be met in the labour market. This is likely to be an increasing source of conflict in the near future, mainly because of the high proportion of adolescents in the total population and the relatively no-growth economy. In the long term this stress might diminish if predicted demographic changes occur and the proportion of young persons in the population is markedly reduced.

Alongside a general shift towards the tertiary ('human services') sector of employment there is a change in the relations between paid and unpaid work. The latter will not only receive more recognition, but will also tend to be institutionalized. This relates to the basic question of the meaning of work which itself is acquiring pluralistic definitions. These might well vary not only by country but by region.

What is the importance of work in relation to the time devoted to it? Will there really be more time free for leisure activities owing to the situation in the labour market on the one hand, the importance of work in one's life, and a reduction in working hours? If this is the case, constructive channels should be provided for a profitable and creative linkage between working and leisure experiences.

When the labour market is in difficulty, the first to become unemployed are the last hired. At present and in the foreseeable future, these are likely to be the young and women. Both lack experience relative to adult male workers and are for that reason more vulnerable. In the more distant future, however, adolescents will be in a better position due to the extension of recurrent education, which provides the option to re-enter the educational system; women will have reached a percentage of participation in the labour market such that they cannot any longer be considered as a minority, either in number or in the sharing of responsibilities.

Societal policies

There is substantial disregard of the impact on adolescents of public policy decisions at both the state and local levels. Criteria for analysing such impacts should be developed which consider the effects of administrative and legislative policies and programmes on adolescent development in its totality. Such criteria should also be used for the evaluation of effects on adolescent development of any legislation or policy not particularly aimed at adolescents (e.g., minimum wage; energy; adult education; urban planning and housing developments; the development of local television). These short term evaluations ('impact statements') should be weighed in making social policy decisions.

Another weakness in policy making is the absence of information about the adolescent's attitudes, preferences, wants, and behaviour. In this connection national efforts should be undertaken to establish social indicators related to the status and functioning of youth. These should permit cross-society comparisons and provide indications of local variation according to early, middle, and late adolescence, gender, parental roles, occupation, and the like. Such programmes should include the collection of information about attitudes and behaviour related to (the future of) marriage and family; work; leisure and education; youth organizations; the future of society; and socio-economic issues such as population, energy, resources and the like. Social indicators may be used to assess the need for new programmes and to assess the effectiveness of those in place.

Another resource for social (as well as for scientific) policy makers would be synopses of existing scientific knowledge about adolescence and the conditions of adolescent development. The generation of such synopses should be institutionalized through co-operative efforts of both the public and private sectors.

On the level of services several initiatives need to be taken:

(a) a range of services should be designed for facilitating normal development instead of focusing, as do most services at present, on deviance and remediation. In this respect special attention should be given to the creation of a new cadre of adolescent specialists who could plan and implement such programmes. Additionally, sub-specialists in adolescence have not been added to existing professions at nearly the rate they have for early childhood and ageing;

(b) the (mis)use of drugs, including alcohol, the problem of venereal disease, and increasing numbers of teenage pregnancies are among the problems that require the accelerated establishment of health education and remedial health services for adolescents;

(c) nutritional information services, including nutrition education programmes for adolescents themselves, should be developed. Obesity and the high incidence of malnutrition (even in affluent families) require such efforts;

(d) in providing services to adolescents every attempt should be made to avoid labelling and the creation of 'cases' with negative connotations and fixed attitudes. For this purpose development oriented educational models are superior to disease oriented medical models;

(e) given the extensive variability in the onset and duration of puberty and the growth spurt, information services should be provided for both adults (parents, teachers and others who work with adolescents) and adolescents themselves on normal variations in physical and sexual maturation.

At present, considerable capital continues to be invested in large scale physical facilities for adolescent programmes. This is a trend that should be reversed. When using existing physical facilities, diversified activities should be organized within them. When planning new buildings, size should be restricted; the facilities should be multiple in order to serve smaller groups within neighbourhoods in more personal ways.

Such neighbourhood centres should be staffed by both professionals and volunteers. A balance between professionals and volunteers will need to be consciously sought in view of the tendency for roles occupied by volunteers to be professionalized. Volunteers will continue to be essential both because sufficient professionals cannot be trained to meet the demand and because volunteers bring resources from their other roles and personal characteristics to their tasks. Professionals need to be trained to respect these important contributions and to share responsibility for the guidance of adolescent activities.

3 Some perspectives on adolescence in modern societies

John P. Hill and Franz J. Monks

The youth movements of the late 1960s gave new life to a perspective on adolescence and youth already widely held. The focus upon adolescents as troubled persons was reinforced. Both research and public policy initiatives were and continue to be justified from this point of view. We wish, at the outset, to dissociate ourselves from this perspective. There is no evidence that adolescence is any more problematic for persons passing through it or for their families than is any other period in the life cycle. The youth movements—or, more exactly, public reports of them—not only raised social consciousness about adolescents and youth but did so in such a way as to reinforce the perspective that adolescence is, universally and by definition, a troubled and troublesome period in the life cycle.

Turning things around a bit, one might say that such a trouble-oriented perspective was applied *to* the youth movements in an effort to render them 'understandable' in just the same way as it has been applied on a more modest scale for many decades to account for adolescent behaviour which in some way departs from the norms of the dominant culture or which is a statutory delinquency. It is difficult to name *any* distinctive adolescent behaviour which some reporter, sage, or both has not pronounced to be the result of 'rebelliousness', for example. This, of course, is an explanation evoked by many for much of the behaviour of activists in the late 1960s. And what was meant was not only opposition to certain social policies and their underlying values but an opposition to adults. The oppositional behaviour has been seen as fundamentally generational in orientation; indeed one of the legacies of the period is the entrance of the term 'generation gap' into the common language. Ordinarily responsible scholars proclaimed the existence of a generation gap as qualitatively different from what had existed before as a canyon is from a crack. A homogeneous 'peer culture' impervious to adult influence was said to exist. We have serious doubts that such interpretations are adequate to explain the behaviour of activists themselves. There is no doubt at all that such perspectives are inadequate for an understanding of typical adolescent development. However, since many readers will bring somewhat similar perspectives to this volume (derived, in part, from their experience of the youth movements), it seemed important that we begin this chapter with some analysis of the problem of generations, youth movements, and matters of diversity and conflict within and across generations, in general. In so doing, not only do we hope to suggest a quite different perspective to guide the reading of the remainder of the chapter but also to point out on what major assumptions and issues we may differ with certain of our colleagues whose work is represented in Part II of this book. Before moving on to this task, a few words about the chapter as a whole are in order.

This chapter is not an official document of the colloquium. While based upon what was written for the meeting and upon transcripts of that meeting, it also has a basis in our own views about adolescent development and our reading of the theoretical and empirical literature in the area. It is our own attempt at an integration of materials from all the sources mentioned above. It is highly selective. We shall try to reflect accurately areas of agreement and disagreement when this seems useful but it is not our intent to take the meeting solely on its own terms and integrate what happened in the light of some 'structure' that emerged from it. The colloquium discussions were not sufficiently focused to make this possible. (Recall that its purpose had been described as 'brainstorming'.) Instead we will present a heuristic model of adolescent development which we believe is helpful in naming, sorting out and making sense of the welter of facts, issues, recommendations, and areas of research reported on in this volume and in the literature. Using this heuristic framework, our aim is to present some perspectives on adolescence in modern societies that may be helpful in shaping both research and policy in the near future.

The problem of generations

Westby and Braungart (1970) asked some late adolescents to write a history of their nation 'from the present to the year 2000'. The organizing themes of the essays ranged from utopian to dystopian. Five conceptions were identified: steady improvement of the society; overthrow of existing structure; steady decline; and sudden cataclysm. The left wing activists tended to be more dystopian than utopian: 34% of the left wingers predicted a linear decline; 15% predicted cataclysm; 13% a progressive drift upward; 10% revolution; and 4% conversion to leftist objectives. The right wingers were more utopian than dystopian: 36% foresaw a drift toward state controls followed by a conversion to conservative principles; 29% hypothesized linear decline; 15% forecast steady improvement; 4% sudden cataclysm; and 1% revolution.

The percentages reported would doubtless differ had the survey been taken elsewhere or today. (It was made in the USA in 1966.) However, the categories certainly seem to be applicable across time and place. Our point in presenting the study is not the documentation of right–left differences in attitudes toward the future (although these are interesting in themselves and might well be replicated cross-nationally). Nor will we make much of the fact that fewer than half of the young people in this study had an optimistic view of the time and place in which they would live out the rest of their lives (although the pessimism of so many affluent young people at a point in the life cycle when fully adult status was imminent must be taken seriously). Here, the differences obtained function to illustrate the *diversity* in consciousness and behaviour which typically exists within generations and, assuming the same range of views in the adult generation, the *similarities* which typically exist across generations. Given the proclivity of scientists and laymen to construe adolescence and adolescents within the bounds of some *Sturm und Drang* framework, differences between generations are more often stressed than similarities between them and, in times of heightened consciousness of youth and adolescence, homogeneity of attitudes and values within a given generation of young people is more likely to be stressed than is heterogeneity (see Mönks and Heusinkveld, 1973).

Mannheim's (1952) discussion of the 'sociological' problem of generations is helpful in understanding these issues. Mannheim saw *generation* as a locational variable that bears considerable similarity to *social class*:

> Both endow the individuals sharing in them with a common location in the social and historical process, and thereby limit them to a specific range of potential experience, predisposing them for a certain characteristic mode

of thought and experience, and a characteristic type of historically relevant action (p. 291).

Mannheim recognized that no individual lives in the total society nor is exposed to the total culture. Thus it follows that the 'social and historical process' will be experienced differently by and have different consequences for subgroups within the same generation. Mannheim (1952) advanced the notion of *generational unit* to describe this kind of diversity-within-similarity:

> Youth experiencing the same concrete historical problems may be said to be part of the same actual generation; while those groups within the same actual generation which work up the material of their common experience in different specific ways, constitute separate generational units (p. 304).

Being born in the same period in historical time does not automatically yield similarities of consciousness; the generational unit emerges only when location by generation is accompanied by a sharing of ideas and values. From this point of view, it is not surprising that Westby and Braungart found that the backgrounds of their two groups of American activists differed markedly. Their right wing activists often came from lower middle- and working-class, Protestant or Catholic families of high ethnic status. The left wing activists most often came from upper middle-class Jewish or non-religious families of lower ethnic status. The socio-political events impinging upon their generation were the same; the adolescents' interpretation of them differed (but in seemingly regular and understandable ways).

Mannheim advanced the notion of generational unit in the context of an analysis of youth movements and social change. He would have explained the youth movement which some of Westby and Braungart's subjects were enmeshed in as the product of a complex concatenation of historical, social and cultural conditions which arises rarely. From this point of view, generational differences emerge in their most pronounced forms as 'youth movements' when societies are free of war or natural calamity, when institutional growth is protracted, and when, therefore, social and cultural change is rapid whether due to science, technology, nationalism, or overpopulation (Braungart, 1975). This congeries of events is hardly a constant of social life, and, therefore, youth movements are irregular and unusual occurrences that are difficult, if not impossible, to predict.

In their chapter in the present volume, Hilde and Leopold Rosenmayr suggest that youth be considered in terms of societal reproduction *and* transformation. 'Youth is to be understood as reproduction because it is the product of socialization . . .' yet it is also to be understood as transformation 'because a certain freedom of selection in the socialization of values is inevitable' (p. 96). Values just appearing in society or those in the process of being revitalized, 'youth values' as it were, are tested by cohorts of young persons, themselves 'just becoming able to accept *and* select among the values accessible to them' (p. 95). Such a selective process, the Rosenmayrs add, occurs in conjunction with the kinds of socio-cultural change enumerated by Mannheim, presumably because crisis and change make new values salient and open access to them. The Rosenmayrs indicate that the selective process is likely to be the result of socialization in the more affluent classes which provide not only greater security but training for decision making, and encourage greater cognitive differentiation of the social environment. Research on the characteristics of the early activities of the past decade certainly substantiates this conclusion (Braungart, 1975; Flacks, 1970).

The college-age activists of the USA in the 1960s, for example, represented a small minority of the total university student population— perhaps as high as 5% (Flacks, 1971)—yet university administrators, journalists, politicians, and scientists routinely behaved as if far larger numbers were involved. A generation gap of astonishing proportions was claimed; widespread alienation was diagnosed; even that old standby, *rebelliousness*, was brought out again to bear the explanatory burden for young people's activism. Paradoxically, it turned out that the vanguard of the radical youth movement were *following* (and not rebelling against or alienated from) the intellectual, libertarian, romantic, compassionate, and idealistic values of their parents (Flacks, 1967, 1970; Keniston, 1968, 1971; Haan, Smith and Block, 1968). The presumed gap was not between the activists and their upper middle-class parents but between the activists' values and those of their less affluent and more conservative countrymen of *all* generations. To a substantial extent, then, it appears that the youth movements gave expression to values abroad in the more affluent and liberal sectors of adult society and were expressed by young persons well socialized to do the job. They involved young people in conflict with dominant institutions in society and were a powerful source of some kinds of social change. Youth movements are important and dramatic but irregular and limited. Magnified by the presence of instant and global communications, they provide a misleading model of adolescence and intergenerational relations involving adolescents. In the first place, only some generational units within any generational cohort are likely to be involved, so that to characterize the total cohort on the basis of the activities and values of select minorities is to commit a serious over-generalization. It is to ignore the diversity of values, ideology, and attitudes present within any given cohort of young persons (as was illustrated by the Westby and Braungart study), a diversity probably as great as that found in the parental generation. Second, the focus upon conflict between youth and society in the youth movement has been over-generalized as well, most particularly to the parent–child relationship. Youth movements provide no evidence for the hypothesis that conflict and rebelliousness are normal features of adolescence (indeed, analysis of them suggests that by their parents' standards, at least, activist leaders are well socialized young persons who have internalized their parents' values and are acting upon them (although not always using means of which their parents would approve). To some extent, the actual data on youth movements, as opposed to the publicity about them, call attention to the social class gaps and the politico-economic gaps in modern societies more than to intergenerational relations. Finally, drawing one's perspective on youth and adolescence from the inflammations of the past decade is also to overgeneralize in still a third way—namely to fail to distinguish between adolescence and youth and therefore to ignore the rather special needs of early adolescents, most of whom shared in movements only to the extent of adopting some of the personal appearance characteristics of the activist groups which diffused downward to students in secondary schools.

Of the papers presented in this volume, our perspective is perhaps most at variance with that of Faessler who argues that there is a 'relationship of conflict' between youth and society. In our view, there is no such relation; there are social conflicts in which youth, as other generations, are involved. The irregularity of youth movements and the involvement of relatively few young people in them does not make them any less important as *social forces* to us than to Faessler but these features do make them less important as models for understanding the diversity of the adolescent experience in its various social contexts. Thus, we can agree that the young people involved in the youth movements 'revealed themselves to be the magnifying mirror of the unconfessed contradictions of society in general' (p. 125) but not that this is characteristic of youth in general (nor that it is necessarily visionary, since the same values are shared by a segment of the parent generation).

We see, then, grave dangers in taking the youth movements of the late 1960s as a departure point for developing science policy or social policy today. Not only does such a stance perpetuate the perspective of adolescence as universally a troubled and troublesome period but it results in a kind of homogenization of adolescence that denies the reality and importance of the diversity of the experience of it and the diversity of the contexts in which it occurs. There may be some universals in the experience, e.g., mass scholarization, but even here it is unlikely that the school experience has similar effects on the behavioural development of young people of vastly different social backgrounds. We shall return to this theme of diversity again and again as it seems to us to be critical for science and social policy not to lose sight of it. We turn now to the heuristic model mentioned above. As we have noted, it is meant to be helpful in organizing information and in revealing areas of ignorance. And it will serve here as the basis for examining some perspectives on adolescence in modern societies.

Dimensions of the heuristic model

The individual brings to the beginning of the adolescent period the residuals of an already complex series of transactions between his bio-psychological make-up and the social world as he has experienced it (primarily through roles played in the family, the peer group, and the school). Whether one conceives of the *residuals of the pre-adolescent experience* as motives, traits, attitudes, values, social habits, or schemata, the point is that the individual has a pre-adolescent history. And much of adolescent development is to be understood in terms of that history and in terms of the continuities that bind adolescence to the childhood that was before it. There is, of course, a fashionable tendency to regard adolescence as discontinuous, as a unique and disjunctive period in the life cycle, whereas, as we shall see below, the available scientific evidence strongly supports another conclusion.

To say that the organism has a history is not to deny but to describe a particular kind of change. Indeed, some of the changes which characterize adolescence occur so universally that they demand our attention as primary phenomena of the period. In our view, there are three sets of *primary changes* and they may be considered in terms of their apparent universality: biological changes, changes in cognitive competence, and changes in social definition. Those biological changes which lead to changes in physical capacities, motor skills, and sexual motivation are sometimes held to mark the onset of adolescence itself. The cognitive changes (most dramatically demonstrated by Inhelder and Piaget, 1958) are not so well known, so apparent to others, and evidently not so universal as the physical changes (Neimark, 1975). Briefly characterized, the changes represent a final freeing of thought from its object with the consequence that reasoning can proceed from 'might be' instead of taking the perceptual givens as its departure point (that is to say, hypothetico-deductive thought becomes possible). The individual can extrapolate the possibilities from a given situation and see the concrete givens as a sub-class of the possible. He can now think about his own thought and reason using propositions. The third kind of primary change, that in social definition, is found in most dramatic form in markedly age-graded societies in which a status position occurring between childhood and adulthood is universally recognized and much of the behaviour of persons occupying the position is defined by norms applied throughout the society. It is frequently held that the *absence* of clear consensus about the position of adolescence in modern societies is problematical.

From the perspective of individual development, the classic problems of adolescence take on their distinctive shape and content from inter-relations among the residuals of pre-pubescent development, the primary changes just briefly characterized, and a third class of events, the adolescent's *social participations*. No adolescent lives in or is exposed to his total culture. The impacts of large social structures and cultures are mediated, as they were in childhood, by the roles played in the family, the peer group, and the school. For some young people, during adolescence and youth, work roles may be added to this list. As adulthood approaches, social structures come increasingly to exercise their effects 'through the imperatives of social position (its demands, constraints, task experience) ...' (Elder, 1975). Thus the adolescent apprehends 'society' and 'culture', at first, largely through social participations in relatively intimate groups and only later through occupying a social class position himself. Nevertheless, since adolescents in modern societies, with their residential ghettoes at all class levels, are segregated by virtue of their parents' social class position, they will be exposed to a selected range of the total culture. (And this is important in the present context because it again highlights the diversity of the adolescent experience in pluralistic, modern societies.)

We have thus far spoken of residuals of prior development, certain primary changes, and adolescent social participation as critical classes of events whose interrelations provide 'the classical developmental problems of adolescence with their distinctive shape and content'. In our view, these problems, the *secondary changes* of adolescence, have to do with detachment and autonomy, with sexuality and intimacy, and with achievement and identity. We shall consider each of these problems later in this chapter, after considering the primary changes and adolescents' social participations in greater detail in the following two sections.

Primary changes of adolescence

Biological changes

The classic explication of the biological changes which occur at and around puberty is that of Tanner (1962). (Tanner has also written a shorter book on the subject expressly for practitioners, 1961.) Among the most direct consequences for behaviour of the biological changes are those having to do with physical capacities, motor skills, and sexual motivation. Strength and stamina increase, meaning an increase in capacity for both work and play. With practice, motor skills improve considerably. The organs that make reproduction possible begin to mature at the time of puberty and, conjointly with cultural influences, lead to pronounced change in sexual motivation. (See, especially, Ford and Beach, 1951; Katchadourian and Lunde, 1972; and the chapter by Hebbelinck in this volume.)

The body as a social stimulus

Among the more indirect consequences for behaviour of biological change are those stemming from the reaction of others to the body as a social stimulus. Parents, peers, and others react not only to changes in stature but in the secondary sex characteristics:

> In male and female human beings they include pubic and axillary (under-arm) hair. Deepening of the voice occurs in both sexes, although it is more marked in the male. Facial hair begins to appear in boys; other body regions including the chest, forearms, and legs may also become more hirsute. The female breast is a secondary sex character and growth of this structure is usually rather rapid at the time of puberty. In males, the shoulders tend to become wider and in females the hips undergo similar alteration (Ford and Beach, 1951, p. 170).

As the appearance characteristics change, so does the stimulus value of the body to others. Assumptions and inferences about overall maturity, interests, attitudes, and desirability as a friend and sexual partner are made by comparing the body-as-observed to cultural norms. The adolescent is one of the most important evaluators of his body as social stimulus.

Variability in onset

One of the most important—and most often ignored—characteristics of the biological change at puberty is the variability in the time of its onset. In boys, for example, the sequence may begin between 10 years and $13\frac{1}{2}$ years with an acceleration of growth in the testes and scrotum. If this sequence is considered to end at the time of first ejaculation, it may be noted that average age is $13\frac{1}{2}$ to 14 but that this may occur earlier or later depending upon when the process began. What should be noted here is that, given two boys of the same chronological age, one may complete the sequence before the other has begun it. One is, therefore, exposed to a totally different set of internal and external stimuli (in the reactions of others) than the other. The studies of the impact of early versus late maturing are among the strangest in the literature of adolescence and reveal behavioural consequences of early and late maturing which persist into adulthood (see, e.g., Faust, 1960; Jones, 1965; and Peskin, 1967). At between 13 and 15, for example, male late maturers exhibit greater talkativeness, activity, lack of uninhibitedness, tension, and bossiness than do earlier maturers. This pattern of behaviour is suggestive of both less maturity and compensatory negative attention-getting. The social advantages of early maturity continue into adulthood past that time when differences in physique are no longer present. In their 30s, early maturers have higher occupational status, are more likely to have supervisory or managerial positions, and report more active social lives (Jones, 1957). The persistent differences suggest that early maturers achieve in a conforming way whereas late maturers' achievements are more idiosyncratic. The early maturer is likely to be conventional in cognitive patterns and attitudes as well. A great flexibility and adaptability is characteristic of the late maturer; he copes with life situations 'with tolerance of ambiguity and of individual idiosyncracies, with perceptiveness, and with playfulness in the service of the ego' (Jones, 1965, pp. 908–909). Thus as Peskin has suggested (1967), it appears that the greater social advantage of the early maturer may be accompanied by a premature closure of self-definition and subsequent conventionality. The approbation of early biological change by peers and adults leads then to the adoption of conventional roles by the adolescent and a consequent identity foreclosure. Put in terms of our model, variability in onset of biological change interacts with cultural concepts of valued body types and gender roles (as these are encountered in the family, peer group, and school) to produce secondary changes in identity.

Secular trends

In so far as the defining and decisive events of adolescence are seen as shaped by the onset of puberty, adolescence itself can be said to have been prolonged over the past decades not only by mass scholarization (see Husén) but by the earlier and earlier onset of the growth spurt and sexual maturation. These changes are documented in the chapters by Hebbelinck and Milani-Comparetti. Less well documented are the behavioural consequences of secular trends for successive cohorts of adolescents, accompanied as both have been by greater relative affluence, the advent of mass communication and consequent diffusion of 'liberal' mores, and decreases in the difference between the chronological ages of parents and their children at puberty. Perhaps the most important point is that secular trends combine with scholarization to prolong the period of transition at *both* ends of the period and it is at the latter end that exclusion from fully adult prerogatives would appear to have its most important consequences.

Cognitive change

The developmental theory of Jean Piaget posits a major and radical change in cognitive organization and ability during adolescence (Inhelder and Piaget, 1958). Piaget deals with the development of modes of cognition over time through the individual's encounter with his environment. Cognitive structure consists of various schemata (internal perceptions of the organization of reality) and operations (possible manipulations of the elements of given realities). As an individual develops, certain changes occur in internal schemata and in available operations. The cumulative effect of these changes is a radical restructuring of the modes of selecting and processing information from the environment.

Before adolescence, an individual's cognition is tied to those objects and events with which he has had direct experience. Piaget terms this the period of 'concrete operations'; these are tied to concrete realities, excluding the hypothetical and the logically abstract. Such operations depend on the personal experience of the individual with the objects or events in question.

During early adolescence a change in cognitive organization may occur. The individual becomes capable of freeing his reasoning from dependence upon the concrete attributes of an object or event. He can now see these attributes as one combination of all the possible combinations of attributes. He can reason about the possible as well as the apparent and apply his reasoning about what might be to what is. He can consider the abstract and the hypothetical. Logical operations such as classification, relationship, reciprocity, and combination can be applied equally well to the abstract as to the concrete. He can operate on hypothetical objects or events which may or may not occur in the real world. He is no longer egocentric; his cognition does not depend on his personal experiences. Piaget has termed this the period of 'formal operations'.

Reasoning, by no longer being tied to the concrete, proceeds by logical isolation of variables and hypothesis testing. Because he is no longer tied to concrete reality, the individual can even 'operate on operations', classifying classifications, relating relations, and so forth. Perhaps the two most important aspects of this cognitive reorganization are that an individual can construct the set of logical possibilities and consider the givens of a real situation as but a subset of all possibilities and that he can think about thought.

The consequences of this cognitive change are extensive for the individual, yet are not the kinds of consequences that are immediately apparent to observers. The adolescent can deal with situations as a whole rather than being caught up by some especially dramatic or otherwise salient feature of immediate perceptual reality. He can consider a situation from many different points of view because he can reason in terms of what might be; in this sense his thought is more flexible. For the same reason, he can entertain many possible explanations of the same set of events. He is ready to see many possible meanings in an object or an event. He can use more abstract concepts—that is, concepts which are more general and free of immediate perceptual givens. He can reason more abstractly, thinking in terms of verbal propositions about objects and events and not only the objects and events themselves. He can, for the first time, think about his own thought.

Although they have been the most studied, the adolescent's new accomplishments are not confined to cognitions of the world of impersonal objects and events. To attach effect to *ideals* (a form of valued possibility); to make interpersonal and social judgements in terms of conditions never seen nor experienced but merely envisaged; and to see the self and others not only in mutual interaction but to see that interaction as in itself subject to the rules and roles of some larger system; and to project one's self into an array of futures (which Mahler argues is one of the hallmarks of the adolescent period): these are some of the more important consequences of being able to look at the world as it could be instead of as it is. There is considerable recent interest in these achievements (Hill and Palmquist, 1974) and the next 25 years of the study of adolescents are likely to focus upon their consequences for the secondary changes of adolescence.

Age at onset of formal operations

Empirical research devoted to confirming Piagetian notions about formal operations is sparse compared to that devoted to the phenomena of the pre-operational and the concrete operational stages. The number of studies has, however, been accelerating over the past few years and there seems little doubt that the kinds of change Inhelder and Piaget (1958) describe do begin to be seen in adolescence (Brainerd, 1971; Dulit, 1972; Elkind, 1961; Kirk, 1972). Inhelder and Piaget themselves studied students in Swiss secondary schools who were preparing for the baccalaureate examination. In this college-preparatory group the onset of formal operations was identified as occurring in 11 to 12 year-olds and their consolidation in 14 to 15 year-olds. In a somewhat less selected group, Peel (1972) reports the modal onset of 'invoking possibilities' as occurring between 13 and 14 (two years later than in Inhelder and Piaget) and consolidation coming only after 15 and often later. Relational concepts pertaining to equilibrium and change whether in biological, social, or physical domains are especially late in emerging (Peel, 1971).

But to say that a new stage emerges at any point in the second decade is to say nothing about its universality. It is fairly well established empirically that formal operations are not as inevitable or universal a step in development as are concrete operations. In a sample of gifted high school students, Everett Dulit found that only 75% of subjects beyond the age of 11 attain formal operations on some of the Piaget tasks (Dulit, 1972; Kirk, 1972; Martorano, 1973). In the light of these data, Dulit has suggested that formal operations are a 'characteristic potentiality' but not a characteristic of adolescents.

The empirical work of the next 25 years will establish to what extent the variability in the emergence of the posited changes (and their seeming lack of emergence even in adulthood in a substantial portion of the population) is a function of methods of assessment and to what extent it is a function of the absence of environmental conditions which aid their development. In the face of this variability, Piaget (1972) has himself argued that formal operations are likely to be found in those areas of activity in which the individual is particularly invested. If the present level of interest in these issues continues over the next two decades, by the turn of the century it is to be expected that a knowledge base will exist for important changes in curriculum and instruction in schools as well as for better understanding of adolescents' comprehension of social relations and social systems.

Changes in social definition

It has been suggested above that changes in social definition at or around puberty be considered primary only if they are universal within a particular society. This is not meant to deny the importance of social definitions and demands upon adolescents in every society but rather to emphasize the special set of circumstances which exists when there is widespread consensus about norms for the behaviour of a given age group. In such age-graded societies, the norms change for all of those who attain a given age and there is not only consensus among the older generation about what the behaviour of the younger groups should be but support from the younger groups during the period of transition as well. Important rituals, the so-called *rites de passage*, are likely to govern the transitions into and out of a particular period.

In modern societies such fundamental changes are not so apparent. Minimal ages for work roles, for universal military service, or for leaving school may mean sudden and formal redefinitions of rights and obligations for individuals. However, our societies do not invest them with universal meaning. Neither do they all occur at the same time or apply to enough realms of behaviour such that a socially shared, new identity is defined in successive cohorts of individuals. It is the absence of such consensual meaning and definitional processes in complex, industrialized societies to which problematic behaviour in adolescence is often attributed (Mönks and Knoers, 1976). Indeed, the diversity of expectations regarding present conduct and the variety of alternatives for future adult roles which impinge upon the individual adolescent in highly differentiated, urbanized, and mobile societies are among the central features of adolescence in modern societies (Mead, 1958). It is in this context that the press for educational reforms, for work apprenticeship arrangements, for greater articulation between school and work experience should be interpreted. In their chapters in the present volume, Husén and Delors place major emphasis on such education for choice in the face of modernization and change.

Mass communication and adolescence

The several references in the previous chapter to the impact of mass communications on the adolescent experience should not go unremarked here. The mass media do provide a series of images of adolescence which colloquium speakers identified, not as indicative of the kind of organic social definition referred to above, but as stereotypes that may exercise undue influence upon parents (particularly first-time parents) of adolescents, as well as practitioners, policy makers, and adolescents themselves. These stereotypes are often based upon overgeneralizations from current events involving minorities of adolescents (as was the case in the early days of the student movements of the late 1960s). Personal habits and appearance characteristics of deviant or protesting groups are widely publicized and manifestations in younger adolescents of the most superficial of these characteristics become the occasion for oppression and discrimination against the young. Witness the preoccupation with teenagers' hirsuteness in the wake of the 'hippie' movement (*and* its disappearance in the wake of adult adoption of the same styles). Attributions of protest, immorality, violence and criminality to teenagers who wore their hair long were not uncommon. On a less extravagant scale, somewhat isolated instances of adolescent 'deviance' in local communities (e.g., drug abuse, crimes of violence) are likely to be overgeneralized to the total adolescent population. As noted in the previous chapter, the colloquium participants endorsed the recommendation that the quality of public debate about adolescence be improved by finding ways to present more information to parents, practitioners, policy makers and adolescents themselves about more typical adolescent development in a variety of social–cultural settings. At present mass communications about adolescence tend both to overdramatize and to overhomogenize the period.

The primary changes do not exercise their effects in a social vacuum. They derive meaning (for others and for the adolescent himself) from the roles adolescents play in the family, the peer group, and the school.

Social roles of adolescents

The adolescent as son or daughter

Changes in family structure
It was the consensus of the colloquium that the family continues to play a strong role in adolescent development although it was recognized that

currently available information does not permit strong inferences about the relations between changing family structures and particular aspects of cognitive and social development. Certain changes in family structure are described by Piotrowski (Chapter 10). Marriage increasingly is coming to be defined in terms of the opportunities it provides for individual development, or 'self-actualization', as opposed to being justified on the basis of its procreative function. The evolutionary trend toward equalitarianism as the norm for all role relationships is reflected in increasingly less autocratic marital and parent–child relations. Concomitant with these two long term trends are substantial increases in maternal employment and in divorce rates. Piotrowski also calls attention to cohabitation and communal living arrangements, making the (perhaps unexpected) point that despite their superficial differences from the idealized nuclear family, these arrangements function *as* families to provide for basic human needs.

Changes in certain aspects of families and family life have occurred, but their magnitude, their frequency, and their effects on adolescent roles in the family are all subject to misinterpretation, distortion, and propagandizing. This occurs owing to the relative absence of sound research on such topics or, when it is present, to its inaccessibility to policy makers, practitioners, or interpreters of family life in the mass media. The prevalence of persons living out the more flamboyant 'alternative lifestyles' has been exaggerated owing to the frequency of their mention in mass media. In turn the family is said to be 'breaking down' and the loss of its functions for the socialization of the young is mourned.

The extent to which one asserts that families have 'changed' in terms of their socialization functions depends in part upon the length of the time perspective one takes. From the viewpoint of the Rosenmayrs (Chapter 5), for example, there has been a striking change in the degree to which families provide the kind of 'information' that young people need for life in adult society. Seen against a time line in which the industrial revolution and universal education for young people are the significant events, it is certainly the case that the relative role of the family in socialization has diminished over the past 20 decades. In a world of many thousands of occupations of interest to both genders, and of varying instigations to marriage, family, and family-like arrangements the socialization of duplicates has come to be dysfunctional.

However, this generalization can be carried too far. The family, whatever its superficial form, still provides a great deal of information about family roles to its younger members and considerable anticipatory socialization for such roles is provided, if only in terms of definitions of gender-appropriate behaviour, whether traditional or less so. And, whether one is to look upon work as the means of 'buying a lifestyle' or as a bearer of intrinsic satisfactions, attitudes toward work certainly must be influenced by the attitudes of the workers in the family. Similarly, if one considers the family to have shifted from a production unit to a consumption unit (a view with which housekeepers of either gender ought not totally to agree), certainly a wide variety of consumer behaviours and attitudes have their beginnings in family life. Indeed one might argue that the socialization functions of the family in relation to consumption have *increased* markedly over the past few decades (television notwithstanding).

Doubtless, in a time frame that begins with the events that set the industrial revolution into train there have been overall decreases in the informational aspects of adolescent socialization in the family of the kind suggested by the Rosenmayrs. These are part of the process that stripped the family as a unit of those economic, religious, social, recreational, and other functions that it played in pre-industrial, 'kinship' societies organized around it. The family is ill equipped to socialize young people for activities in which it no longer itself participates, let alone dominates as a unit. However, it remains a major source of influence on those behaviours and attitudes that parents do model (the best examples being intimate relationships in general, and parenting itself in particular) and, through its social class position, in the opportunities it makes available for the young person. It serves as the means of access for young people to the bureaucratic organizations which provide services to adolescents (see Piotrowski for examples). It might serve better in this capacity if providers of services took pains to strengthen such linkages. In the years before adolescence, the family provides socialization for the development of those personal and social characteristics which make integration into peer group life possible and developmentally fruitful for the young person. Before and during adolescence it can and usually does provide the emotional security and support which scholars of the family have long agreed is a development-sustaining, major, and continuing function of the family. The role of the family in socialization, then, has changed in degree (if one takes the long perspective). But, perhaps more importantly, it has changed *in kind* and this reflects the change in the role of the family in the larger society itself.

In our view, the reports of the mass media about changes in the family serve best to remind us of not only increasing but long-existing diversity in the lifestyles of adults and youth. There is not one 'the family' that is changing in some linear way. There are many kinds of families in modern societies that are changing in many ways. When what appears to us as a particularly avant-garde, bizarre, or simply new family arrangement is publicized, the conclusion of rapid social change may be advanced. Given the family and individual history of the persons actually involved, change may be illusory. (Recall the similarity of the early activist leaders in the USA to their own parents yet the dissimilarity of both to their working-class observers.) The possibility we wish to suggest, then, is that much (certainly not all) of what we interpret as alarming and rapid change is, instead, the increasing exposure to mass viewing of diversity, or pluralism, in modern society. There is 'real' change to be sure but, in our view, in relation to the family it is not so rapid or dramatic as it is made out to be. The pursuit of equalitarian norms is a long-lived trend in modernizing societies, for example, and likely to continue to characterize the next 25 years as well. There is evolution, not revolution. From this perspective, recent and anticipated changes in adolescent socialization probably can best be characterized as changes in *kind* rather than *degree*. It is not that parents have ceased to be influential in the lives of their sons and daughters. It is that through their own lifestyles, they model *different* kinds of behaviours than did their own parents for them or than do parents 'on the other side of town' or in other neighbourhoods. Through what they sanction in the behaviour of their sons and daughters (e.g., activities that shape individual personality as opposed to loyalty to the kinship group), they socialize their children to different values, attitudes, and behaviour than did their own parents or than do parents in other neighbourhoods.

Socialization in the family

The above examples call attention to the two most marked means of socialization in childhood: modelling (or *imitation*) and direct tuition, or *reinforcement learning* (that is, socialization which depends upon the consequences that the physical and social environment provides for the behaviour emitted). These processes as such have been little studied in adolescents (particularly in relation to the primary changes). However, phenomenological studies of adolescent attitudes toward parental sanctions and toward parents as models strongly support the generalization that parental influence on decision making concerning future occupational achievement, as opposed to transitory peer group customs, is stronger than that of the peer group (Brittain, 1963; Kandel and Lesser, 1972). Both the Rosenmayrs (Chapter 5), Piotrowski (Chapter 10), and our reading of the colloquium proceedings remind us of the critical importance of familial support for learning. (The great majority of the variance in school achievement continues to be attributable to parental and socioeconomic variables.) There are other examples.

As Hartup (Chapter 11) points out, adolescent use of marijuana is affected not only by peer usage but by parental usage of psychotropic drugs as well. Similarly, Kooy (1972) recently reported that certain liberal and equalitarian attitudes toward sexuality were characteristic of adolescents. These attitudes represented a change from traditional values; however, it was found that the adolescents' parents themselves held the non-traditional values. As a final example, one might point again to the value agreements characteristic of the activist youth leaders and their parents. There is evidence, then, that what from the viewpoint of the larger or dominant society may be traditional *or* non-traditional values and behaviours continue to be strongly influenced by parents. The presence of what may be seen as deviant or non-traditional values in adolescents and youth, then, should *not* be taken as evidence of the breakdown of socialization in the family as it so often is in dealing with adolescence.

The study of the witting and unwitting consequences that parents provide for their adolescents' behaviour and the study of the models their own behaviour provides for adolescents has not proceeded much beyond using the paradigms of research done in early childhood. Research on basic socialization processes in adolescence needs to be done which takes the primary changes of adolescence into account. Certainly the individual who is now capable of taking many perspectives into account at the same time is likely to respond differently to parental sanctions than the child who cannot. Effective interventions with adolescents, not only on the part of parents but of other adults as well, depends upon our increased understanding of such processes.

In a similar vein, any inventory of important but undone research on adolescent development would include the study of the effects of divorce and maternal employment on adolescent development. Indeed, studies on effects during childhood are so few in number that it is unclear whether age at which maternal employment begins is at all important in accounting for the effects of unemployment. As was pointed out at the colloquium, however, those studies which have been done have failed to turn up *negative* effects of employment on cognitive or social development. Indeed, Piotrowski reports that children of working mothers might be advantaged in that the latter are more likely than non-working mothers to make time expressly for activities with their children as opposed simply to monitoring their behaviour while doing other things. In this area, as in many others, however, it is not clear whether the child perceives the situation as one in which greater attention is being received let alone whether such primary attention has any of the beneficial effects assumed for it. We raise this point both because it is important in itself and because it illustrates another serious gap in family research—that is, studies which simultaneously examine aspects of family structure or employment *and* developmental outcomes. The more usual procedure is to investigate the first and *assume* certain effects on child or adolescent development and behaviour.

Socioeconomic status and family influence

One of the major aspects of diversity in the adolescent experience has to do with socioeconomic status. The socioeconomic status of the family determines the opportunities for learning and development within the family. The Rosenmayrs (Chapter 5) document some of the differences between working- and middle-class adolescents in the development of cultural interests and activities, for example. Differences such as those reported should give pause to those who think of the adolescent experience in some homogeneous way, usually that associated either with theories equating normality and mental health with the absence of symptoms in upper middle-class neurotics or deviance and illness with the 'acting-out' behaviour of delinquents. If research is to be relevant to social policy over the next few decades, it seems essential that investigations of adolescence be based upon conceptions which take sociocultural diversity as a given. These must be studies which do more than measure simple differences between adolescents of varying social status on a few isolated variables. Such investigations (which are legion in the annals of the study of early childhood) have two major deficiencies important for the development of social policy. In the first place they invite interpretations based upon deficiency models, that is, interpretations in which the responses of the middle class become the norm. The characteristics of working- or lower-class adolescents come to be defined in terms of the *absence* of middle-class characteristics as opposed to the *presence* of attributes which may be advantageous within such a subculture and indeed, in society in general (either as it is or as it might be). Second, studies that simply compare adolescents of varying social class levels in regard to one or more attributes do not provide much in the way of advancement in knowledge, whether judged by canons of science or social policy. Such studies should always include variables within the same design which permit either the explanation of, or the reduction of possible explanations for, the differences observed. It is difficult to know how to go about effecting some social change, no matter how desirable, without some knowledge of *why* the differences found are maintained. In so far as different values (e.g., a greater degree of fatalism in working and lower classes, a tendency to believe that events outside one's own control play the major role in one's life) and different child-rearing strategies (a greater authoritarianism in working- and lower-class families) are characteristic of varying social class levels, effects of maternal employment and divorce may well have differential effects on adolescent outcomes, achievement striving, for example.

The adolescent as peer

The youth movements of the late 1960s called public attention to the possible existence of a youth society or youth culture independent of adult society. Actually this issue had surfaced about five years earlier in the social science literature with the publication of Coleman's *The adolescent society* (1961). In the absence of actual studies of parents, Coleman asserted that:

> The adolescent lives more and more in a society of his own. He finds the

family a less and less satisfying home. As a consequence, the home has less and less ability to mold him (p. 312).

The past 15 years have seen many studies of the issues sparked by Coleman's work and by the attention to youth culture and counterculture instigated by the youth movements and the widespread publicity about them. Over and over again, these studies have documented the existence of 'adolescent societies' and the importance of peers as social influence agents. However, the studies have also demonstrated repeatedly that the connections between adolescent societies and adult society are far more robust than those postulated by Coleman and others.

The most comprehensive empirical response to Coleman's thesis is that of Kandel and Lesser (1972) who studied adolescents and their parents in Denmark and in the USA. Their findings confirmed those of other investigators. As had Brittain (1963), they found that 'there is no doubt that with respect to future life goals, in both countries, parental influence is much stronger than peer influence' (p. 183). As had Coleman, they found that the adolescent social climate did not often reward intellectual achievement in high school, 'but peers have less influence on adolescents than parents with regard to future educational goals' (p. 166). As had Douvan and Adelson (1966), they found that close and harmonious relationships with parents were the rule and not the exception, even while the adolescents were well integrated into adolescent peer groups. In neither society was there evidence for an adolescent society totally differentiated from that of adults. And, as had Hollingshead's (1949) classic community study of adolescence argued, Kandel and Lesser's data

> argue against the 'exclusive' view—the assumption that the stronger the rejection of adult standards, the stronger the acceptance of peer standards and, conversely, the stronger the commitment to adult standards, the less the need for accepting peer influence. Our data lead to a contrary view: In critical areas, interactions with peers support, express, and specify for the peer context the values of parents and other adults; and the adolescent subculture is coordinated with, and in fact is a particular expression of, the culture of the larger society (p. 168).

Earlier Hollingshead had put the matter in a slightly different way:

> *The social behavior of adolescents appears to be related functionally to the positions their families occupy in the social structure of the community . . . Children's be-*

havior patterns are established primarily by their early experience in the family and secondarily in the neighborhood; and similar experiences in the family and neighborhood mold children into similar social types because their learning in both areas tends to be strongly associated with class (p. 444).

In view of these data, one may ask why the notion that adolescent and youth societies are independent cultures (or, indeed, countercultures) has been so widespread and so persistent. Kandel and Lesser (1972) suggest one reason:

The young ... express more openly and often more effectively the internal divisions that exist within society at large. It may be less threatening to adults to attribute differences to generations when they actually emanate between race, class, or interest lines within adult society itself (p. 185).

We present this information not to deny the influences of peer relations upon development in adolescence and youth—far from it—but rather to suggest that peer influence must be viewed in the light of the broad and diverse familial and sociocultural contexts in which it occurs. There have been and continue to be *many* adolescent and youth cultures as there are adult cultures, not only those of the type identified with the youth movements. In his chapter, Hartup describes some aspects of the diversity in peer relations during adolescence. But his major contribution is the demonstration of the importance of peer relations in terms of the more universal and facilitative functions they serve for human development, a point likely to be ignored in science and policy making which begins with the assumption that peer influence is necessarily antagonistic to that of adults.

Peer relationships and peer influence obviously do not begin in adolescence. From early childhood onward, the range of social relations gradually expands, and children are presented with the opportunities and dangers for personal development of group membership, acceptance, acquaintanceship and friendship, status and power, and conformity. During early adolescence these matters, objectively and subjectively, take on a new colouration and importance owing to the primary changes of adolescence. Physical and sexual maturation provide new bases for evaluation and acceptance and individual differences in maturation, and as was seen above in the studies of early and late maturing adolescents, may have profound consequences for subsequent development. The onset of formal operations may provide, for some, a new basis for evaluating conflicting perspectives of parents, other adults, and peers of diverse backgrounds and different values. As Hartup (pp. 171–175) points out, important consequences may follow for the development of aggression, sexuality, intimacy, and morality. Individual differences during early adolescence may mean that earlier established relations of prestige and acceptance in a given neighbourhood or school-related peer group shift markedly. Unfortunately, what might be done to facilitate development during early adolescence, given the primary changes and the variability which characterizes them, is often lost sight of in social policy making which is more responsive to real (or imagined) historical trends than to questions about individual development. In the remainder of this necessarily brief exposition of peer relations, we will first focus on such historical changes and second on highlighting some of the consequences of peer relations for development.

Age-grading, age groups, and age segregation

In every society known to scholarship, age (along with gender) is a primary basis for differential behaviour expectations. How the life cycle is partitioned varies from society to society but the partitioning is spoken of as *age-grading* and of the phases in the life cycle to which differential expectations apply is referred to as an age grade. In some societies, social life is organized in such a way that most of the important interactions among individuals occur between those in the same age grade. In such societies we have *age groups* and not only age grades. Eisenstadt (1956) has suggested that age groups are particularly common during the phase we call adolescence. Adolescent or youth groups are characteristic of non-kinship societies—that is, those societies in which the major roles, political, economic, and social, lie outside the family. Membership in the society as a whole is direct and does not come about by virtue of one's membership in a particular kinship, descent, or family group. Modern, highly industrialized, and urbanized societies constitute the most extreme example of non-kinship societies.

Why should youth groups emerge under these conditions and not in kinship-based societies? Eisenstadt (1956) argues that the norms young persons learn in families are particularistic, whereas the norms required to govern behaviour in adult roles in a non-kinship society are universalistic. The distinction is:

> Whether individuals are treated as members of categories or as special cases ... To say that children learn the norm of universality is to say that they come to accept being treated by others as members of categories *in addition to* being treated as special cases as in the family (Dreeben, 1967, pp. 40–41).

For society, the function of youth groups is to provide continuity from generation to generation by training young persons in universalistic values. For the individual, the function of youth groups is to provide socialization for adult roles which cannot be learned in the family unit. Three kinds of youth groups are to be found in modern societies: schools, youth organizations, and spontaneous groups.

The advent of nearly universal secondary education and the growth of higher education has provided the occasion for the segregation of young persons from adult society: '. . . the high school has performed an important, although originally unintended and unforeseen, function in promoting socialization by the peer group' (Coleman *et al.*, 1974, p. 27); at the level of higher education, the existence of university and dormitory communities serves the same function and, indeed, has been credited as playing no small role in the facilitation of recent youth movements (Flacks, 1971). Whatever the superficial and time-bound social and political consequences of such segregation, it may be argued that schools and their associated youth groups provide a variety of arrangements for the learning of universalistic norms. All children in a given class are given a single set of tasks to perform. Age, a universal category, is the basis for assignment to a particular classroom. The transition from one grade to another associates each age-grade category with a set of arrangements that differs markedly from the child's interactions in the family where, even though in the category *child*, the young person is likely to hear behaviour justified on particularistic grounds of family membership. Equalitarian values are likely to be stressed more than in the familial context. Perhaps most importantly, schools provide the occasion and the site for the development of 'informal' (non-adult-organized) and yet often highly structured peer groups and the arena for a variety of spontaneous peer relations outside the immediate supervision of parents and other adults.

Organizations for adolescents and youth, ranging from scouting groups which include early and middle adolescents through organizations for youth affiliated with political parties, segregate the young from their elders (relative to allowing participation in the society through association with and through the family in social life). At the same time, they provide occasions for informal and spontaneous interaction as do schools. Some colloquium participants stressed the apparent decline in appeal of these organizations for young people. Organizations for younger adolescents very often do not acknowledge their biological or cognitive maturity or the diversity of pre-adolescent experience. The programmes of young people's political organizations, being dependent upon adult interests, often do not provide opportunities for the examination of conflicting ideologies or for the initiation of activity that might train people for active citizenship roles. As Hollingshead (1949) pointed out:

> The youth-training institutions provided by the culture are essentially negative in their objectives, for they segregate adolescents from the real world that adults know and function in. By trying to keep the maturing child ignorant of this world of conflict and contradictions, adults think they are keeping him 'pure' (p. 149).

Age groups associated with school or youth organizations in modern non-kinship societies do seem to differ from their counterparts in primitive or traditional non-kinship societies. In the latter, membership in a youth group is legitimated by the larger society and the youth group is usually allocated some important role in it, the warrior role, for example. The entry into the new age grade and age group is likely to be celebrated by some initiation rite that symbolically confirms the individual's new status in the society and recognizes his newfound sexual and physical maturity (or its imminence) as well as his status in the new role. These conditions do not obtain in modern societies. As Eisenstadt has remarked, the situation is a paradoxical one. On the one hand, modern societies may be characterized by a 'consciousness of youth' and increasing industrialization everywhere brings with it an increasing concern about the problematic nature of adolescence and youth. On the other hand, adolescent and youth groups are less likely to be assigned legitimate roles. Both the school and the organized youth group focus on preparation for life, not on life itself. There is no *job* to do, as there is in the universalistic primitive or traditional society and there is no universal legitimation or celebration entailed in achieving the new status and the new identity connected with it (Eisenstadt, 1956). Spontaneous groups, on the other hand, offer a kind of life in the present instead of a promise for the future. And, unlike the school or organized groups, they are likely to give explicit recognition to the young person's physical and sexual maturity. Many contemporary efforts at the development of social programmes for the facilitation of adolescent development are attempts to substitute participation for preparation. Unfortunately their effects upon the development of adolescents who are growing up in varying contexts are not well known and not much investigated, however critical they are both for scientific understanding and for policy making.

Peer relations and development during adolescence

In the above discussion we have noted frequently that school and organized youth groups have increased and prolonged opportunities for spontaneous peer interaction. We turn now to a brief examination of some effects, or possible effects, of such interaction on development during adolescence. In his chapter, Hartup makes a useful distinction between surface structures of peer behaviour and those basic, universal dimensions which underlie it. The surface structures, of which 'lifestyles' are a good example, are somewhat ephemeral, changing from cohort to cohort and sometimes even within cohorts, but are nonetheless important: 'The salience of these structures cannot be over-stated. Adolescents themselves are preoccupied with them, parents obsess overtly about them, and they furnish endless amounts of copy for editorial writers and television broadcasters' (Hartup, p. 181). It is often the minutiae of day-to-day life in and customs of the peer groups that are the subjects of conflict in the family, presumably in part because changes in the customs and rituals of young people's peer group lives are taken as symbols of profound social change when in fact they are characteristic of the cohort only and, if that, only during the adolescent years. (The relative stability of social, political, and economic institutions in most highly industrialized societies from generation to generation suggests that each new generation could not have gone to the dogs.) Hartup suggests that the surface elements of peer relations will continue to change rapidly over the next few decades and that the range of diversity will increase. A greater pluralization of lifestyles is to be expected in society, in general, and will certainly be reflected in the adolescent experience and society's consciousness of adolescence.

Social preoccupation with what changes in adolescent surface culture presage leads to insufficient attention in policy making to the deeper dimensions of life with peers: the effects peers have had, have, and will continue to have—whatever the superficial changes in peer relations—upon the modulation of aggression and sexuality, the development of intimacy and, perhaps the development of principled moral judgements. With regard to the latter, for example, we have already noted Eisenstadt's (1956) argument that universalistic norms, e.g., egalitarianism, require the relatively egalitarian, 'peer' nature of adolescent and youth groups for their development. Piaget (1932) has also argued that an egalitarian morality does not develop in an authoritarian institution like the family. The interest of policy makers and practitioners in changes in the more superficial aspects of adolescent peer cultures threatens to crowd out continuing support for developing and disseminating basic knowledge about the underlying processes and dimensions of peer relations, to retard building the knowledge base about precisely those issues which would be critical if we wished to understand how to facilitate development as opposed to remedying adolescent trouble.

Cross-age interaction
Recent years have seen a number of programmes designed, at least in part, to reduce age segregation of adolescents by arranging interaction with both younger (cross-age tutoring) and older persons (apprenticeship, community action, volunteering in nursing homes for the aged). We believe that such programmes can have value for adolescents. Among other things, they can contribute to the fund of information the adolescent has about the variety of life careers possible in a highly complex society and thus they can facilitate later choice. However, it does seem to us that often the programmes are encouraged and promoted on the basis that they decrease opportunities young persons might have to spend with peers and that they therefore decrease the risk of some kind of 'contamination' by peers. The pull of peer relations for most youngsters during adolescence is probably too great for programmes devised on this value

base to be effective. And where the programmes are effective, it is to be hoped that this is not at the expense of practising how to live with one's own age-mates—and not in the sense of sociability alone, although that is important too, but in the sense captured by the notion of the secondary changes of adolescence. There is no serious scholar of the period (with the possible exception of the Freuds) who has not seen peer relations as *indispensable* in some way or another to dealing with the major issues of adolescence: whether it be the integration of sexuality and intimacy into the gender role (Sullivan, 1953); the transformation of identity (Erikson, 1968); or the development of autonomy (Douvan and Adelson, 1966). Indeed, as Hartup points out (pp. 177–180), there is some evidence that poor peer relations during adolescence presage subsequent social and psychological pathology in adulthood.

The adolescent as student

We have already noted (as do Husén, Delors, and the Rosenmayrs in their chapters) the historical ties between the emergence of 'mass scholarization' and the major phenomena of adolescence itself. Both the summary report of the colloquium and Husén's chapter describe what we and other colloquium participants see as major features of secondary schools today and some of their effects on adolescent development. The chapters by Husén and Delors describe the history, recent trends, and some of the 'alternative futures' of the relation between school and work. We do not wish to reiterate or reintegrate this complex set of issues here. Instead we will make three points: first, that there is little research information available to support claims for non-cognitive effects of school programmes for adolescents; second, that an important and complex policy issue for the near future is the extent to which schools should and can build effective programmes of non-cognitive education; and third, that research on the conjoint effects of family, peer group, and schooling will be required for framing sensible policy.

Effects of schools on development

There are numerous studies available in educational journals of the effects of various curricula, instructional practices, and institutional arrangements

3

on intellectual development, attitudes toward schools and education (see Husén), and performance on achievement tests and simple cognitive learning tasks. However, the literature on effects of various schooling arrangements on other developmental or behavioural outcomes at the secondary level is sparse indeed. In preparing to write this chapter, for example, one of us surveyed the last 10 years of publication of a prestigious journal of educational psychology and found that only about $7\frac{1}{2}\%$ of the pages published during that period were given over to studies that dealt with any outcome of schooling other than some kind of intellectual achievement itself (and only a handful of the papers with adolescents). That this is not an artifact of sampling is suggested by a similar survey of *Child Development Abstracts and Bibliography* (which regularly abstracts some 200 journals relating to development); in this case, only 0.39% of the articles over the past decade dealt with effects of schooling on non-achievement-related variables. Outside the important but narrow realm of cognitive development and achievement, there is little information on effects of schooling on development. This is an important omission not only for our basic understanding of schools as a context for development but for social policy as well.

Consider the common argument that the authoritarian cast of secondary schools is inimical to the development of autonomy; Boocock's (1972) assertion that passivity is universally a primary feature of the student role is cited in the recent Report to the President (of the USA) from the Panel on Youth (Coleman *et al.*, 1974) in support of the general argument that schools are not effective in preparing young persons for adult roles. A variety of policy changes is advocated. What is striking here is the absence of any evidence (to our knowledge) that shows even a modest correlational relation, let alone a causal one, between some kind of educational arrangement and the development of autonomy. Furthermore, there appears to be no evidence that secondary schools are any more authoritarian in terms of child-rearing than are parents or other socialization agents, while there *is* substantial and consistent evidence, recently reviewed by Hill and Steinberg (1976), for a negative relation between parental authoritarianism and the development of autonomy during adolescence. (And this is true whether the measure of autonomy is assertiveness in parent–child interaction, feelings of self-confidence and trust in personal judgements, or perceived independence.) Our point here is not that we believe that schools have no effect, or a lesser effect than parents, but only that more information is required if a sensible policy is to be framed. As has been the case in dealing with real and imagined changes in the nature of the family and their effects on adolescents and with real and imagined changes in the peer group and their effects on adolescents, so it is with the schools: there has been greater scientific and public interest in documenting the changes than in actually studying their effects upon critical aspects of development. Those who are normally fastidious in their empirical analyses of institutions and institutional change (or, if not scientists, in their call for 'hard data' on which to base policy) appear sometimes to be less demanding of information about the actual effect on development of the posited changes.

Athletic programmes, recreational programmes, sex-education efforts, parenting education—extracurricular and curricular activities of various kinds—are traditionally justified, supported, or opposed on the basis that they change attitudes, develop self-confidence, self-understanding or mis-understanding; promote self-esteem and greater social responsibility; or teach cooperation, teamwork and self-discipline. The plea for the partici-pation of young persons in creating their future was made repeatedly in the colloquium, featured in Mahler's paper, and the major, general recommendation of the Panel on Youth's report is based on a similar rationale. We urge that the future bring not only increased opportunities for participation but increasing opportunities for the serious study of its effects on behavioural development.

As Dreeben has put it in his critique of the Panel's report:

The third straw man is the pervasive and tacit assumption, running through the Panel's discussion of issues and presentation of alternatives, that there is something wrong with the way youth now makes the transition to adulthood. Indeed, this may be a correct assumption; the problem with it is that it remains tacit. For if there is one point about which the Panel might have sought empirical evidence, even if sketchy or indirect, it is whether present arrangements—based on the preemption of youth by school and the segregation of youth from those different in age—impede maturity, exact undue psychological costs, narrow perspectives, and create the in-capacities that the Panel would have us believe, its proposed alternatives might restore. Without this crucial evidence, the Panel's argument crumbles, and its recommendations become little more than interesting talking points (Dreeben, 1974, pp. 45–46).

Objectives of schools for development

The dichotomy we have suggested above in considering what we know and do not know about *effects* of schooling—that between cognitive and achievement-oriented outcomes and other developmental outcomes—may also be considered in terms of the *objectives* of schools at the secondary level. As was noted in the previous chapter:

> Criticisms of and demands made upon the school systems are: it is excessively knowledge centered, with overemphasis on cognitive goals, neglecting to foster and develop affective aesthetic, ethical and other aspects of personality . . .

The extent to which schools should take on programmes designed to foster the latter kinds of development will be a major social policy issue in the decades ahead. This seems likely to be true in the USA as well as in many European societies. In the former case, schools have already taken on such programmes and the Panel on Youth has suggested that they divest themselves of them. Heyneman's (1976) recent summary of the Panel's recommendations is helpful:

> The point is what to do about the process which has hoisted the plethora of noncognitive functions into the school: the teaching of driver's education, a boggling array of sports, metal shop, environmental, ethnic, career, and sex education, all taking place under one institutional roof commonly accommodating several thousands of adolescents at a given time. The members of the Panel on Youth suggest, and there is sufficient evidence to take them seriously, that: (1) the schools' most efficient function is the transfer of academic skills; (2) that the school itself should be honed down and expected to do primarily what it does best; while (3) other experimental institutions be developed to specialize in whatever local variety of noncognitive experiences the parent and child wish to negotiate with the help of vouchers. One by-product might be the opportunity to have smaller public schools, which are, by all agreement, nicer places to be. Thus the expectations attributable to the 'school' could become consistent with what it does best (p. 35).

The fundamental question raised by the Panel's recommendation is whether the school *can* devise programmes that meet both kinds of objectives within the same structure. Bureaucratization and the hierarchical organization of large schools and school systems along with opposition between school and home culture may militate against meeting non-cognitive objectives. There is now a body of literature which shows, for example, that there are far greater opportunities for participation and leadership in small high schools than in large ones for individual adolescents (e.g., Barker and Gump, 1964). More students participate in more, different activities in the smaller schools than in large ones and the satisfactions they report are those of active participation (increases in confidence, cooperative skills, leadership schools) as opposed to passive observation. In terms of cultural conflicts, educational programmes which make sense to some parents and community leaders may not to others (e.g., sex education). Traditional cognitive objectives may motivate teachers in a community of affluent parents who view self-development as more important. Under such conditions, controversial programmes may not be included at all or, if so, offered in such sterile, 'non-ideological' and 'cognitive' ways as to vitiate their effectiveness for the stated non-cognitive objectives. Some increased social experimentation in the facilitation of adolescent development appears important within the next few decades. It seems undesirable either to 'hone down' the school without other available options in place or to embark on a course which adds non-cognitive programmes on a large scale to an institution which may not be able to meet non-cognitive objectives.

The school and other institutions

As we have pointed out before, schools provide occasions for the formation of peer groups and other forms of peer relations. The positive impact of peer relations on many aspects of non-cognitive development has been well documented (see Hartup) while there is clear evidence that some kinds of peer associational networks undermine achievement and achievement striving in students of all ability ranges (Coleman, 1961). (In the many schools where academic success is not a criterion for membership of peer groups of the highest status, the average gap between ability and actual achievement is likely to be greater, for example.) Paradoxically, then, we have two sets of institutions in a symbiotic relation, each of which may support different, and conflicting goals. We can find no studies in which both sets of influences are examined within the same design. Whereas, above, we complained about the lack of available information on the impact of schools on non-cognitive developmental outcomes, our point now is that schools do not exercise their effects in a vacuum. Both our understanding of adolescent development and social policy regarding adolescence and youth will profit in the coming decades from considering the interrelations among the various contexts for development and their conjoint effects upon it. This is true not only for the peer group and the school but for the family and the school as well. From increased understanding of the fit between school culture and various home cultures in given communities may come the only viable solutions to questions of a non-cognitive role for the schools.

Thus far, we have considered the primary changes of adolescence (biological, psychological, and social) and the adolescent son or daughter, peer, and student roles. We have argued that society and culture as the adolescent knows them are mediated by the expectations, sanctions, and models that these three forms of social participation provide. (We have not considered here some less universal adolescent roles, those of worker and citizen, for example, but their potential significance is made clear in many of the following chapters. Indeed, demands for wider participation in these roles are hallmarks of current policy proposals, as we have noted above.) The transformations in adolescent behaviour which have most caught the eye of students of the period and which preoccupy social observers (and critics) of the period are secondary to, that is, the resultants of, complicated interrelations among the primary changes and the adolescents' social participations as these impinge upon the biopsychological make-up the individual brings to the adolescent era. We turn now to a brief consideration of some of the more important of these secondary changes: autonomy and detachment, sexuality and intimacy, achievement, and identity. In large measure to take as a general policy objective the *facilitation* of adolescent development—as opposed to remedying the problems adolescents are seen as creating for society—is to commit oneself to an increased understanding of these secondary changes and to examine critically how changes in institutional arrangements might affect them.

Secondary changes of adolescence

Detachment and autonomy

Although a posited change in emotional ties to parents at puberty is the key feature of at least one part-theory of adolescence (A. Freud, 1958), and the problem is an important one in its own right; empirically, we know next to nothing about the process of detachment itself. This conclusion stands in sharp contrast to the speculations in the media, in textbooks and in policy making based upon the assumption that a unitary trait, motive, or need called *independence-striving* underlies much of adolescent behaviour. What evidence exists on the matter provides no support for and, indeed, contradicts such a claim (Hill and Steinberg, 1976). Ignored in discussions of what might constitute a 'normal' transformation of the relationship to parent figures at and during adolescence and youth are the degree of emotional bonding common in the society before adolescence; and the community's definition of what constitutes an appropriate relationship with one's parents when one is an adult. For example, normative emotional development in working-class communities in London as described by Young and Willmott (1964) includes frequent contact among adult family members of different generations. What is needed are studies of *transformations* in emotional ties at and during adolescence and youth in varying social contexts instead of speculations about some universal underlying need.

Similarly, if we wish to facilitate the process we need to learn how detachment, or emotional autonomy, might relate to independence of decision making (behavioural autonomy), the acquisition of principled moral thought (moral autonomy) or the development of a sense of personal values (value autonomy). At present the best-informed hypothesis is that the latter two forms are characteristic acquisitions of the youth period rather than of adolescence (Kohlberg, 1973; Douvan and Adelson, 1966) and they may therefore depend in some way upon the acquisition of the earlier, more external, forms.

The literature is particularly lacking in sound measures of autonomous behaviour in adolescents themselves (as opposed to the presence of many scales which tap the tendency of parents to grant autonomy, generally as this is seen by the adolescents). From what may be pieced together, it appears that extreme permissiveness or extremely authoritarian parenting facilitates continued dependence upon parents and slavish peer conformity (Devereux, 1970; Douvan and Adelson, 1966). But in the more modal case, it is not at all clear what the interplay is between increased responsiveness to peers as attachment objects, as models, as reinforcers of independent decision making and changes in responsiveness to parents. Whatever the process, it seems clear that adolescence is a more pacific period in contemporary society than would be predicted were the psychoanalytic hypothesis that rebelliousness is the avenue to autonomy the most useful one (Douvan and Adelson, 1966).

Over the next quarter century, we suspect that the major public policy and scientific questions related to the development of autonomy in adolescence will have to do with the nature of schools and the impact of the school experience. As we have noted above it has been suggested that passivity is a primary characteristic of the student role everywhere (Boocock, 1972). Indeed, secondary schools have not been without critics who assert that the continued reinforcement of obeisance to authority is what they are best at (see, for example, Friedenberg, 1967). The question ahead seems to be whether we can diversify the school experience and design new, complementary institutions that facilitate autonomy. The American President's Scientific Advisory Commission's Panel on Youth (1973) has made several suggestions in this regard. These have two characteristics in common: the promotion of incidental learning, learning not 'packaged' in ways which invite the assumption of traditional student–teacher roles; and the creation of roles in which adolescents bear increasing responsibility for the lives of other persons.

Sexuality and intimacy

Reiss (1973) has characterized the changes in sexual attitudes and behaviour over the past seven or eight decades as expressions of an increasing equalitarianism in gender roles:

> The human sexual relationship is becoming less one of male satisfaction of body-centered sexuality supported by masculine peer groups. It is becoming more a part of an equalitarian relationship that involves more than just physical attraction. Physical attraction as a base for sexuality will, of course continue as long as humans exist. A great deal of human sexuality will be

done simply for pleasure. The point I am making is that there will increasingly be mutual pleasure and not a double-standard emphasis on masculine pleasure . . . There is then a bimodal development wherein equalitarian sex without affection grows in popularity but so does equalitarian sex with affection (p. 260).

One striking manifestation of change is the increase in premarital sexual activity of women. For example, the proportion of women in the USA who had sexual intercourse by the age of 20 increased markedly in the 1920s and again between 1960 and 1965. Presently available data (Sorenson, 1973) suggest that within the next two years it will have become statistically deviant for young women not to have had sexual intercourse before the age of 20 (Bernard, 1975). In the USA, at some point in the 1970s, the percentage of marriages that end in divorce seven years later will exceed 50%. As Bernard (1975) puts it, 'In the lives of today's teenagers the stable life-long marriage may become deviant' (p. 240). While the rates of change probably vary with the nation involved, it is improbable that European nations are immune from these trends. Given these trends, the absence of upgraded programmes of education for responsible sexuality in the next quarter decade might well lead to far more widespread and serious public health problems (venereal disease, teenage pregnancy, infant mortality) than we now face in relation to teenage sexuality. Furthermore, our developmental understanding of sexuality and sexual behaviour is inadequate. For example, we have not found a single study which focuses on the relation between prepubertal gender role socialization and onset of sexual activity and its incorporation into the gender role. Effective educational efforts cannot be designed without some better understanding of sexual development.

The substantial changes in the onset and circumstances of sexual activity in adolescence have been accompanied by changes in sexual attitudes as well. These are threefold: greater openness about sexuality; a belief that sexual behaviour is more a matter of private than public morality; and an emphasis on affectional context. As the trend toward equality in sexual relationships continues, further changes in gender roles can be anticipated. By and large, males continue to bring a 'body-centred' orientation to heterosexual relationships while females bring a 'person-centred' orientation; thus 'dating and courtship may well be considered processes in which persons train members of the opposite sex in the meaning and context of their respective commitments' (Simon and Gagnon, 1969, p. 46). But does equalitarianism mean that we shall see earlier socialization and cultivation of males' capacities for intimacy?

Achievement

Achievement traditionally has been a more central issue for males than for females in adolescence (Douvan and Adelson, 1966). While the trend toward equalitarianism means that for some (mostly upper middle-class girls), career and marriage is the adaptation of choice, for most females, visions of the future relate more to the marriage role than to achievement in the world of work (although work is often considered as the means to buying a lifestyle as opposed to offering intrinsic satisfactions. See the chapters by Delors and Piotrowski). Gender role socialization prior to adolescence, then, exercises major influence upon adolescent conceptions of achievement and identity, including vocational development. Given the steady increase in the number of women in the labour force with young children (which has exceeded 50% now in a number of nations), it seems probable that some of the gender differences which characterize the literature on achievement motivation and achievement behaviour will change in nature and that some may disappear altogether.

Achievement behaviour, that is, behaviour in situations to which some standard of excellence is applied, is multidetermined. It results from the interactions of abilities (skills, competencies), achievement-related personality characteristics (e.g., need for achievement, fear of failure), and situational factors (e.g., probability of success, availability of extrinsic rewards). Given traditional socialization patterns, boys appear to be more motivated by intrinsic rewards than do girls; girls' performance is more likely to be under the control of extrinsic factors, including fear of social disapproval. Indeed, it has been suggested that a key issue for early adolescents is the conflict between social acceptance and achievement; meeting the standards of excellence preferred by adults may constitute a negative qualification for peer group acceptance. Coleman's (1961) data offer quite striking confirmation for this position, particularly for girls.

Little is known about the usefulness of these laboratory and school-based findings in explaining or understanding achievement behaviour in other settings. This, in turn, means that we have little developmental appreciation of the continuities and discontinuities in achievement behaviour from childhood through adulthood. The problem to which this kind of understanding needs to be brought to bear in the next decades is the meaningfulness of work:

> Learning is work. Caring for children is work. Community action is work. Once we accept the concept of work as something meaningful—not just the source of a buck—you don't have to worry about finding enough jobs. There's no excuse for mules anymore. Society does not need them. There's no question about our ability to feed and clothe and house everybody. The problem is going to come in finding enough ways for man to keep occupied, so he's in touch with reality (Helstein, cited in Terkel, 1972, p. xxii).

The continued segregation of adolescents and youth from adults in general, and from adults of other social strata in particular, prevents the exploration of the diversity of meanings in work and hinders, as lack of exposure to options, the development of rewarding sources of satisfaction in achievement.

Identity formation

One of the most influential conceptions of adolescence is that of Erikson (1968). In his view, what we have called the primary changes of adolescence bring about an 'identity crisis', a period of disequilibrium in the individual's conception of self, in its continuity over time and its coherence. The consequences are a preoccupation with who one is in the eyes of others, a 'trying on' of roles in social interaction with others in order to judge their 'fit', and a temporary sense of not belonging or not being able to 'take hold' that Erikson has labelled 'role confusion'. The resolution of the crisis results in the formation of an identity at a new level of equilibrium and, therefore, the restoration of the sense of coherence of the self and continuity over time. The process is acknowledged by Erikson to require the kinds of cognitive competencies that Piaget would label formal-operational:

> . . . identity formation employs a process of simultaneous reflection and observation, a process taking place on all levels of mental functioning, by which the individual judges himself in the light of what he perceives to be the way in which others judge him in comparison to themselves and to a

typology significant to them; while he judges their way of judging him in the light of how he perceives himself in comparison to them and to types that have become relevant to him (Erikson, 1968, p. 22).

The resolution of the identity crisis is seen by Erikson as the central developmental task of adolescence and this view has been echoed in many secondary sources on the period. In view of the indispensability of very sophisticated cognitive competencies to identify formation at this level and the strong possibility that such levels of competency are not attained by great numbers of individuals in adolescence, if ever, the universality of the crisis and its resolution is somewhat suspect. The origins of the concept in psychoanalyses of upper middle-class adolescents and youth may yet turn out to limit its applicability severely. (It is precisely middle-class youth who are more likely to develop the cognitive skills requisite to the kind of self-examination Erikson has in mind.) Those lower- and working-class persons, particularly those reared in and resident in well integrated urban ghettoes, are unlikely to have a history of role participations which requires them to take multiple points of view. Lacking role taking experience, they fail to develop the multiple perspectives that lead to a sense of self as described by a William James or an Erik Erikson (cf, e.g., Gans, 1962). (It is interesting to note as well that Piaget considers the assumption of adult roles to be a key environmental event in assumption of formal operations.)

The next two decades should see the further empirical study of this issue. The argument that much of the social learning important to adolescence requires broad and diverse role taking opportunities—to use the more common word, increased *participation*—would be much strengthened should it turn out that role taking exercises a strong influence upon the process of identity formation. A better understanding of the process of identity formation might also help policy makers and the developers of programmes for young people to differentiate the more effective kinds of participation from the less effective.

Adolescence in prospect

In planning this chapter, we were faced with a choice between concentrating upon the future-oriented aspects of the colloquium and dealing with some perspectives on adolescence which seem to us to underlie much policy and programme development in relation to the period. We opted for the latter. We concluded that efforts on behalf of adolescents in the near future are more likely to be shaped by current underlying assumptions about the nature of this period than by a set of what might or might not be sensible predictions about adolescents and the conditions for adolescent development at the turn of the century. In addition, we have provided a simple heuristic model which we consider helpful in ordering many of the phenomena of adolescence, in revealing gaps in present knowledge as it might relate to social or scientific policy now and in the near future, and in revealing contradictions between what is known about adolescent development and how the period is represented in public debate. In this section, our aim is to summarize some of the major issues upon which we have touched.

Social change

Beset with the titillating scraps of information about diverse lifestyles that pour from the mass media, we are likely to mistake what is merely 'news' for rapid, profound, and society-wide change. The nature of the family has been changing for centuries in modernizing societies (along the dimension of increasing equalitarianism of role relations, for example), yet news of cohabitation or communal living is exaggerated in public debate as indicative of some new profound and widespread breakdown in the family's capacity to socialize its young. In societies suffused with rapid communications it is easy to mistake views of diversity for some kind of overall change and to frame social policy accordingly.

To the extent that Jeugdprofiel 2000 succeeds in trying to change the conditions for young people's development in the next few decades, we would hope that its attempts, and those of others, can and will be based upon more systematic information about the rate and extent of change in those social institutions that provide the major conditions for adolescent development. Second, however such information is gathered, it is important not to aggregate it in such ways that the modal contexts a society provides for rearing its adolescents are lost sight of. Policy makers (to say nothing of scientists) must know a good deal more about the plurality of sociocultural milieux in which adolescents develop in any given society. Finally, it seems to us important that policy makers be aware of the increasing number of such contexts, that is, of the predicted growth in diversity, and sensitive to the possibility that 'news' about one or many such contexts may not be indicative of any linear and profound change, but of increasing diversity of lifestyles instead.

Changes in adolescence

Just as we believe that misguided policy is likely to result from mistaking news of diversity for widespread change, so we believe that there is even greater danger in mistaking one age cohort's distinctive social encounters for a profound and widespread change in the nature of adolescence itself. It should be clear by now that we read the evidence for the strength of youth cultures and for the magnitude of the generation gap as much weaker than is commonly believed. We do not think that the evidence supports any argument for substantial change of the sorts implied by these concepts in the nature of *adolescence* itself in the past decade. (The aggregation of many more persons beyond the secondary school level in university communities probably has had some important effects on *youth*, however.) Therefore, defining social policy in relation to adolescence in terms of the youth movements of the late 1960s seems to us to be a hazardous course, not because the movements did not suggest some possible changes but because they involved a minority and non-representative sample of young people. The recent spate of policy proposals on adolescence and secondary education in the USA, including the Panel on Youth report, are facing strong criticism:

> The reports are very important as reflections, indications of the mores, concerns, anxieties, the preoccupations of a decade. . . . They convey a selective *Zeitgeist* of an era. It is a truism that we are always fighting the previous war. Were we to act on many of the policy assumptions and recommendations of these reports, we would be perpetuating and increasing the myth of a pathological, homogeneous age group which requires solely problem-oriented interventions.
>
> And what *is* the problem? Is the problem a heterogeneous clientele? a lack of fit between institution and age group? bureaucratization? a shrinking labor market and a large birth cohort? drugs? pregnancy? suicide? No, the problem is youth activism of the Vietnam era, that is . . . the *overt* protest of middle-class youth . . . The 'problem' was the disturbing and not the disturbed adolescent (Lipsitz, 1976, pp. 3-4).

As is often the case in dealing with adolescents, the 'problem' was taken at face value and defined in terms of its consequences for society rather than for adolescent development. In addition, next to no evidence was provided that the 'transition to adulthood' was being accomplished with any less effectiveness than it had been before. We would suggest that such inadequacies in policy analysis follow from a kind of general readiness in modern societies to accept arguments whose general outlines are that adolescence is by nature problematical and is always getting worse. A marked increase in scepticism toward any such views might contribute in the next few decades to more sophisticated analyses of what the problems in fact are that require research or action.

Diversity and homogeneity

Basing social policy on events distinctive to one cohort of adolescents not only may mistake a cohort difference for a basic change in adolescence itself but, as we have noted above, may also mistake the characteristics of one generational unit (that part of a generation which responds to its sociohistorical context in a uniform way) for the generation as a whole. The range of political opinion among adolescents and youths must be at least as great as among their elders, given intrafamilial continuities in voting behaviour from generation to generation; however, one would not have known this from reading the newspapers during the late 1960s. The tendency to stereotype adolescents extends beyond the illustration provided by the youth movements. As the sociocultural milieux for adolescent development are many and varied in any given society, so is the experience of adolescence. Another set of criticisms of the Panel on Youth Report, for example, focuses upon its lack of attention to the development of other than white, middle-class males (Heyneman, 1976). Indeed, it is also to be noted that if adolescent and youth policy is to be justified in terms of preparation for adulthood, then the plurality of adult life careers in society must also be taken into account. Which of the many modal adulthoods in any given society is the proposed policy to foster?

What we have called the secondary changes of adolescence are referred to in many sources as developmental *needs* or *tasks* of adolescence and their being met or solved are seen as preconditions for psychological health or maturity. We do not regard them in this way and believe that to do so results in defining health or maturity in middle-class terms (that being the segment of the population on which the best-known conceptual treatments are based and on which most data exist). Neither social science nor social policy can move very far in their contributions to the facilitation of adolescent development in the next few decades without a greater investment in analysis of the diversity of the experience of adolescence in contemporary societies.

The de-dramatization of adolescence

We have referred frequently to the tendency to see the adolescent period in terms of conflict, whether internal, between parents and their offspring, or between the younger generation and larger social institutions. And, about as frequently, we have stated that the knowledge we have of the period suggests that it is not so conflictful for the great majority of adolescents as it is so often said to be. Modern societies' receptiveness to the dramatization of adolescence is a topic for consideration in its own right. Adults, for example, frequently judge adolescents as having more negative views toward them or views discrepant from theirs than is actually the case (see Hess and Goldblatt, 1957). Attitudes toward adolescents among various sectors in modern societies might well be systematically explored to provide a basis for improving the quality of public debate *vis-à-vis* adolescents. The extent to which envy, fear, and hostility toward adolescence are pervasive in modern society—and in what sectors—might well shape the kinds of informational programmes educators ought to be directing toward parents, citizens, practitioners, and policy makers.

Mass media treatments of adolescents frequently sensationalize events involving them, particularly criminal violence, and the reports invite over-generalization to larger groups of adolescents as well. This form of drama-tizing is pervasive enough that counter-educational efforts ought to be de-veloped and directed toward the audiences identified in the preceding paragraph. Such efforts would take as their objective the general improve-ment of the quality of public debate about adolescence with the under-standing that such a de-dramatization of the period among the general populace may be essential for mounting programmes designed to help those adolescents who do have problems of adaptation, and even more im-portantly, to facilitate development as opposed to solely coping with trouble.

We have suggested that relatively few programmes or policy changes on behalf of adolescents are likely to be instigated by some appeal to the facilitation of development as opposed to the remedying of some problem. We believe that the former approach deserves serious consideration in the decades ahead and have pointed out that this requires an investment in greater understanding of what we have called the secondary changes of adolescence. 'How might the social institutions of our society be changed to facilitate development in early adolescence?' seems to us the most important question for policy analysis and public debate in the decades ahead.

Having said this, and in the context of some of our other remarks, we would hasten to add that we are not blind to the problems of adaptation faced by many subgroups of adolescents in all our societies. In tracing out any of these problems, we are struck with the absence of analyses and policies which face up to the role of the absence of facilitative services in creating 'the problem' in the first place. In addition, problems encountered in adolescence are often seen as uniquely *adolescent* and interpreted in terms of some intrapsychic conflict as opposed to attempts to understand the role of enduring contexts for development—family, peer group, school—and situational factors in their determination. Unsupported and old-fashioned trait-like 'explanations' are not unpopular even when they simply consist of labelling the problem in question as another instance of misguided independence-striving or rebelliousness. Those adolescents who do have problems deserve more sophisticated attention than this form of blaming the victim. Improvement in the quality of public debate would require re-education away from such simple-minded universal *Sturm und Drang* conceptions and toward some appreciation of the interactions between pre-adolescent experience, the adolescent's social participations, and what we have called the primary and secondary changes of adolescence.

Research and policy

Throughout this chapter, we have commented frequently on the relations between research on adolescence and social policy relevant to this age group. It seems suitable to conclude by summarizing some of these comments in the form of four kinds of action that seem important in the decades ahead.

First, we endorse the suggestion of the colloquium that means be found to make synopses available to policy makers of information about adolescent behaviour and development and the contexts for it in policy-relevant areas. What was envisioned here were background papers dealing not only with up-to-date information about the demographic characteristics of youth and the contexts for their development in any given society but also papers which reviewed the current state of knowledge about policy-relevant aspects of development: e.g., adolescent sexuality, autonomy, the impact of schools on non-cognitive development.

Second, the colloquium agreed that means should be sought for responding to particular public policy proposals in terms of their probable consequences for adolescent development. Here the focus would be upon the impact on development of alternatives actually under consideration in any given situation (as opposed to the background information suggested in the first proposal). Such 'impact statements' would provide analysis of the issues in question in terms of the information available in the literature. Upon which groups in a given society could lowering the school leaving age have its most profound effects? Of what sorts? What does available information suggest would be the effect of some major modification in school size or organization? What might the consequences of increased participation of certain kinds be for specific aspects of adolescent development (e.g., creativity, autonomy, achievement motivation)?

Third, provision should be made in the implementation of policy for the evaluation of its consequences. Such 'action research' (and its absence) figured strongly in our discussion of the 'participation' issue, for example. Similarly, the effects of attempts to introduce non-cognitive educational programmes into the schools, counselling of various kinds, for example, should require such accompanying research.

Fourth, and finally, we have pointed to a number of areas where basic research presently has little to offer policy makers and where investment in the next few decades might pay off handsomely. First among these areas is the impact of organizations upon development (particularly schools, where we know next to nothing about their non-cognitive and non-achievement-related effects). Greater support for the study of what we have called the secondary changes of adolescence is warranted, particularly in relation to non-middle-class non-male populations. And, in addition, change and diversity in the family requires greater monitoring and carefully designed investigation, particularly of that sort which builds change or variation *and* its consequences for adolescent growth, development, or behaviour into the same design.

References

Barker, R. H. and Gump, P. V. 1964. *Big school, small school*. Stanford: Stanford University Press.

Bernard, J. 1975. Adolescence and socialization for motherhood, in Dragastin and Elder, *Adolescence in the life cycle*. New York: Wiley.

Boocock, S. S. 1972. *An introduction to the sociology of learning*. New York: Houghton Mifflin.

Brainerd, C. J. 1971. The development of the proportionality scheme in children and adolescents, *Developmental Psychology*, vol. 5, pp. 469–476.

Braungart, R. G. 1975. Youth and social movements, in Dragastin and Elder, *Adolescence in the life cycle*. New York: Wiley.

Brittain, C. V. 1963. Adolescent choices and parent–peer cross-pressures, *Amer. Soc. Rev.*, vol. 28, pp. 385–391.

Coleman, J. S. 1961. *The adolescent society*. New York: The Free Press.

Coleman, J. S. *et al.* 1974. *Youth: Transition to adulthood*. Washington, D.C.: Office of Science and Technology.

Devereux, E. C. 1970. The role of peer group experience in moral development, in J. P. Hill, *Minnesota Symposia on Child Psychology*, vol. IV, pp. 94–140. Minneapolis: U. Minn. Press.

Douvan, E. and Adelson, J. 1966. *The adolescent experience*. New York: Wiley.

Dreeben, R. 1967. The contribution of schooling to the learning of norms, *Harvard Educational Rev.*, vol. 37.

Dreeben, R. 1974. Good intentions, *School Review*, vol. 83, pp. 37–48.

Dulit, E. 1972. Adolescent thinking à la Piaget: The formal stage, *J. Youth and Adol.*, vol. 1, pp. 281–301.

Eisenstadt, S. N. 1956. *From generation to generation*. Glencoe, Ill.: Free Press.

Elder, G. H. 1975. Adolescence in the life cycle: an introduction, in S. H. Dragastin and G. H. Elder (Eds)., *Adolescence in the life cycle*. New York: Wiley.

Elkind, D. 1961. Quantity conceptions in junior and senior high school students, *Child Develop.*, vol. 32, pp. 551–560.

Erikson, E. 1968. *Identity, youth and crisis.* New York: Norton.

Faust, M. 1960. Developmental maturity as a determinant in prestige of adolescent girls, *Child Develop.*, vol. 31, pp. 173–184.

Flacks, R. 1967. The liberated generation: Explorations of the roots of student protest, *J. Soc. Issues*, vol. 23, pp. 52–75.

Flacks, R. 1970. Social and cultural meanings of student revolt: Some informal comparative observations, *Social Problems*, vol. 17, pp. 340–357.

Flacks, R. 1971. *Youth and social change.* Chicago: Markham.

Ford, C. S. and Beach, F. A. 1951. *Patterns of sexual behaviour.* New York: Harper.

Freud, A. 1958. Adolescence, *Psychoanalytic Study of the Child*, vol. 16, pp. 225–278.

Friedenberg, E. Z. 1967. *Coming of age in America: growth and acquiescence.* New York: Vintage.

Gans, H. J. 1962. *The urban villagers: Group and class in the life of Italian-Americans.* Glencoe: Free Press.

Haan, N., Smith, M. B. and Block, J. 1968. Moral reasoning of young adults: political and social behavior, family background, and personality correlates, *J. Personality Social Psychol.*, vol. 10, pp. 183–201.

Hess, R. D. and Goldblatt, I. 1957. The status of adolescents in American society: a problem in social identity, *Child Develop.*, vol. 28, pp. 459–468.

Heyneman, S. P. 1976. *Toward interagency coordination: FY '75 Federal research and development activities pertaining to adolescence.* Third Annual Report, the Interagency Panel for Research and Development on Adolescence. Washington, D.C.: Social Research Group.

Hill, J. P. and Palmquist, W. J. 1974. Social cognition and social relations in adolescence: a precursory view. Paper read at the meeting of the Eastern Psychological Association, Philadelphia.

Hill, J. P. and Steinberg, L. 1976. The development of autonomy in adolescence.

Paper prepared for the Symposium on Youth Problems Today. Madrid: Fundacion Orbegoza Eizaguirre.

Hollingshead, A. B. 1949. *Elmtown's youth.* New York: Wiley.

Inhelder, B. and Piaget, J. 1958. *The growth of logical thinking from childhood to adolescence.* New York: Basic Books.

Jones, M. C. 1957. The later careers of boys who were early- or late-maturing, *Child Develop.,* vol. 28, pp. 113–128.

Jones, M. C. 1965. Psychological correlates of somatic development, *Child Develop.,* vol. 36, pp. 899–911.

Kandel, D. B. and Lesser, G. S. 1972. *Youth in two worlds.* San Francisco: Jossey-Bass.

Katchadourian, H. A. and Lunde, D. T. 1972. *Fundamentals of human sexuality.* New York: Holt, Rinehart, & Winston.

Keniston, K. 1968. *Young radicals.* New York: Harcourt, Brace and World.

Keniston, K. 1971. *Youth and dissent.* New York: Harcourt, Brace, Jovanovich.

Kirk, J. K. 1972. *Relationship of analogies and Piagetian formal operational tasks.* University of Pittsburg: Unpublished manuscript Thesis.

Kohlberg, L. 1973. Continuities in childhood and adult moral development revisited; in P. H. Baltes and W. K. Schaie (Eds.), *Life-span developmental psychology: personality and socialization.* New York: Academic Press.

Kooy, G. A. 1972. Jeugd en sexualiteit tegen de jaren zeventig. Wageningen: Veenman.

Lipsitz, J. 1976. Comments on 'Youth in transition'. Symposium presented at the meetings of the American Educational Research Association, San Francisco.

Mannheim, K. 1952. The problem of generations; in Mannheim, *Essays on the sociology of knowledge.* London: Routledge & Kegan Paul.

Martorano, S. 1973. The development of formal operations thinking. Paper presented at the meeting of the Society for Research in Child Development, Philadelphia.

Mead, M. 1958. Adolescence in primitive and modern society; in E. E. Maccoby, T. Newcomb and L. Hartley (Eds.), *Readings in social psychology,* pp. 341–349. New York: Henry Holt.

Mönks, F. J. and Heusinkveld, H. G. 1973. De mythe van de generatiekloof; in J. de Wit *et al* (Eds.) *Psychologen over het kind* 3. Groningen: Tjeenk Willink.

Mönks, F. J. and Knoers, A. F. M. 1976. *Ontwikkelingspsychologie*. Nijmegen: Dekker & van de Vegt, pp. 180–205. (German edition *Entwicklungspsychologie*. Stuttgart: Kohlhammer.)

Peel, E. A. 1971. *The nature of adolescent judgment.* New York: Wiley.

Peskin, H. 1967. Pubertal onset and ego functioning, *J. Abnor. Psychol.*, vol. 72, pp. 1–15.

Piaget, J. 1932. *The moral judgment of the child.* New York: Harcourt, Brace and World.

Piaget, J. 1972. Intellectual evolution from adolescence to adulthood, *Human Develop.*, vol. 15, pp. 1–12.

Reiss, I. L. 1973. *Heterosexual relationships inside and outside of marriage.* Morristown, N.J.: General Learning Press.

Simon, W. and Gagnon, J. H. 1969. On psychosexual development; in D. A. Goslin (Ed.), *Handbook of socialization theory and research.* Chicago: Rand McNally.

Sorensen, R. C. 1973. *Adolescent sexuality in contemporary America, personal values and sexual behaviour.* New York: World.

Sullivan, H. S. 1953. *The interpersonal theory of psychiatry.* New York: Norton.

Tanner, J. M. 1961. *Education and physical growth.* London: University of London Press.

Tanner, J. M. 1962. *Growth at adolescence.* Oxford: Blackwell.

Terkel, S. 1972. *Work: people talk about what they do all day and how they feel about what they do.* New York: Pantheon.

Westby, D. L. and Braungart, G. R. 1970. Activists and the history of the future; in Foster and Long, *Protest! Student activism in America.* New York: Morrow.

Young, M. and Willmott, P. 1964. *Family and kinship in East London.* Baltimore: Penguin.

4 Adolescents' ethics and morals in the year 2000

Fred Mahler

In organizing an international colloquium on 'adolescence in the year 2000', Jeugdprofiel 2000 is significantly participating in the rapid increase in recent years of research on the future time perspective and orientation of young people. *The future*, a general human problem, is above all a problem of adolescence and youth. The present generations will not only live the future as their own present, receiving it from the adults' hands as a completed work, but will also invent and build it up themselves as an open work. Mankind's present responsibility towards the future is great; not only must we prepare youth for the future but we must also build up those premises which will permit them to be the authors and the masters of it (Jungk and Galtung, 1969).

In recent years we find more and more theoretical and empirical research works in which the relations between adolescents and the future are investigated (e.g. Gillespie and Allport, 1955; Guillaumat, 1964; Hosia, 1970; Ikonnikova and Lisorski, 1972; Mönks, 1967; Ornauer, Wiberg, Sicinski and Galtung, 1974; Wallace and Rabin, 1960). The present paper is a contribution to the delineation of some theoretical, methodological, and empirical aspects of such investigations considered as a specific field of future studies. Our main hypothesis is that the propensity towards the future, characteristic of adolescence, is a system peculiar to that age. It has, however, distinct features dependent upon the social, cultural, and concrete historical environment. It is a system the knowledge and shaping of which are decisive in the building up of the future man as man of the future.

Man is by his very condition time bound. Not only in the sense that he exists *in* time, but also in the sense that he exists *through* time. The emergence of the future as an open field of possibilities, as a territory of projects, choices and decisions, and, therefore, as a domain of deliberate and conscious praxis, is the product of man. Man's most remarkable Promethean invention is that of the future as a conscious act. And, at the same time, man is man precisely by his prospective dimension. If man is generally a prospective being, the young individual, by his very bio-psychosocial peculiarities, is characterized by a relation to the future whose specific features are: prospective scope; prospective distance; prospective liberty; and prospective mobility. Adolescence means the birth of the consciousness of man as a future oriented, and future creating, being (Mahler, 1972a). The discovery of future and the development of an active and self-conscious position and behaviour toward the future is the most important and relevant trait of adolescent existence and maturation. The first and last objective of education and of all social policies should be to ensure that young people accept their responsibility to think of the future and to shape it in terms of their aspirations and needs. We believe that the defining attribute of studying adolescence from the prospective point of view is the gauging of the relation between young persons' present and their projected status and role. Man's first conscious relation with the future and his first self-made options occur then and adolescents experience the discovery of their actual status and role and, at the same time, the projection of their desired status and role (which may become reality if social opportunities permit).

The moral problem in future studies of adolescence and youth

In the context of our own subject, i.e. adolescents' ethics and morals in the year 2000, we must stress that studies concerning youth attitudes, aspirations, expectations, and ideals about the future are more and more morally concerned and ethically oriented. This means that the value-free approach and the axiological neutrality that have characterized these studies in the past are coming to be avoided. In such concepts as L. K. Frank's (1939) 'time perspective', E. Spranger's (1955) 'Lebensplan', R. Bergius' (1957) 'time sense' and 'time perception', F. R. Kluckhohn's and F. L. Strodbeck's (1961) 'time orientation' or H. Erikson's (1949) 'collective-ego-time-space', we find a growing interest in the moral aspects of adolescent future orientation.

At the seminar on 'The Youth of the Future and the Future of Youth', which was held as part of the 3rd World Future Research Conference in

Bucharest (Mahler, 1972b), two explanations of this phenomenon were offered. On the one hand, there is the strong confrontation of adolescents and youth with the moral problems of what has been called 'the crisis of contemporary civilization' (UNESCO, 1975), the need to define new values raised by the dilemmas of living in consumer oriented societies.

On the other hand, interest in the moral aspects of adolescent future orientation is a reflection of an evolution in future studies themselves (Apostol, 1975; Botez, 1971; Malita, 1975). An axiological orientation asserts itself ever more powerfully as an answer to the unilateral, economistic, or technocratic tendencies that were threatening to reduce the study of future to a means of maintaining the social *status quo*. The humanistic, axiological orientation, often fruitfully inspired by Marxist philosophy, consists in a critical effort to reappraise future studies, especially by emphasizing the preponderance of ends over means, of intentionality over processuality, of values over facts, and of the ideal over the real.

One of the most important theoretical and methodological premises of any research concerning these problems is the understanding of the principal objective economic, social, political and cultural determinants of future orientations of young people and their relations to the subjective ones. As K. Mollenhauer (1971) writes in his introduction to Kasakos' study, time perspective must be analyzed simultaneously from the subjective point of view of the individual's perceptions and orientations and from the objective point of view of the opportunity structure of individuals, groups and classes. In fact, the future will not be the result of the absolutely free will of individuals or groups and of their expectations and aspirations but of the actualization of the objective potentialities, of the realization of the possibilities included in reality. This does not occur spontaneously but is a process realized only with the active participation of the human historical forces, guided by human needs and ideals and therefore by moral value orientations, and by individuals' own conceptions about the future ethos and about the future in general.

Thus, the future evolution of ethos and of adolescents' moral orientations in the perspective of the year 2000 can be considered only in the light of the concrete historical situation it will materialize in, and will vary with the kind of social system, region, and country in question. However, modifications in the future ethos will not be the automatic result of socio-economic transformations alone, but also of options for certain future ethical models. (Present ethical confrontations make the bases for the new models apparent.) Without attempting to undertake such a study here and now, we wish to refer to one of the major features of youth's moral profile and to the probable directions of its future evolution.

From marginality to participation

Young people's social and ethical orientation depend, to a large extent, on their status in society. Undoubtedly, young people's social status varies in different sociopolitical systems or even within the same system, depending on relations among classes, on level of economic development, and on political and cultural situations, traditions and the like. A global problem, materialized in different ways depending on the social–historical context, is the marginal status of adolescence and youth. This is a problem whose interest lies in its implications for future social participation and commitment. Indeed, analysis of the prevalent features of contemporary young people's ethical orientations soon reveals a continuum of positions from the pole of social–political and moral commitment to the pole of alienation and accompanying political passivity and moral scepticism. The problem is which positions will assert themselves in the perspective of adolescents in the year 2000: commitment or non-commitment, activism or passivity, militant idealism or uninvolved scepticism?

Certainly the evolution of the positions adopted will be determined by a multitude of economic and political factors (generally macrosocial) as well as educational influences. The social status of adolescence and youth and its evolution will continue to play an important role. Thus, a specific characteristic of adolescence and youth, even in modern society, although with different reasons and in different forms, is the maintenance of marginal status. Given the greater immaturity of adolescents compared to that of the adults, in many societies the former occupy a marginal status. *Marginality* has a polyvalent meaning. In the light of a possible Marxist interpretation (Mahler, 1970), we define it as having to live under circumstances other than those of the society or of the respective social group in general, with fewer rights, responsibilities, possibilities of assertion, and participation in social life and social decision making.

What is the relationship between adolescence and marginality? While the adolescent's task in society is both to train himself and to participate actively in the life and work of society, marginality implies the separation of young persons from society and their removal from a real participation in civic life and social decision. This creates a specific consciousness ruled by a feeling of isolation and frustration and there arises the conviction that society belongs only to adults. In this universe young people are not permitted social or self assertion and social expectations regarding work and social life come to be seen as repressive. This kind of situation can (and has) cast some young people into a 'moral revolt' which enables them to reject not only the shortcomings of society, but society itself. Consequently, young people are led towards a utopian pattern of building their own world, a subculture characterized by its own rules of life and behaviour and by its own specific ethical values and customs. It is a world of isolation of the young from adults, often aimed at the replacement of work by a playful attitude, of social rules by anarchy, of integration by absolute liberty. Many of these tendencies express marginality and contribute to its maintenance. They represent a more or less conscious refusal to pass over the barriers of social maturity (viewed as integration into adult society). Sometimes such young people manifest until a fairly mature age a lengthened stubbornness in order to preserve their adolescent status and role.

Contending youth movements express the contradictions young people experience between marginal status and the various roles they already play or want to play in society. The relations existing between denial and projection, prevalent in the ethical mentality and behaviour of these young people, are a particularly good illustration of their ambivalence. While the value of these movements to youth has to do with the power of opposition and repudiation, their weakest point is that they do not lead to a constructive solution and a projection of the future.

What are the future possible, probable, or desirable tendencies in the evolution of marginality and its correlated ethical orientations? The rarity of young people in a society with a low rate of population growth is, and is still supposed to be, more and more replaced by a youth 'density' (if not everywhere, at least in larger areas decisive for the average increase of population). The percentage of young people attending schools of various kinds will increase significantly and, consequently, the inactive young population will increase. The contradiction between the objective situation of starting work at an older age, and the subjective wish of young people to assume responsible roles much earlier will increase. The access of young people to social, economic, and family responsibilities will be further delayed. Rosenmayr (1968) has dealt amply with the contradictions existing between the way modern industrial society stimulates the need for immediate achievement and yet delays the moment of youth's entering into the activities of professional life. In his view, youth access to adulthood, the process of maturation, involves the achieving of a new status which ensures personal independence and authority.

Adolescence continues to increase in length in modern civilizations. In the future we shall see a permanent increase of its upper limit while at the same time puberty and an earlier onset of physiological maturity will probably decrease its lower limits. All these processes suggest the possibility of increasing youth's marginality in the future. But must this possibility be considered as a probability? On the contrary, the necessity of considering youth as a real factor in social change requires the removal of, or a maximum reduction in marginality. Youth is generally considered to be the age of ambiguity; one is no longer a child yet not an adult. (See, for example, Coleman, 1961; Eisenstadt, 1956; Erikson, 1959; Hornstein, 1966; Tenbruck, 1962.) The umbilical cord which used to bind one to the family is already cut but the bridges towards participation in the broader society are not yet built. This ambiguity explains why so many thinkers and policy makers hesitate to accord to youth a status of its own. A child is not an immature grown-up, but still a child, a being living in a particular world with its own standards and specific values. Youth, on the contrary, does not have such a definite status. The young person lives in the direct vicinity of the adult but is seen as his unaccomplished copy, as an underdeveloped adult.

Youth cannot be explained as an age in which the individual is still a child and, at the same time, already an adult. Youth is neither a perfected childhood, nor an unperfected maturity. It is a qualitatively new stage of life, a point generally not much insisted upon by the paternalist theories. Like the child, the young person is training himself for work and life; but unlike the child, this training becomes in adolescence and is in youth a process in which the young person consciously participates as an active subject. Although he is often outside the economic process, the young person cannot and should not be excluded from the activity of social life. The lack of a full economic responsibility need not be accompanied by the lack of social responsibilities. On the contrary, it should be made up for by work activities parallel to learning, by giving youth a civic education, requiring real practice in the exercise of its rights and its social and political obligations in addition to sound knowledge of them.

From this point of view, it may be possible to change marginality and the ethical orientations correlated with it into participation and commitment. Many problems of education and behaviour of youth in the contemporary and future world are attributable to marginality and they could be better solved by reconsidering the ways of approach and solutions.

Given the requirements demanded by the progress of civilization and of the technical and scientific revolution, society has to spend an ever-increasing amount on training and education of young people. It is obvious that young people are aware of and acknowledge this effort. However, this should not be regarded as a philanthropic act, as a grant suitably accompanied by guilt feelings. Adolescents and youth should be conscious that the conditions created for their training *are* due to society, but are the duty of the latter.

Apart from the requirements regarding a polytechnic education—which includes in school curricula the assimilation of knowledge and the shaping of habits for various productive activities—the necessity of training young people for work by work is being stressed more and more. Both school and extra-school ways of direct productive activity are not only supplying them with useful knowledge and habits, but are contributing to the shaping of their moral profile, helping at the same time in multiplying social relations and in the acquisition of new comprehensive life experiences. They are also giving adolescents and youth the satisfaction of the status of effective participation in society's progress.

Without neglecting and, on the contrary, by respecting, the specificity of adolescent and youth value orientations, various educational efforts are concerned with the removal of the negative effects of their subcultures, which generally maintain segregation and marginality. A dialogue between the generations can be achieved only through a definite participation of young people in the ensemble of the cultural and spiritual life of society. This must include the opening of their subcultures to that society.

With reference to the civic and social aspect of the role and status of youth, we can stress the complexity of problems concerning their removal from the social forum. Such segregation gives birth to *anomie* or to a state of latent or open revolt, in contrast with the striking tendency present in other countries towards a fully responsible commitment of young people in social and political life. Besides civic rights, there is a positive need to stimulate young people's active participation in public life, both formal and informal. The characteristics, the effects, and the tendencies belonging to marginality cannot be considered outside the analysis of participation in the social and political structure. In all these domains the status and role of marginality can and must be replaced to an ever larger extent by the status and role of social participation. Only this will ensure the substitution of the frustration and the disarming consciousness of lack of commitment by the tonic feeling and ethical orientation of commitment to the progress of society. Due to the social and political structure, to the new relations between generations, and especially, by bringing into play the dynamism of youth in the economic and cultural development, socialism is creating a new status for youth as participants in the progress of society. The status of marginality of youth is therefore not an inevitability, but the result of some political and economic circumstances, of some social relations and ideological influences. It may and could be eliminated by an adequate change in youth's status and role, but this must be based on a new understanding of their social traits and on incorporating this understanding into relations between young people and adults, beginning in early adolescence.

Towards an ethics of social commitment

The emerging emphasis on youth participation and on the equal rights and responsibilities of young people in society encourages not only the reduction of marginality but the assertion of new moral orientations characteristic of an ethics of social commitment. We are referring mainly to the concrete context of the contemporary Romanian socialist society in order to show the emergence of such a new ethical orientation. Certainly, these characteristics are influenced by the socio-economic, political, and educational conditions of the social context, by the assertion of new principles of socialist ethics and equity in a society open toward the future, and by the subsequent accelerated rate of social and economic development which builds up a new civilization (Beller, Miros, Popescu and Zamfirescu, 1969).

The opinion of adolescents about the future ethos expresses a point of view, in some respects positive and in other respects critical, about the moral principles and norms existing in society, and in the real present behaviour of young people. At the same time, it also reflects the adolescents' outlook on the future *possible* evolution of morals as well as the *desires* ideal image of these. We may find an appropriate example of this approach to the moral side of adolescents' future orientation in various studies carried out in Romania by the Youth Research Centre (Mahler, 1972b; Bazac, Dumitrescu, Mahler and Radulian, 1974). The world towards which most adolescents aspire is not that of a 'consumer society' in which men's alienation leads to a degradation of values and a depreciation of ideals. Adolescents want a world in which industrialization and automation are accompanied by the optimization of social relations through the assertion of the ideals of social equity and justice.

Denying scepticism, the majority of the adolescents we studied expressed their faith in ideals. Their desire is to have, and to act according to, a humanistic ideal. For most, the future ethos does not mean the giving up of the ideal but, on the contrary, a permanent aspiration towards the ideal. In the future society doing away with poverty and the reshaping of human relationships in a world of progress and of a new economic and political order will lead to the replacement of hunger and of the pursuit of material welfare by a 'hunger for ideals' and a pursuit of values.

In spite of the presence of some pragmatic orientations in a minority of the adolescents, an orientation towards the social ethic predominates. Many of the subjects of our investigations consider the future neither a simple moral justification of narrow material interests, nor an ascetic repression and diminution of these. The future ethos, denying both individualism and gregariousness, will achieve the Kantian imperative of 'man as end' not only at the level of philosophical speculation of social élites, but at those of praxis and common man.

Among adolescents' life projects, be they accompanied or not by a social ideal, work, professional activity or career no doubt occupies a privileged place. Since in Romania the high rate of economic development has been incorporated into the everyday effort towards the improvement of life quality, young people centre their destiny round a profession, whose free choice is guaranteed and whose mastery is ensured. For many young people, success in life depends on the choice of a profession corresponding to their aptitudes and aspirations, and on specialization, effort, and passion for one's activity. (Of course, some of the adolescents we investigated expressed their conviction that chance might play a more important part.) Most adolescents prefer an ethos which, based upon the values of work and social equity, make effort and competence the criteria for success. To the perspective recorded in other surveys and, in particular, to the 'drop-out' type of behaviour which denies work as fundamentally alienating, the investigated teenagers oppose the perspective of transforming Sisyphean labour into a creative Promethean activity. The ethos of future society as foreseen and forecast by the young people we refer to, is not opposed to work as such, but to its alienating and degrading forms. The future ethos is one of creative work that ensures the fulfilment of man's personality. And, if alongside the increase of labour productivity and the new social relations, man's free time will also increase, this will not cancel the virtues of work and diminish the personality of *homo faber*, but will complete it with the virtues of leisure and of *homo ludens*, within the ideal of *homo artifex*.

Man's 'massification' (that is, his depersonalization by the reduction of autonomy to heteronomy and by the replacement of originality by standards and of individuality by common behaviour) has been prophesied by numerous scientists but it is not regarded as a certainty by adolescents. It has been argued that scientific, technical, and technological development, the increasing institutionalization of education, and the impact of the mass media involve the possibility of man's becoming 'unidimensional'. If this is a danger, avoidance calls for a 'pedagogy of option' (Mead, 1952) which places the subject of the educational process in the position to select values and behaviours autonomously concomitant with self-education.

As a corollary, we can assert that one of the characteristics of the future ethos is the right to personality. Founded upon a society of justice and equity, embarked upon steady material and spiritual progress, the future is called not only to help man to accomplish a multilateral personality, but also to stimulate the formation of multiple personalities, i.e. diversified individualities too. As an alternative to a world of depersonalization, owing to the confusion of values or the authority of norms, the future ethos will appear as plenary assertion of varied and multiform personalities accomplished in spite of, or precisely due to, their superior value orientation.

Ethical forecasting and public policies

The dimensions and the values of the ethos in the year 2000 are undoubtedly more numerous, more complex, contradictory (and more susceptible to change) than could have been explored in our paper. However, it is essential to underline the value of the hypothesis and methodology of studying adolescents' projective options and of correlating the present status and role with the future ones so as to contribute to the study of adolescents' future orientations. The study of moral options and aspirations, in the light of the relation between the present and the projected status and role, opens a relatively objective possibility of analysis, including a quantitative and a mathematical interpretation. Prospective, prognosis and planning aim ever more at replacing the exclusively economic and technological viewpoint, based mainly upon extrapolation of present possibilities and present tendencies of development, by a truly scientific and humanistic conception. The majority, if not all the researchers of the future, naturally consider it to be a reality different from that of the present. But from this very general agreement, their positions go quite different ways. For many, the future is but a more or less straight extension of the present or even of the past. Of course, it is seen as change but is mainly conceived of as simple growth, an accumulation of elements congruent with those already in existence. For these researchers the future of the present is in the past, and the future of the future lies in the present. At the theoretical level, continuity is asserted; methodologically, extrapolations are used. Axiologically, the consequence is a preponderance of achievement values. Forecasting and, particularly, planning are seen as depending on present needs and aspirations, possibly amended due to a probable and predictable quantitative growth. The character of future research is, in this context, predominantly *descriptive*.

Opposed to this there is the direction of thought in which the future

4

represents mainly a *transcendence* of the present, a qualitative change (and not a quantitative accumulation). In 'continuation' of the past and present, there is not only one single future, but 'possible futures' or 'futuribles' (de Jouvenel, 1964). For better or worse, what we have to do in the present is to see the germs of these possible futures. Thus, there are not only several futures of a present, but also desirable or undesirable ones. The incomparably more important place that values and the axiological judgement play in this way of seeing things is obvious. To the apparent or relative axiological neutrality of the theory of the future as a one-way continuation of the present, of the ideals as a mere development of the given, to all these the tendency we are referring to opposes the *moral commitment* of future studies. Among several possible futures, each having its own value dimension, there must be a *choice*. The future of the present and, particularly of the future, does not lie in the past and not even in the present (although the future remains bound both to the past and the present) but mainly in the chosen future. In the light of this kind of future investigation, discontinuity is asserted at the theoretical level, and innovation at the methodological one. The consequence at the axiological levels is, in this case, the preponderance of accomplishment values. Forecasting and planning depend not so much on present tendencies and on the present features of aspirations and expectations but on the desirable values of the future. In this hypostasis future research is predominantly *normative*.

The experience of confronting prognoses with reality as well as the critical analysis by future sciences of prognostication itself has shown one chief shortcoming: the technical unidimensionality of planning whenever human aspirations are not taken into account. A scientific and humanistic outlook on planning implies the consideration both of the determining objective elements and those linked with the requirements and perspectives of social development and the assertion of personality. Planning cannot disregard the active role of the subject in its relation to the object, of the conscience in its relation to social existence, of values and ideals in their relation to human activity. Thus, future sciences are ever more determined to consider the problems of social and moral dynamics and to develop a specific 'moral perspective' (Fourastie, 1968). The object of this axiological forecasting is ultimately the *future ethos*.

The scientific interdisciplinary prospective study of the tendencies of moral development and of the dimensions and values of the future ethos may use critically the results of public opinion surveys. However, as numerous authors remark, surveys of public opinions about the future are principally significant for the assessment of the dominant traits of present-day thinking. They offer premises for the approximation of tendencies whose ulterior occurrence is not only possible but also probable. Since even the studies on the prognosis of economic development admit variants and record an ever greater differentiation and shading, the prognosis of ethical development is probabilistic *par excellence*. What is more, since in the field of morality there is not only the possibility but also the necessity of *varied* and even *divergent values and behaviours* and since their social determinations are in a complex way *mediated*, the prognostication of the future ethos calls for elimination of all traces of homogeneity, schematism, and mechanism. Considering the importance of the prospective studies about the *future ethos* as an auxiliary but significant element of the general forecasting, including economic and social planning; and the specific difficulties and requirements of any prospective study in this field, it is imperative to elaborate a number of hypotheses and methodologies, including formalized models for the prospective study of ethical dynamics.

Our main conclusion is the necessity to emphasize more and more the moral component of the researches about adolescence, youth and the future as one of the most important conditions of their efficiency in the shaping of public policies and in the improvement of young people's own participation in the building up of a new and better world. An essential problem in the investigation and shaping of the future, and particularly in the formation of morals, is to regard it as an open study and action, forever perfectible. Certainly, today's options and decisions will inevitably influence, sometimes in essential fields, the way of living of the younger generations in the year 2000 and their own way of conceiving the future. Therefore, an exigence is the orientation, on a scientific–humanistic basis, of these options and decisions so that they may correspond to the largest possible extent to the needs and aspirations of the people of that time. But, at the same time, they must be studied and adopted in such a way that they cannot 'colonize' the future, but ensure instead the highest possible freedom to future generations in shaping their own futures. This presupposes that the present models of the future, putting the aspirations in agreement with the objective possibilities and tendencies, should be shaped as *open alternatives.*

At the same time we have to keep in mind that the world of the year 2000 will be a world of change even more than is the world of young people at present. Subjective components of behaviour will have to be more and more developed in order to ensure for young people the conditions to adopt themselves to rapid changes and also to give them opportunities to exert an influence upon the transformations themselves.

Young people are the future in the present. Therefore the interdisciplinary and prospective investigation of adolescence and youth, their dynamics as a 'factor of transformation' (which investigation we may call *iunology*) becomes imperative. The world whose future we now consider is the world in which today's young will be living tomorrow. This world must correspond to their own plans in life, to their ideals, to the dimensions and values of the future ethos they desire, one which offers them the possibility not only to dream of the future but also to participate effectively in building it. For young people 'tomorrow's world' must be not only a dream but also an appeal and an action programme, not only a part in a scenario already made by others, but a work whose authors should be the young themselves. Relating adolescence and youth to the future demands granting the status and role due to them now, that of conscious historical subjects who participate actively and responsibly in social decision making.

References

Apostol, P. 1975. *Calitatea vietii si explorarea viitorului.* Bucuresti: Editura politica.

Bazac, D., Dumitrescu, I., Mahler, F. and Radulian, V. 1974. *Geneza si dinamica idealului in adolescenta.* Craiova: Ed. Scrisul romanesc.

Beller, N., Miros, L., Popescu, V. and Zamfirescu, V. 1969. *Tineretui si idealut moral.* Bucuresti: Ed. Academici.

Bergius, R. 1957. *Formen des Zukunftserlebens*, p. 59. München: Barth.

Botez, M. 1971. *Introducere in prospectiva.* Bucuresti: Centrul de informare si documentare in stintele sociale si politice.

Coleman, J. S. 1961. *The adolescent society.* New York: The Free Press.

Eisenstadt, S. N. 1956. *From generation to generation.* New York: The Free Press.

Erikson, E. 1948. Childhood and transition in two American Indian tribes. In: C. Kluckhohn and H. A. Murray (Eds.), *Personality in nature, society and culture.* New York: Knopf.

Erikson, E. 1959. Identity and life cycle. *Psychological Issues,* vol. 1, no. 1.

Fourastie, J. 1967. *Essais de morale prospective et politique.* Vers une nouvelle morale.

Frank, L. K. 1939. Time perspectives. *Journal of Social Philosophy,* vol. 4, pp. 293–312.

Gillespie, J. M. and Allport, G. W. 1955. *Youth's outlook on the future.* New York: Doubleday.

Guillaumat, M. 1964. *Reflexions pour 1985.* Paris.

Hornstein, W. 1966. *Jugend in ihrer Zeit.* Hamburg: Marion von Schröder Verlag.

Hosia, E. 1970. *Future prospects of the youth.* Tampere.

Ikonnikova, S. N. and Lisorski, V. T. 1972. *Tineretul despre el insusi.* Moscova: Editura Agentidei de presa Novosti.

Jouvenel, Bertrand de 1964. *L'art de la conjecture.* Ed. du Rocher

Jungk, R. and Galtung J. 1969. *Mankind 2000.* London: Allen and Unwin.

Kluckhohn, F. R. and Strodbeck, F. L. 1961. *Variations in value orientations,* pp. 13–15. New York: Knopf.

Mahler, F. 1970. *Tineret—dezvoltare (de la marginalitate le angajare).* In: *Fineretul-factor de schimbare,* p. 43. Bucuresti: Centrul de cercetari pentru problemele Fineretu-lui.

Mahler, F. 1972a. Youth and moral options, *Revue internationale des sciences,* Paris, vol. 2.

Mahler, F. 1972b. *The prospective dimension of juvenile personality.* Paper for the 3rd World Future Research Conference, Bucharest. See also *Paideia III,* 1973, pp. 123–138.

Malita, M. 1975. *Cronica annului 2000.* Bucuresti: Editura politica.

Mead, M. 1952. *Coming of age in Samoa.* New York: The New American Library (1st ed. 1928).

Mollenhauer, K. 1971. Vorwort in Kasakos, G. *Zeitperspektive, Planungsverhalten, und Sozialisation. Überblick über internationale Forschungsergebnisse*, p. 7. München: Juventa Verlag.

Mönks, F. 1967. *Jugend und Zukunft*. München: Barth.

Ornauer, H., Wiberg, H., Sicinski, A. and Galtung, J. 1974. *Images of the world in the year 2000*. The Hague: Mouton.

Rosenmayr, L. 1968. Esquisse d'une sociologie de la jeunesse, *Revue internationale des sciences sociales*, vol. 20, no. 2, pp. 319–351.

Spranger, E. 1955. *Psychologie des Jugendalters*. Heidelberg: Quelle und Meyer.

Tenbruck, F. 1962. *Jugend und Gesellschaft*. Freiburg: Rombach.

UNESCO. 1975. *Finalités et théories de l'education*. Genève: UNESCO.

Wallace, M. and Rabin, A. I. 1960. Temporal experience. *Psychological Bulletin*, vol. 57, pp. 213–236.

5 The social plasticity of youth

Hilde and Leopold Rosenmayr

The purpose of this paper is to contribute to the complex problem of forecasting the development of youth up to the year 2000 from two points of departure: the historico–sociological analysis of the position of young people in European history, and the different forms of manifestation of youth in different social strata. Both historical sequence and vertical class differences will be discussed to demonstrate the eminent variability of the phenomenon of youth and thus its historical, social, and cultural nature.

The historical and futurological analysis of youth

An age status, generally, is an artifact grounded in biological facts, moulded by social forces such as the division of labour, the diffusion of information, education, medicine, and ideologies and norms (including chronologically defined ones). Out of all this the individual arrives at some degree of synthesis of his personal status. By 'youth' we understand a sequence of age statuses which can be grouped in two subsets, adolescence on the one hand and young adulthood on the other, as we explain in more detail later in this paper. The theoretical and conceptual basis of the present work has been selected to demonstrate both continuity and change as we shift our focus from history to the future. Our definitions should also provide a basic perspective on youth policy; at least they should help to avoid short term errors in the establishment of aims of a youth policy for the future. Youth (in the twofold meaning just mentioned, and with labels which depart from those of the editors as explicated in Chapter 1) will be considered as a product of societal reproduction as well as a force in social transformation. The degree to which young people cleave to reproductive channels or paths of transformation depends on the historical constellation and on the class structure.

The socialization of youth takes place within the context of tensions between different historical forces: on the one hand they are taught the limits of freedom and on the other hand taught to value it. Thus youth must not be considered as a separate race somewhere on the sidelines of social life but as the historical moment of societal reproduction and transformation. Youth is to be understood as 'reproduction' because it is the product of socialization and can only be understood within its societal framework and the cultural contents offered to it. Youth is to be understood as 'transformation' because a certain freedom of selection in the socialization of values is inevitable. The better the cognitive and emotional basis for decision making provided during childhood, the more degrees of freedom there are during the following period. In addition, typical connections develop between 'young' values (i.e. values just appearing in society, or being revitalized), and young cohorts, just becoming able to accept *and* select among the values accessible to them. Therefore youth must be analyzed in terms of the forces determining society through symbols and through their actual power (élites) as it is exerted in the leadership of institutions and organizations. Among the liberal upper class, educated young people have recently exhibited more intense social criticism than did their parents when they were young. The security provided by progressive, well-to-do parents and the cognitive and aesthetic differentiation typical of such environments probably account for this finding. Basically, we may consider the criticisms of this minority as an instance of 'protest as a type of conformity', as Allerbeck (1971) has aptly termed it. (Probably the best and most comprehensive review of the numerous studies on protesting youth so far is a work by Braungart (1975) which consolidates the results into a set of theses.)

In dealing with the concept of social transformation we must bear in mind that the cultural spectrum of an epoch is subjected to a selective process by each new cohort of young people at a certain point in their development during and after puberty. However, this heightened value sensitivity, 'the prevalence of the value experience', suggested by Bernfeld (1923) does not apply equally to all social strata of youth. It applies mainly to a certain favoured type of development of youth and occurs particularly in conjunction with certain types of sociocultural change. According to Mannheim (1928) a 'new access' to culture is opened up by 'social shifts'. The historico-social process of the 'new access' constitutes a fresh constitution of values after childhood. The function of the cohort as an 'access-opener' in the social system increases if the system is under crisis; if, for example, it reorganizes because of internal and/or international ideological and power changes (including those in occupational and political systems). In the USA, for example, the coincidence of the Vietnam War on the one hand and the civil rights movement and the student movement on the other saw an intense and widespread 'access-opener' in a crisis of the total system.

Sociological analyses of youth have little predictive power if the general social horizon is not taken into account. The young can be understood only within the degrees of freedom granted to them and as motivated by the cultural contents which were and are offered to them. These degrees of freedom (or the lack of, or incapacity for, control by 'adult' society) enable the young to create or at least adopt a brand of attitudes and lifestyle whereby reproduction becomes transformation. The position of youth in society must be considered the product of historico-social dynamics. Youth sociology should therefore be reconsidered as or even replaced by theory and research on the relation between society and youth and on special problems of youth in the light of a theory of age groups, cohorts, and generations of historical society. If this demand is combined with a theoretical basis including in its view *all* age groups of society, then the attitudes and behaviours of successive generations will be studied in a *relational analysis*, as they are confronted with each other in social institutions. Inter-cohort relationships within the family, in the educational system, in political organizations—conflicts between the principal dominant cohorts as one contracting party (parents, teachers, professors, foremen, masters, chairmen, etc.) and their counterparts in youth—require analysis in order to permit the determination of the position of youth in society, past and future.

The changing position of youth in history

In a recent volume, an attempt has been made to develop the historical sociology of youth as a subfield of youth studies and to integrate it with empirical research on present-day youth problems (Rosenmayr, 1976). The attempt revealed that historical research on problems of youth in society is extremely fragmentary and that generalizations toward a more global typology are not yet possible.

For purposes of a historical sociology of youth as well as for its futurological aspect, we find it difficult to define adolescence as a period, phase, or stage which begins around puberty and ends with the assumption of responsible work and family roles and to consider youth as a period between adolescence and adulthood. As Ariès (1962), Gillis (1974), and others have shown, *adolescence did not exist* until the nineteenth century when mass scholarization set in. The individual up to marriage and up to the assumption of more independent work roles was treated as an 'infant in the clothes of adults', the status of the student presenting some exception. Youth up to the seventeenth and eighteenth centuries cannot be considered a period following adolescence as there simply was no adolescence. Specific age was not a dominant feature, for example, of the medieval university. The age of the students varied greatly: children, grown-ups, and the elderly sat there together. 'Puberty' in itself, as Bernfeld (1923) has shown theoretically and as has been documented by masses of data on body size, menarche, and the like has proved to be dependent on economic and social factors as far as its onset and development are concerned. The necessity to subdivide groups of young people by age or to differentiate within the phase which is generally called youth is not in question. Such a subdivision in adolescence and young adults has been suggested (Rosenmayr, 1964b) and further elaborated (Rosenmayr, 1972) in the following way.

The lower age limit of 'youth' as a social group is frequently defined in terms of the onset of sexual maturity—which of course occurs at different chronological ages. However, even this definition does not appear entirely convincing, for instance because children of 11 or 12 may already adopt a behaviour pattern characteristic of teenagers by 'dating' before they reach sexual maturity. The concept of youth cannot be adequately pinpointed in biological terms or with strict reference to age, but must be defined with reference on the one hand to empirically frequent forms of behaviour (attaining dimensions assumed to be relevant) in a roughly determined age range, and on the other to the existence of individual, social, and economic limitations to which grown-ups are not subject. This definition of youth in terms of status should be subdivided by the terms 'adolescents' and 'young adults'; young adults being defined as having already reached certain positions which are not yet open to adolescents. On the other hand, young adults do not, any more than adolescents, yet enjoy full adult status with the access to full sexual, family, household, professional and political rights which this confers.

Initially these axioms complicate matters because they imply that in every society which is studied, the terms 'adolescent' and 'young adult' must be accurately defined with reference to social, economic and legal status criteria: this entails costly procedures when it is desired to make intersocietal or intercultural comparisons. However, these axioms are a prerequisite for the sophisticated and sociologically useful attribution of individuals to social groups or theoretical collectives, which should then yield meaningful information on behaviour, attitudes, and the like. It seems to be more appropriate to call students 'young adults' as they, in several dimensions, have assumed adult roles (as citizens, members of an institution, voters, etc.), certainly not 'adolescents' (or individuals in a period of adolescence) on the grounds of not having yet assumed 're-sponsible work' or family roles. (For a further elaboration of this position see Rosenmayr, 1972.)

Kenneth Keniston has recently used the term 'young adulthood' to denote those 'whose place in society is settled, who are married and perhaps parents, and who are fully committed to an occupation' (Keniston, 1975, p. 7). Keniston rejects the notion of protracted or stretched adolescence when such marital, parental, and occupational commitments are *not* present. Instead he prefers using the term 'youth' to characterize what he feels is 'the emergence on a mass scale of a previously unrecognized stage of life' (p. 8). We agree on the newness of the 'mass scale' yet not on the previous non-recognition or non-existence of this stage of life which in our mind was reserved to certain élites. We have some doubts that this *ad hoc* descriptive and restrictive usage of the term 'youth' is even adequate for the sociological analysis of the present. It is certainly not legitimate for the sociohistorical perspective and tends to freeze perspectives for the futurological approach. We shall provide some reasons below why the phenomena which Keniston describes (the mass access to traditional school education with accompanying varying positions of emancipatory and/or political processes) and for which he usurps what in our theoretical conception should remain a general and principally open term, namely 'youth', will be a very transitional phase of late industrial or early post-industrial society.

The basic theoretical assumption here is that the nature of *any* age group within the structure of the age stratification system of a given society in a given period of history depends upon certain macrosocial influences. Thus the duration, position, or quality of youth (adolescence and young adulthood) in any given society depends upon the systems of production and of representation, and on the training and education to perform the tasks in the social and economic division of labour. Youth further depends on the aims and values of the political system and on the access to and production of ideologies. Historical and/or futurological research must use these categories (division of labour, political system, ideology) for analysis, treating them both as interacting and as simultaneously acting categories.

The family and other systems of emotional significance such as friends and peer groups have significance in structuring the personality in interactive identification and projection processes (see Hartup, Chapter 11). Although such groupings and institutions are constitutive for the individuality of the person which emerges from them, they, as social units, are shaped by and depend on the larger social structures like economic, educational, power and ideological systems. (The use of these categories is intended to be equally important for the analysis of historical as well as 'contemporary' or future relations between youth and society. Their application is largely independent of the methods applied, be they historical, experimental, field research of an observational or questionnaire type, or case studies.) It is further assumed that periods and phases of historical and societal development have to be considered as mutually interconnected open units yet *not* in a sequence of a linear progress, e.g. in the sense of a continuously growing power of youth in society. Recent gains in certain power positions of youth in educational systems cannot be used for linear assumptions and extrapolations of global further development in this respect. If we compare youth in both forms conceptualized in this paper (adolescents and young adults) we find it characterized by certain traits of 'non-incorporation' and lack of status (status deficiency) as compared to the masses of the 'adult' population. They are somehow similar to the elderly retired population in this respect yet they differ from the latter in some ways and in some groups by their more frequent alliance with new historical forces, a matter we have dealt with as an instance of transformation.

In prehistoric times the degree of self-organization of youth outside the family or comparable social institutions was low and societal independence of youth did not exist. The development of a notion and ideal of society in post-archaic, early European cultures goes hand in hand with a special definition of youth and informal youth organizations. Periods connected with empire building and the continuation of systems of dominance produced formal definitions of age status and youth organizations functioning as recruitment and selection mechanisms.

The development of the classical Greek city state saw the emergence of a specific role for young people, with the idea of education fostered by an urban upper class founded on acquirable property. A measure of freedom was allowed and the virtues (*aretai*) cultivated in young people; but the subordination referred to above was still maintained. The civilization of the city state at its apogee finds its classic expression in Plato's *Republic:*

> When the father is wont to become like a child and fear his sons, and the son to become like a father and neither to feel shame before his parents nor to fear them, in order forsooth that he may be free . . . the teacher . . . fears his pupils and flatters them, while pupils despise their teachers . . . and in general the young seek to resemble their elders and contend with them in word and deed, while the elders condescend to the young and are all wit and jollity, imitating the young lest they should appear curmudgeonly and despotic . . . all this softens the soul of the citizens so that they resent even the merest hint of servitude and will not stomach it . . . in the end . . . they disregard even the laws . . . for they lead to excessive servitude (Book 8).

The process of education to the status of an independent citizen able to put forward his opinions with the help of rhetorical and logical arguments and acquire a leading position in society necessarily means that a part of life must be set aside for this education. This represents an important step towards the development of a concept of youth.

By contrast, the factors governing Roman attitudes to youth included a cult based emphasis on the family as an institution and the absence of a private or public school system. Thus nothing comparable to the informal youth groups of Socrates and Plato could develop. Characteristic of

Rome, instead, was a respect for 'advanced years' inevitable in a society where military and political experience and achievement were held in particularly high esteem. There was therefore an upper stratum of young people who accepted established authority, belonged to the *collegia uv enum*, and prepared themselves for a political career.

The European Middle Ages saw the first unfolding of a socially stratified youth: young knights, artisans, students. Youth included the long span from approximately the eighth year of life up to the end of the period of apprenticeship and/or the moment of marriage. The medieval students were the first type of youth which was at some time deviant as well as recognized. The birth of the modern state in the sixteenth century led to the development of princely schools and knightly academies responsible for the training of government officials. The graduates of these educational establishments constituted generation based communities of persons with administrative and political influence. In conjunction with the courtly ceremonial of the day, this system provided much of the basis for young adult subcultures. The gallant or courtly way of life became the ideal of upper-class youth and markedly influenced the life of young members of the burgess class.

Important changes in the condition of youth set in with the Enlightenment and the following period of romanticism in Europe. The young man in the texts of literature and philosophy became a quasi-divine figure mediating salvation to the world. The selected sincere youths, transgressing conventions and outmoded norm systems, many of them stemming from the bourgeoisie or even lower classes, entered into science, philosophy, history and poetry. Youth was often both subject and object of hero worship. Rousseau in his *Emile* had created the basis for an educational philosophy of the young by demanding an extension of the period of education (termed 'moratorium' in the twentieth century) so that 'culture', which Rousseau conceived of as a liberating force, could really be transmitted.

During the nineteenth century youth gained some recognition by its participation in the movements of national defence, political constitutionalism, freedom of the press and of the expression of opinion. Yet none of these revolutions in the 1930s and 1848 were youth revolts. The last decade of the nineteenth century saw the more general introduction of scholarization for the masses of the population in Europe and the

USA and the abolition of child labour. *Mass scholarization created the problem of adolescence.* Those who came out of school at the age of 13 or 14 had been formed and prepared in a certain way. They presented a type different from the developing 'children' that had remained in either their own or another family for occupational training as had been the case before.

The beginning of the twentieth century saw a prospective identification with the young: they were considered the bearers of the future, a future which meant an optimistic prolongation of the then present, promising structures of further development. Therefore youth was tended and furthered, yet at the same time held in control because the structure of norms and values of at least certain ideological groups was to be perpetuated and no reason for fundamental changes within this area accepted. 'Youth' took on some meanings of a revisionist social philosophy couched in promising yet sometimes rather vague expectations. It never was a 'revolutionary' concept until the revolts of the 1960s.

The Youth Movement, particularly strong in England, Germany and Austria, also set in with the beginning of the twentieth century. Churches and the new pedagogical forces of reformist teachers catered especially for the new social age stratum, *adolescence*. The special aspirations for the future of society attached to adolescence was one of the origins of youth research in the world, as it originated in Central Europe and in the USA practically at the same time (Rosenmayr, 1976). The scientific interest in youth clearly began with an interest in adolescence, the new type of a protracted phase of childhood coinciding with physiological puberty: problems of socially and psychologically extended or protracted puberty, however, were soon also discovered (Bernfeld, 1923). It was not until the student revolt of the 1960s that a new meaning could be attached to the prolongation of education and formation.

As we proceed in the history of post-industrial society towards the third millennium, we are confronted with change in all areas. Change seems to have become an obsession. For Central and Western Europe, political, technological, and economic changes during the last half century have become obvious; changes in the moral system only slightly less so (see Mahler, Chapter 4). The rate of becoming aware of these changes was comparatively slow but more recently has accelerated. At the beginning of the third millennium we may expect a change in the

consciousness of change. The role of youth within this accelerated process of growing was up to now a protagonistic one. Whereas in the
nineteenth century, in the wars against Napoleon, in the revolutions of
1848, youth just did its part, in the 1960s youth fought for its own
interests. It was *their* status in universities and schools they wanted to
improve.

Youth as a stratified subsociety

Instead of a systematic summary of pertinent sociological literature
demonstrating the stratification of youth (available in Rosenmayr, 1976)
we will present data from a series of our own researches comparing
middle-class youth (high-school students whom we will call 'pupils')
with young workers (apprentices) in Austria. Lower-class youth has a
stronger tendency to adopt adult status; and seems more forward in
regard to independence in practical matters of everyday life; interactions
and common activities with parents are less frequent than with pupils;
and parental control is weaker (Rosenmayr, 1963; Rosenmayr *et al.*,
1966). Adolescents receiving a full secondary education advance more
quickly in respect of a kind of critical independence ('intellectual autonomy'). Middle-class youth receiving secondary education feels more 'at
home' in cultural systems of symbols extending into the fields of literature
and art and is less frequently induced to escape boredom by engaging in
any activities offered by only casual stimuli of the peer group or the
mass media.

We found that pupils, as compared to apprentices, are controlled to a
greater extent by their parents with regard to movie going, dating, and
dating partners. It seems to be the apprentices, however, who are more
liable to negative sanctions, especially all rough forms of punishment
(Rosenmayr, 1963). As far as family relations go, discussion appears to
be the dominating medium of control for the parents of pupils. In the
working classes, socialization has a firmer footing in more supervisory
forms of control. Aggression and its social presentation are shaped
differently according to social stratification.

What seems to be particularly important is the type of progress which
the two groups of adolescents make in their different processes of cultural
maturation. Table 1 illustrates the two types.

Table 1   Reading habits

	Apprentices		Pupils	
Age	15	17	15	17
Low and middle standard fiction				
Adventure stories	43	24	19	7
War novels and stories	16	23	7	9
Historical novels	7	13	20	15
Detective stories	11	9	13	10
'Fact' books	14	17	16	14
Literary novels, poetry	9	14	25	45
	100%	100%	100%	100%
	(N=269)	(N=335)	(N=354)	(N=350)

Source: Rosenmayr *et al.*, 1966, p. 145; see also Rosenmayr, 1970c, p. 173, for an English version.

Instead of asking respondents to state what type of book they liked best (as most of the very numerous reading surveys in German-speaking countries had done), we asked them to give us the title of the last book they had read. The several hundred titles thus obtained were then classified by: subject matter; the age group for whom they appeared suitable; literary standard; and whether the story had been turned into a film. (The quality criteria we used were made explicit.) Table 1 above shows only the results for literary standard. We considered 'literary standard of last book read' an indicator for the dimension we termed 'cultural level'. We believe cultural level to be distinct from, although not orthogonal to, the dimension of 'literary age'. Between the ages of 15 and 17, the percentage of pupils reading books of high literary standard increased as much as from 25% to 45%. Among the apprentices, the table reveals no such marked development. Here the impact of continued education is evident.

The pupils' development toward a higher literary standard of the books read depends mainly upon the influence of the school. Yet schooling received accounts only partially for this influence. In the selection of books for private reading, the exchange and borrowing of books among classmates is important too. That the majority of pupils come from families with a high cultural level probably has a strong 'group effect' (to use Lazarsfeld's term) on the book reading choices of peers from less cultured families. Participation in other media, for example, the frequency of visits to theatres, concerts, art exhibitions, and also the types of newspapers and periodicals read, seems to be much more directly influenced by family habits and thus depends a good deal on social origin.

Our extensive comparisons with data on adolescent reading collected in the 1920s suggest that parallel to the well known acceleration in physical maturity, an acceleration in 'literary age' also seems to have taken place during these last three decades. That is, certain types of books are being read by comparable groups at a somewhat lower demographic age now than 30 or 40 years ago. Concerning movie going habits, Table 2 shows a development towards higher quality for pupils than apprentices (Rosenmayr, 1966).

Table 2 Films of high rated quality as seen by apprentices and pupils

	Apprentices		Pupils	
Age	15	17	15	17
	15	12	24	34
	(N=303)	(N=400)	(N=355)	(N=344)

Source: Rosenmayr *et al.*, 1966, p. 189.

A comparison between pupils and apprentices also shows that the former are relatively more interested in such topics as religion and politics. And the difference grows larger as the young persons grow older. Privileged adolescents experience a differential development of cultural interests and an expansion of cultural activities, while the underprivileged experience stagnation.

Let us not forget that the uprise of new ideas among adolescents was almost solely an affair of students who very often, in the name of class egalitarianism, joined their peers in (quasi-)revolutionary ideas. Growing up in privileged adolescence results in encouragement and guidance to solve problems in a specific way. It supports the motivation to engage in leisure activities which satisfy culturally higher aims. Such processes might also be referred to as the development of the cultural capacity of selecting. They may be documented in newspaper- and book-reading habits, in musical taste and activities. Privileged adolescence gives the young more numerous changes of development over a relatively long period. Apprentices, however, are both more exposed to and more influenced by those elements of popular culture (Rosenmayr *et al.*, 1966, pp. 1–10) which are directed toward speed and ease of immediate wish fulfilment.

Upper middle-class youth is further characterized by patterns of deferred gratification, self-reliance, and planning one's future. Deprivation, on the other hand, is characterized by a lack of history and a lack of future orientation, planning ahead, etc. Unfavourable conditions lead to a sticking to the limited horizon of the present; they show up in the inability to defer gratifications. In order to describe some traits of this attitude of general apathy or short range living we use the term 'fatal immediacy' (Rosenmayr, 1970).

We find that fatal immediacy in various forms is still present within industrialized societies with well organized school systems. We observe interlocking networks of disfavouring conditions which intensify early disadvantages. It is likely, however, that expanding welfare institutions, growing nationalization of industries, and the rising proportion of schooling on broad national levels will diminish the preponderance of class structures. Or, they may move on to a different level, beyond conflicts over property and control of a basic income level. Multidimensional participation according to various types and levels of interest will become more important than unidimensional membership in well defined strata.

The capacity of youth as a factor of (or in) social change, as an active agent in historical and social process, depends on the rise of the influence of mass education in the secondary school system and universities. The growing impact of the mass media on the imagery of childhood, adolescence, and youth has de-institutionalized socialization processes and will continue to do so. The beginning of the twenty-first century will see less programmed and more off-hand socialization processes than those that have been characteristic of closed (or at least well defined) institutions. This leads us immediately to the futurological view.

Trends in the future development of youth in society

Industrialization brought about the rise of the importance of an inter-dependent school system as the dominant factor for the *content* of socialization. The family became more and more limited to early emotional interventions, to transmission of securities and anxieties, guilt feelings, achievement attitudes and the like. The structures transmitted by the family were elaborated and filled by the contents and orientations mediated by the school system; this was true at least for the petite bourgeoisie, the majority of the masses migrating to the cities, and for the proletariat (see Husén, Chapter 12). The growth of the latter (during the last decade of the nineteenth century) soon became influenced by the organizations of their class.

The crisis of the self-definition of the young, their quest for autonomy and self-determination arising as a social force in the mid-1960s has strongly affected the role of the school and led to the questioning of its centrality. Socialization becomes more based on mass diffusion when the socializing forces are hidden in organizational nuclei of the movie making and TV producing world, and in the (quasi-)political weeklies which create certain needs and dependencies in the regular consumers of their products. Socialization of youth was already in some phases of the student revolt more *directly* linked with the progressive political opinion leader élite. The filters and sieves of the family and of local environment rank second only in importance.

The family will continue to exert a relatively amorphous emotional backing and at least retain linkage, some socialization, and allocation functions. The 'living space', the area of cognitive and interactional realization of family ties has been and will further be limited in highly industrialized or post-industrial society. The general rapid decrease in the birth rate of industrial nations since the 1960s is both a result and a cause of changes in family solidarity.

The period of 'youth' in its future meaning will have to cover the socio-economic necessity of prolonged preparation for complex functions in the upper strata of the division of labour pyramid plus the quest for autonomy in this period of transition into 'fuller adulthood'. The original bourgeois philosophy (since Rousseau) has been to defer gratification in order to obtain autonomy. Self-reliance and the qualifications to determine one's career were the aims for which immediate social and sexual satisfaction had to be postponed and the consequent frustration withstood. The increased extension of youth (almost into the early 30s for individuals with ambitious professional career goals) and the growing general social crisis of normative structures in relation to authority, sex, self-control, and the like will have important effects. Further permissiveness and pluralism will ultimately lead to the rejection of the notions of deferred gratification and of moratorium and to their replacement by the ideas of participation and determination.

New social channels (such as the anticipation of marriage patterns in long-lasting, heterosexual, premarital, dyadic friendships) for gratification are now sought on a broader basis. The discussion of actual behavioural change in sexual areas of the young during the last decade is not closed yet. It can no longer be affirmed, however, that the verbalization of sexual problems is the main change in this respect (Rosenmayr, 1976). 'Sex with love' becomes more and more acceptable even outside the general norm structure. The 'double standard' which permits the male a promiscuity denied the female is receding and will continue to do so. Sexual activity in the female will be denounced less in the future.

Looking ahead to the beginning of the twenty-first century in Europe and the USA we offer the following prognostic points and preview.

1. During the next decades a reduction of the proportion of youth will take place in industrialized societies.

The prognosis of this trend ought to be supplemented by a comparative age structure prognosis showing differential developments and thus backing our thesis of the socio-economic dependency of the phenomenon of youth (see Figure 1).

Demographic projections for the coming decades, as presented also by N. B. Ryder for the USA (1974), show that because of the decrease in the birth rate the percentage of adolescents and young adults in the total population will stagnate and the ratio of the population aged 14–24 to the population aged 25–64 will decline from 0.449 in 1970 to 0.423 in 1980 and 0.332 in 1990. It remains to be seen, however, whether the percentage of adolescents in the developed industrial societies of Europe and the USA will be stable after the beginning of the twenty-first century, or whether we are to expect a cyclical fluctuation in the percentages of adolescents in the total population. The prognosis for the German Federal Republic is given in Table 3 as an example for Western Europe.

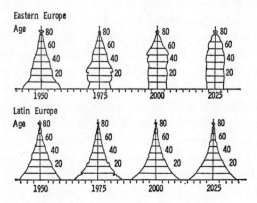

Figure 1. Age structure changes in Eastern Europe and Latin America, 1950–2025. Source: Mesarovic and Pestel, 1974.

Table 3   Expected growth of the population aged 0–20 in the Federal Republic of Germany, 1969–2000 (in 'ooos and as a percentage of the total population)[a]

	1969		1980		1990		2000	
	'ooos	%	'ooos	%	'ooos	%	'ooos	%
Population age 0–20	18 846	31.2	20 488	32.7	20 488	32.7	22 313	32.4
Total population	60 463		62 638		65 392		68 947	

[a] Source: *Gesundheitsbericht—Deutscher Bundestag*, 1970, p. 23.

2. Some further reductions in the importance of the informative content of family socialization are likely to occur. In addition, we can probably also expect a change in the intensity of solidarity within the family. A crystallization of functions of emotional and basic economic support by the family and its linkage functions may be expected.

3. As a result of the growing emphasis on development throughout the lifespan, and on the pressing problems of the middle aged, the elderly,

and of the very old, a de-emphasis on youth as a special force or group in society will occur.

4. Historically, youth has been the first phase in the human lifespan expanded as a prerequisite for coping with a more complicated system of production and information in society. This expansion (through a pro-longed period of education) had profound repercussions. Contrary to historic youth movements and to the tenets of those youth organizations which remained integrated within society even if they proclaimed the character of an insular utopia, the new political youth of the mass universities demanded changes in the basic assumptions and mechanisms of the social system. Their successes remained to be assessed. Structural changes in the universities in Central Europe through legislation were some consequences of the student revolt; a reinforcement of left wing intellectualism and a broadening of leftist influence in the mass media were some of the consequences of the anti-authoritarian breakthrough.

5. Future development will see a much more general expansion of the education to other age groups. The notion of permanent education thus will de-dramatize the unique position of youth in this respect. Youth, historically, will have been a forerunner in the processes of obtained autonomy.

6. The position of youth at the beginning of the twenty-first century will probably also be more integrated with other age groups on account of new systems of combination between learning, schooling and work (Coleman, 1974). The importance of an age-homogeneous school system and culture will diminish.

7. The notion of generation will decline in importance owing to a greater inhomogeneity in socialization, a lesser stability of value systems over the lifespan, and a more complex bouquet of political and administrative loyalties. Similarity of attitudes of individuals cooperating in groups on account of belonging to the same age cohorts of the same class will, accordingly, be less common. New types of solidarization will therefore have to be reckoned with and should be studied increasingly (see Eisenstadt, Chapter 6).

8. As a consequence of these developments, new concepts of youth policies and youth research geared towards an anticipation of future

development rather than being formulated on premises based on the present are urgently needed.

9. In spite of temporary drawbacks due to economic recessions, the 'leisure world' will continue to expand and the territory for independence of youth from traditional lifestyles will be increased thereby. Leisure and cultural transformation will take on more political significance and structures of society will be defined increasingly in terms of leisure and cultural activities.

10. The notion of politics will develop in a paradoxical fashion: bureaucratization and abstract planning will increase as well as initiatives of a personal, local and more spontaneous type. Youth will be engaged predominantly in the second type and will thus perform transformational functions for society.

References

Allerbeck, K. R. 1971. Eine sozialstrukturelle Erklärung von Studentenbewegungen in hochentwickelten Industriegesellschaften. In: K. R. Allerbeck and L. Rosenmayr (Eds.), *Aufstand der Jugend?* München: Juventa.

Ariès, P. 1962. *L'enfant et la vie familiale dans l'ancien régime*, Paris, 1960, transl. into English: *Centuries of childhood: a social history of family life.* New York: Vintage Books.

Bernfeld, S. 1923. Über eine typische form der männlichen Pubertät, in *Imago*, vol. 9.

Braungart, R. G. 1975. Youth and social movements. In S. Dragastin and G. Elder (Eds.), *Adolescence in the life cycle.* New York: Wiley.

Coleman, J. S. 1974. *Youth: Transition to adulthood.* Chicago and London: The University of Chicago Press.

Gesundheitsbericht-Deutscher Bundestag, Bonn, 1970.

Gillis, J. R. 1974. *Youth and history, tradition and change in European age relations 1770–Present.* New York/London.

Gisser, R. 1974. Modell der natürlichen Bevölkerungsentwicklung in Österreich 1971–2000, in: *Statistische Nachrichten*, vol. 5.

Keniston, K. 1975. Youth as a stage of life. In: R. J. Havighurst and P. H. Dryer (Ed.), *Youth: the Seventy-Fourth Yearbook of the National Society for the Study of Education*, Part 1. Chicago: National Society for the Study of Education, pp. 3–26.

Mannheim, K. 1928. Das problem der Generationen, in: *Kölner Vierteljahrshefte*, Bd 2, 3.

Mesarovic, M. and Pestel, E. 1974. *Mankind at the turning point*. The second report to the Club of Rome. New York: Dutton.

Rosenmayr, L. 1963. *Familienbeziehungen und Freizeitgewohnheiten jugendlicher Arbeiter*. Wien: Verlag für Geschichte und Politik.

Rosenmayr, L. 1964a. Sozialbeziehungen und Milieu als Faktoren in der Pubertät männlicher Jugendlicher, in: *Österreichische Ärztezeitung*, vol. 19.

Rosenmayr, L. 1964b. Economic and social conditions influencing the lives of young people, in UNESCO, Annex V.

Rosenmayr, L. 1970. Cultural poverty of working class youth, in: P. Townsend (Ed.), *A concept of poverty*. London: Heinemann.

Rosenmayr, L. 1972. Dimensions of the concept of 'Youth', in: L. Rosenmayr, New theoretical approaches to the sociological study of young people. *International Social System Journal*, vol. 24, no. 2.

Rosenmayr, L. 1976. Schwerpunkte der Jugendsoziologie, vol. 6. In R. König (Ed.), *Handbuch der empirischen Sozialforschung*. Stuttgart: Enke.

Rosenmayr, L., Köckeis, E. and Kreutz, H. *Kulturelle Interessen von Jugendlichen*. München: Juventa.

Ryder, N. B. 1974. The demography of youth, in: J. S. Coleman *et al.*, *Youth: Transition to adulthood*. Chicago and London: The University of Chicago Press.

6 Cultural settings and adolescence and youth around the year 2000*

Samuel N. Eisenstadt

How will the cultural context as it will develop by the year 2000 affect the characteristics of adolescence and youth in that period? The very posing of this question assumes that we are able to foresee or predict future social and cultural developments to some degree for that span of years. But any such enterprise is inevitably beset with many difficulties, the greatest of which is not necessarily the lack of knowledge but rather our inability to specify exactly what knowledge might be relevant for it.

Some basic assumptions

Any such specification is based on two interconnected sets of—often implicit—assumptions. One set is our assumptions about the nature of society and of social and cultural processes. The other is that we necessarily extrapolate from some events or trends in the past and the present and we assume that these will somehow continue or recede. There is no way out of these constraints. The only way to proceed is to make these assumptions as explicit as possible. My analysis of the possible impact on adolescence and on youth of the cultural context as it might develop in the year 2000 will be based on the assumption that some social and cultural processes have, both in the Western and the non-Western world, moved away from the initial premises of Western modernity. These processes are related to what has been called the development of the post-industrial society and they will indeed continue. Of course, this assumption may not be the case at all. These processes may recede either 'back' to the

---

*The analysis presented here is a further elaboration of theories initially attempted in Eisenstadt (1957, 1962, 1971, 1974).

initial premises or turn into some entirely new social and cultural situations. But our analysis will be based on the general assumption of the continuation of such processes. And we shall attempt to indicate some of the contradictions and problems related to the formation of adolescence and youth which may arise out of the continuation of these processes.

The decomposition of the initial paradigm of Western modernity

As has been so often stressed in the literature, the central initial focus of European modernity has been the exploration of continuously expanding human and natural environments. That their destiny, their directions, and even mastery could be attained by the conscious effort of man and society was unquestioned. The central premise was the possibility of active formation of crucial aspects of social, cultural, and natural orders by conscious human activity and participation. The fullest expressions of this attitude could be found in the breakthrough of science and of the scientific approach into the parameters of the cultural order. The premises were that the exploration of nature by man is an 'open' enterprise which creates a new cultural order; that the continuous expansion of scientific and technological knowledge can transform both the cultural and social orders and create new, external and internal environments; and that these offer endless opportunities for human exploration and, at the same time, can be harnessed to man's social, cultural, intellectual vision and technical needs.

Accordingly, the special characteristics of European modernity were initially focused on attempts to form 'rational' cultures, efficient economies, civil (class) societies and nation states where the tendency toward rational expansion of all aspects of cultural and social life could become fully articulated. Actual developments throughout the world, first in Europe and later elsewhere, did not bear out the assumptions about the possibility of such automatic expansion of all aspects of social and cultural creativity. It is true that the Western world has witnessed a continuous, unprecedented increase in standards of living and in material abundance, thus living up at least to some of the promises inherent in the vision of continuous institutional expansion, yet many contradictions have developed in the process.

Expansion in one sphere of social life did not necessarily assure parallel expansion in other fields, or the growing participation of various groups and strata in the social and cultural order; nor did it necessarily and automatically provide these groups with fuller 'meaning' in their different spheres of life. These contradictions were rooted in the fact that all such processes of expansion were connected with continuous changes in the distribution of power, in the structural organization of different institutional spheres, and in the modes of access to them. Hence with expansion came processes of structural dislocation, of exclusion of different social groups, various dimensions of human existence, and attributes of human endeavour from the central domain of society and cultural life. Tendencies toward such contradictions, to the dissociation between different aspects of such expansion, were already incipient in the late nineteenth century. It was only later, after the first major economic and sociopolitical crises of modern Europe, and after the attainment of many of the initial goals of broadening the scope of participation and access to the sociopolitical centres, that these tendencies to dissociation between the different elements of the original charismatic vision of European modernity became more fully apparent.

The problematic aspects of these trends are brought out most fully in developments in those spheres in which development has been seemingly continuous and unhindered. The expansion of science and technology was the epitome of continuous innovation and expansion of rationality. The 'scientific' components of a general world view have continuously permeated social life in contemporary society, increasing the awareness of broader strata. And the results of technological scientific development have affected daily life through, for example, the expansion of consumer possibilities, the spread of nuclear weapons, and the increase of environmental pollution.

But at the same time the growth of the specialized knowledge could not always become fully integrated (as was to some degree predicted in the initial vision of European modernity) into the general 'world views' in a meaningful way for all social groups. There was a growing feeling of dissociation between the growth of such specialized knowledge and the broader cultural paradigms of the emerging cultural tradition and of the actual experiences of the broader strata. At the same time, the very potential power of scientific knowledge as well as the premises of the initial charismatic vision of European modernity tended to sharpen the feeling that such dissociation is illegitimate.

Changes in the situation of adolescence and youth

These processes gave rise to combinations of continuously mutually re-inforcing developments. New types of movements and of protest emerged on the one hand and structural and cultural discontinuities and contradic-tions on the other. This combination created the new societal and cultural frameworks which shape, and will probably continue to shape, the new contours of adolescence and, above all, of youth.

Within the new movements of protest which developed from around the 1950s on, there took place a marked shift in the orientation and foci of protest. Demands for greater participation in national–political centres, attempts to influence this participation, and attempts to influence socioeconomic policies began to give way to new directions. The most important of these directions were: first, attempts to 'disrobe' these centres of their charismatic legitimacy and perhaps of any legi-timacy at all; second, continuous searches for new loci of meaningful participation beyond existing sociopolitical centres and concomitant attempts to create independent new centres; and, third, attempts to couch the patterns of participation in their centres not so much in socio-political or economic terms but more in symbols of primordial or direct social participation.

Many of these new orientations of protest were directed not only against the bureaucratization and functional rationalization connected with grow-ing technology, but also against the supposed central place of science and scientific investigation as the basis, or even one of the bases, of the sociocultural order. Each of the new orientations denotes an important aspect of what Weber called the demystification of the world. Here, demystification has become focused around the possibility that the attain-ment of participation in the social and cultural centres may indeed be meaningless. Thus the centres may lose their mystery and the King may be naked indeed.

Side by side with these new movements of protest, there tended to develop in many contemporary societies in general, and in the highly developed and industrialized ones in particular, a whole series of structural and symbolical discontinuities and contradictions. These were much more variegated than those which developed in the first stages of modernity as a result of fusions between closed traditional familial structure and more specialized and universalistic occupational and political systems. Discontinuities and contradictions tended to become transposed beyond the direct opposition between family and educational and occupational sectors to the different sectors of the society through which youth passes. The major foci of such discontinuities and contradictions became much more diversified. They included discontinuity between the family and the educational and occupational spheres; between the family and educational institutions, on the one hand, and the occupational sector on the other; between the productive and the consumer roles in the economic sector; between the values and orientations inculcated in the family and the educational institutions and the central collective symbols of the society, between the premises of these symbols and the actual political roles of the parents and younger people alike (see Husén, Chapter 12; and Delors, Chapter 13). Thus they came to cross-cut family roles themselves.

Impacts of social and cultural transformations on adolescence and youth

These new types of discontinuities tended to impinge most intensively on the social and cultural situation of youth and on the concrete manifestations of youth problems and protest. Several such repercussions of these discontinuities should be singled out. One is that the span of areas of social life that the specific youth or student culture encompasses has tended to expand continuously. First, it has extended over longer periods of life, reaching, through the impact of the extension of higher education, to what before was seen as early adulthood. Second, it tends more and more to include areas of work, of leisure time activity, and of many interpersonal relations. Third, the potential and actual autonomy of these groups, and the possibility their members have of direct access to work, to marriage and family life, to political rights, and to goods of consumption have greatly increased, while their dependence on adults has greatly decreased.

Thus, paradoxically enough, the growing direct access of young people, both adolescents and youth, to various areas of life has given way to a growing insecurity of status and self-identity and to growing ambiguity of adult roles. This insecurity and ambiguity tends to be enhanced by the prolongation of the span between biological and social maturity and by the extension of the number of years spent in basically 'preparatory' (educational) institutions. The growing dissociation between the values of educational institutions and future, especially occupational and parental roles of those participating in them, exacerbates the insecurity. And the ambiguity is heightened by the fact that for a long period of time many 'young' people have no clear occupational roles or responsibilities. They may be dependent on their parents or on public institutions for the provision of their economic needs while, at the same time, they constitute an important economic force as consumers and exercise full political rights. These discontinuities very often tended to culminate in a crisis or weakening of authority evident in the lack of development of adequate role models and the erosion of many of the bases of legitimation of existing authority.

As a result of all these processes the possibility of linking personal transition to social groups and to cultural values alike, to societal and cosmic time, so strongly emphasized in the 'classical' youth movements and observable, to some extent, even in the earlier looser youth culture, has become greatly weakened. In general, these developments have depressed the image of the societal and cultural future and have deprived it of its allure. Either the ideological separation between present and future has become smaller or the two have tended to become entirely dissociated. Out of the first of these conditions has grown what Riesman has called the cult of immediacy; out of the other, a total negation of the present in the name of a future entirely different from the present and totally unrelated to any consciousness of the past.

In many societies, the new states of Asia and Africa or Russian postrevolutionary or European welfare states, this tendency is intensified by the fact that the new generation of youth and students face not only reactionary parents but also successful revolutionaries who have become part of a new 'establishment'. Here youth has to face a new collective reality, one that evinces all the characteristics of a bureaucratized establishment, but at the same time presents itself as the embodiment of revolutionary collective and spiritual values. These tendencies were also closely related to the reversal relation between the definition of different age spans and the possibilities of social and cultural creativity. Youth became more and more seen not only as preparation for the possibilities of independent and creative participation in social and cultural life, but as the very embodiment of permissive, often unstructured creativity, only to be faced later on with the constants of a highly organized, constricting, meritocratic, and bureaucratic environment.

Student rebellion of the 1960s

These various developments culminated in the most dramatic way in the outburst of student protest in the late 1960s. The rebellions were characterized by a very unique combination of generational conflict with intellectual antinomianism and were focused in an attack on the university. The university was perceived as the major focus of legitimation of modern social order. The attack on it indicated dissatisfaction with its own internal arrangements and with its function as one mechanism of occupational and meritocratic selection but these were not the sole reasons. Taking the university as the object of attack emphasized a denial that the existing order could realize the basic premises of modernity: the effort was to establish and maintain an order which could do justice to the claims to creativity and participation in the broader social order and to overcome the various contradictions which have developed within it from the point of view of these claims. It was in the attack on the university that the new dimensions of protest, the negation of the premises of modernity and the emphasis on the meaninglessness of the existing centres and the symbols of collective identity, became articulated in the most extreme way.

These dramatic events have passed away, leaving a legacy of apathy and discontent and, also, continuous potential unrest. Under certain conditions the attacks may re-occur but even if they do not, the continuation of the various structural processes analyzed above will have far reaching consequences for the emerging sociocultural context. The structural discontinuities, the new orientations of protest, the memories and symbols of the dramatic occurrences of these rebellions will, in their turn, have important consequences for adolescence and, above all, for youth.

Possible direction and impact of cultural and social changes

These consequences will be evident in some of the new cultural contours. First, they will be seen in a growing emphasis on spheres and dimensions of life which were largely neglected in the original vision of European modernity: among these are aesthetic concerns and solidarity in the domain of consumption, leisure, and privacy. Second, these processes will increase the dissociation between different types of knowledge and cultural creativity.

There can be little doubt that the growth of specialized technical knowledge will continue and that in many ways such knowledge will become an even more powerful instrument and influence in economic life. Yet with all its growing 'practical' importance, such knowledge will tend to become more and more conceived as a very special, segregated type of knowledge, or as an important and powerful instrument in the technical analysis of choices between different types of values. It is doubtful whether it will be seen as flowing automatically into the mainstream of the cultural order, as becoming automatically a part of tradition and creativity, as open to everybody's participation. Only some of its components will become integrated within the general parameters of the cultural tradition. Other types of knowledge—such as the aesthetic, the contemplative, the mystical or the like—will tend to become more and more autonomous and distinct, and they may become to some degree organizationally and structurally separated from the centres of specialized knowledge, dissociated from them; and yet accepted as fully legitimate. As a result of all these processes a new type of association among social structure, culture, and different levels of political activity and organization will develop.

Adolescent substructures

The major channels and loci through which these new developments might be institutionalized will probably be loosely, yet continuously connected, structural enclaves. Within them the new cultural orientations, emphasizing the possibility of the extension of individuality beyond the more bureaucratized, meritocratic, occupational, and administrative structures, will be developed and upheld. These enclaves may become

5

centres of various subcultures, of which those connected nowadays with adolescence and youth are the most outstanding. Some people may participate in them fully, others in a more transitory fashion. Within these enclaves, different types of knowledge may develop either in more 'rational' self-explanatory directions or into more 'irrational', aberrant, and purely expressive ones. Many of these tendencies may be contradictory, many mutually reinforcing. Which of them will predominate depends on specific constellations of the various conditions specified above.

But, however strong such dissociation between different types of cultural activity and between different collectivities will be, the segregation between different cultural orientations will necessarily be structured in a different way than in traditional society. It will probably be based on the continuous flow of (very often the same) population through different structural and organizational enclaves within which these different types of cultural and social orientations can be organized. Hence the tension between them will constitute a continuous and permanent aspect of the contemporary social and cultural scene.

One impact of these tensions will be the development of new foci for continuous protest which will add, in both organizational and symbolic terms, to the available reservoir of models, traditions and movements of protest in modern societies. A second impact will be the continuous search for new loci of meaningful participation beyond the existing centres, and concomitant attempts to create new centres which would be independent of existing ones. Third, attempts will be made to couch the patterns of participation in these centres not so much in sociopolitical or economic terms, but in symbols of primordial relations or of direct social participation, thus returning to many elements of anarchist and romantic traditions.

The more extreme of these movements, and especially those of the students, will constitute continuous reservoirs of new types of revolutionary activity. This will be fed and reinforced by the continuous spread of modernity throughout the world and by the problem and aspiration it raises. Most of these movements and ideologies will, at least initially, be leftist oriented. The predominant leftist orientation of most modern student movements thus will continue, but the degree of their organizational proximity to leftist, socialist parties will greatly vary and, on the whole, will probably be rather ambivalent and discontinuous. However, given their great predilection against any 'establishment' centres and organizations as their basic ideological and antinomian orientations (mostly fully seen, as has been mentioned, in their revolt against the university and the transitory nature of their membership) it will be only in some of the exceptional conditions that these revolutionary groups and activities will develop into fully fledged organized, continuous, political organizations, or parties that work within the existing political frameworks. They will, however, constitute nuclei of new international enclaves of various political and cultural subcultures with highly mobile and changing populations that will cut across national and state boundaries and provide rather continuous 'irritants' to the existing frameworks.

All these developments will provide the basic sociocultural framework within which youth will be 'formed' during the coming decades. These developments will probably reinforce the tendency toward extending the youth moratorium as well as strengthen the growing emphasis on youth as the carrier of 'pure' values. Accordingly young people will also continue to act as continuous carriers of various subcultures and it is they who will constitute the most active forces in the various structural enclaves analyzed above. But it is exactly here that some potential, rather contradictory tendencies may develop, the ultimate results of which are as yet difficult to predict. The root of these possible contradictions lies in the fact that all the processes and tendencies analyzed above, if indeed they become actualized, will, paradoxically, lessen the symbolic as well as the structural differences between the adult world and that of youth in the strictly 'chronological' or biosociological sense. 'Youth' will become more and more a symbolic dimension which can be attached to age groups. Thus, while the original structural discontinuities which gave rise to these new symbolic definitions of youth may indeed continue— yet the very development of these symbolic expressions may perhaps give rise to a blurring of these differences—thus also minimizing the original cultural discontinuities.

Moreover all these new symbolic dimensions, as well as structural enclaves and organization will become, in the coming decades, parts of the 'establishment' which the new generation of youth will face, thus necessarily losing much of their attractiveness for 'rebellion'. The study of the repercussions of these possible developments is still very much before us but we should address our attention more and more to these possibilities.

References

Eisenstadt, S. N. 1957. *From generation to generation*. Glencoe: Free Press.

Eisenstadt, S. N. 1962. Archetypal patterns of youth, *Daedalus*, vol. 91, no. 1, pp. 28–47.

Eisenstadt, S. N. 1971 (May). Generational conflict and intellectual antinomianism, *The Annals of the American Academy of Political & Social Sciences*, vol. 395, pp. 68–79.

Eisenstadt, S. N. 1974. *Tradition, change and modernity* New York: John Wiley.

7 Youth in the year 2000: the problem of values*

Marc Faessler

'Is there a life before death?' could be read on the walls of the Sorbonne in May 1968. Once again, young people were putting to Western society the essential question touching the basic aims of its social project and the values underlying it. At the same time those same young people, who were considered as a sector of the general process of social integration, revealed themselves to be the magnifying mirror of the unconfessed contradictions of world society. The fundamental question concerning the meaning of life strikes at the very heart of the technocratic and functional pretension of our society, masking under the hegemony of planning and growth the desperate nihilism of its search for possessions. Between youth and society there is thus a relationship of conflict. On the one hand, young people are the expression and the mirror of forces, of social processes, and of value conflicts that contribute towards shaping the face of our society. On the other hand, however, by revealing through their destructive behaviour the existence of other possible alternatives within a society pursuing its own ends, youth makes manifest the implicit and debatable choices of those ends. The conflict, then, is about values, if we understand this term in the broad sense of a motivating factor orienting the social conditions governing the exercise of freedom and self-realization. A problem of social ethics arises which is not concerned with the working out of an idealistic scale of values, but with the possibility or impossibility of articulating a socialization imposed by virtue of a certain view of man and traditional aspirations about what form the necessary rupture and protest should take.

* Originally prepared in French. English translation by G. Luton.

The question of youth thus turns into a question of the ability of a society to change itself in order to give the right of expression to new values.

Looking into the future (futurology) is a difficult art. It runs the risk of being no more than a sociology of illusion or a prophecy of the imagination. We shall therefore confine ourselves in this paper to situating the phenomenon of 'youth' in relation to the most probable trends of our future in the Western world and to evaluating the significance of certain conflicts of values in our society.

The planet of the young in the orbit of post-industrial society

In speaking here of 'youth' or 'young people' we refer to the social group constituted by young adolescents and young adults who are going through the phase of socialization and integration common to everyone, thereby often showing behaviour which society finds difficult to understand. The term 'the planet of the young' (Duvignaud, 1975) has been used to emphasize three striking social phenomena: the constitution of young people into specific groups, their emergence as a vital agent in their own socialization, and their tendency to form a subculture. Many sociological studies (e.g. Arnold, Bassand, Crettaz and Kellerhals, 1971) have demonstrated that a radical change has taken place in the psychological and social induction of young people into society as a whole. The pressure of urbanization has provided a material basis for the formation of groups and of spaces reserved for young people. New agents of socialization (the mass media) have increased their influence and supplanted or broken the old agents (family, school, church, etc.). Finally there has been the break brought about between the space–time of leisure left to the initiative of the young and the space–time of schooling, jealously kept under the dependence of standards defined by society. A 'young environment' has thus grown up which, for the first time in the history of our society, has become an environment of specific reference in which young people, confronted with the criteria and values of the adult world, build up their own style of life and give expression to their own values. It is evident, however, that this marginalization, this situation of relative 'apartheid' experienced by young people has not come about in complete independence of society as a whole. The room given to leisure, for example, in which the young invest a good proportion of the attributes that belong to them, is largely underpinned by the ideology of 'happiness' implicit in an economy of affluence. The result is an unstable situation in which the aspirations of the young and the instigations of society interpenetrate in the quest for an identity that may range from over-conformism to the protesting rejection of the system, via critical awareness of social inadequacies. In consequence, the integration and socialization of young people are marked by a conflict of fundamental values in the realization of their own personalities. As agents of their own socialization, the young evaluate the importance accorded to relationships and exchange, with the emphasis on the search for a meaning in life, placing stress on creativity and spontaneity. As the object, however, of a socialization imposed on them from outside by the agents of society, young people find themselves called upon to comply with the social imperatives opposed by contradictory images of happiness, by an ideal of rational and functional efficiency and by decision structures in which force and not participation is the governing factor.

At bottom, then, the question is: will the future of our society in the 25 years that separate us from the year 2000 aggravate or resolve this conflict? No one can make any definite predictions. The planet of the young may adjust to its orbit and remain at the distance it has taken up, tempered by the force of attraction of our post-industrial society. It may also leave its present field of gravity to take up the trajectory of other revolutions. . . .

Given the general trends of our society, the first alternative seems to us (unfortunately?) more probable. True, the idea of growth is nowadays being challenged; space and energy are becoming scarce commodities, the environment has to be safeguarded, the problems of birth control, famine and armament are being tackled at a worldwide level, the male-female relationship is being radically transformed, and the consequences of biomedical research have to be controlled. But the very solution of all these urgent problems, whether in a capitalist or a socialist system, involves a concentration of economic power and a control of development that can only strengthen even more the values of integration based on technological specialization, efficiency, and functionalism. Although severely criticized and even described as 'thoughtless', the Hermann Kahn report and that of the Hudson Institute on the measurable characteristics of the year 2000 seem to us, without necessarily agreeing with the premises on which they are based, to present a realistic, perhaps over-realistic, picture of the future:

> Industrial income will be roughly fifty times higher than that in the pre-industrial period.
> The majority of economic activities will have left the primary sector (agriculture) and the secondary sector (industrial production) and have passed to the tertiary and quaternary sectors (i.e. the services sectors).
> Private enterprises will have ceased to be the principal source of technological and scientific reaction.
> The laws of the market will undoubtedly play a less important role than those of the public sector and of social bodies.
> Industry will probably be controlled by cybernetics. Progress will be governed principally by educational systems and the technological innovation at their service.
> The factors of time and space will no longer play a dominant role in the problems of communication.
> The gap in a post-industrial society between high and low incomes will be narrower than that which we know today in the industrial society (Servan-Schreiber, 1967, pp. 44–45).

The aspect in these future evaluations that seems to us to merit emphasis is the emergence of a quaternary sector comprising services that will progressively become disengaged from the laws of the market, such as research institutes, foundations, and non-profit organizations; these will perhaps be capable of creating, side by side with the exigences of global society, islands of creativity where, in relatively modest social confines (lodgings, buying cooperatives, rural communities, artists' settlements, etc.) people can live out countermodels satisfying other aspirations and based on values other than those that are indispensable to the profit seeking world. In this hypothesis we are heading towards a dichotomous society, accentuating the break between personal and collective life, but in which the possibility of self-realization will be available in the extent to which people are prepared to renounce an identification with the global project of society—a real plurality of possible futures. To some extent this is what is taking place in the counter-cultural movement in the USA. Whole communities are living in a subsistence economy based on the values of artisan simplicity and on a return to nature, their only financial resources being allowances from public assistance.

The following is the significant text of an intervention on the part of Roszak during a consultation organized by the 'Church and Society' Department of the Ecumenical Council of Churches:

> For some people—economists, academics, government planners, trade union elites and futurologists—post-industrialism implies that we have crossed the Himalayan summits of permanent abundance . . . the post-industrialized being these privileged peoples who have won the right to live happily ever after. They have their needs but gorge themselves on the milk and honey of affluence . . . and they put up with the minor inconveniences of belonging to a 'developed' economy: the bomb, a ravaged environment, traffic jams, the idiocy of the life of consumption, the super-sonic pace of the jet age, ulcers, ever-increasing neuroses, anonymity in the crowd . . . But there is another, more radical manner of conceiving of post-industrialism, and that is to pass beyond the industrial society to a new cultural era, transcending the material and spiritual inequalities to discover the disciplines of life that are purifying: moderation of appetite, simplicity of taste, the quiet contemplation of nature, the company of parents and friends, everything that industrial society has come to consider as intolerably primitive or ascetic . . . This second interpretation seems to me to explain better young people's rejection of the most highly developed societies . . . These spoilt children of the comfortable middle classes have grown up enough to despise their generous parents and to renounce their affluence. These remarkable young people are, I believe, the pioneers of an authentic post-industrial culture (Roszak, 1970).

We shall not conceal the hypothetical character of these views of the future, which seem to suppose that the present contradictions of monopoly capitalism (unemployment, inflation, deterioration of the terms of trade) will be, if not resolved, then at least surmounted. But even if these views are only partly true, they draw our attention to the possible importance to young people of new poles of identification offering them, in their quest for self-realization, values and models that are closer to their deepest aspirations. Without them, young people are condemned to fantasy projections, to political impotence in mini-groups, or to the public mystification of idols of all kinds. Their socialization and integration thus become one form or another of compromise.

Some conflicts of values

At first sight one might be tempted to believe that man is only important to our society in his capacity as a producer of economic goods. Taking a closer look, however, we see a more complex and contradictory configuration of entreaties and attractions presented to modern man—and to the young in particular—of very different views of the world, carrying almost diametrically opposed images of happiness.

Society needs qualified technicians. It is therefore going to develop a primary image of happiness based on the values of professional qualification and of social success by their own merits, an image of service to the advancement of science, progress in which can only make mankind happier. The happiness proposed is thus essentially a participation in the realization of technological advancement, in scientific success, and in the functional rationality of ingeniously conceived products and systems. The be-all and end-all of existence is to contribute one's stone towards the building of the common edifice. But to guarantee its internal cohesion, society also needs citizens who are aware of their responsibilities. It will therefore produce, superimposed on the first, a second image of happiness based this time on the traditional values of the family, on the democratic ideal and respectability. Happiness here is associated with social success gained through the will, through work, and through the respect of principles. The purpose of existence is above all the exercise of one's responsibility towards the community and its institutional authorities. And finally, society—and more particularly our affluent society of today—has to sell and get rid of its products. Given these economic exigences, society will therefore propagate a third image of happiness, associated with the values of comfort, of pleasure and of easy living. Happiness is suggested to be present abundance, well-being, the discovery of new sensations, the endless possibilities of consuming goods and services and of enjoying life. The aim of existence is hedonistic: to live intensely for today.

Young people are subjected to the pressure of these three contradictory images of happiness which impose themselves with greater or lesser intensity depending on the agents of socialization that propagate them. Sensitive above all to the third and the first, young people nevertheless remain critical of them. For their experience of life makes them intuitively aware of what these images conceal: the social mechanisms of success with their train of scholastic selections and class privileges, the absence of human warmth, competitiveness, the reality of the operation of power in official institutions, the inadequacies of family relationships, social injustice, and so on. Torn between their personal aspirations, the social solicitations to adopt this or that way towards happiness and the contradictions of the system which they experience in their own lives, young people adopt an attitude of quest, in which dreams and illusions are not entirely absent.

It has often been postulated that our society has encouraged the creation among young people of an image of themselves through which they get a wrong idea of the world as consisting in the acquisition of objects promoted by advertising:

> The dialectic between the necessity of integration, the necessity of autonomy and the necessity of identity will acquire its full dimension in the object. In appropriating the object we become integrated, but at the same time we affirm ourselves as autonomous and as persons, we create ourselves. The whole ambiguity of this 'creation' derives from the fact that it is primarily a copy, a plagiarism of the numerous social stereotypes that tend to reduce the meaning to the object, life to the thing. The identity we build for ourselves is thus nothing but the exact sum of the objects we possess (Arnold, Bassand, Crettaz and Kellerhals, 1971, p. 67).

The validity of this postulate seems to have been demonstrated. But it seems to us to isolate young people artificially from a fundamental psychosocial relationship, namely that which links them with the wishes of their parents, where any conception of happiness puts down roots whose importance cannot be underestimated. The success or failure of a life project wished by parents is the most pregnant experience that a young person can have. He draws from it the inner strength to respond by conformism or to break with the ideal values of his social environment. Now, the ideal of life entertained by many parents, modelled on the images of happiness just described, is not apparently attractive to their children today. Hence their frantic quest for something else or some other way, which is not simply a manifestation of adolescent instability, but a passionate search for coherence in life. The happiness intuitively sought by many young people, which dominates the evaluation of family and relationships, is often bound up with communal experiences which our society does not readily tolerate, since they challenge the validity of the ends that motivate the lives of their elders, and undermine the ideology indispensable to the proper functioning of the system. Whether or not this conflict of values can be resolved in the future therefore depends to a great extent on the ability of our society to comprehend and reconcile other experiences of life than those for which it is itself responsible. It boils down in fact to allowing young people a happiness different from that which it would define itself.

But there is more to it than that. Young people involuntarily participate in the myth which our society has built around the idea of youth, which publicity invests with a value capable of attracting so many things. This myth is a powerful denial of death, of old age and of suffering. It creates a situation that simply dodges the issue of human mortality, a situation which does not deceive young people, made uneasy by mounting violence and the apocalyptic predictions of certain ecologists. This is implicit in their searching for mutual and community relationships. It goes even further than that; they are attacking frontally and are thus entering into conflict with two major values of the reigning ideology: individualism and the institutional taking in charge of what is considered as 'creating a problem' in society. It is true that our society constantly endeavours to persuade us that only individuals exist. However, young people, who essentially live in groups, argue that the individual is just an illusion, a convenient bureaucratic abstraction, and that man only really exists in reciprocity, through mutual recognition, through sharing, through meeting one another, through the establishment in this way of a human communion which man cannot do without. They thus reject the prevailing idea that everyone's life is an individual project, making suffering, disease, and death itself something which belongs to an individual's solitude in the face of his destiny. And they challenge the power which society constantly arrogates to itself to 'take things in charge', by severing from his environment and individualizing the person taken in charge (the sick person, the old, the handicapped, the young delinquent, etc.). The young have a strong aspiration, no doubt rather utopian, to take themselves in charge, to guide and counsel one another, to present a common front to all that is negative in existence and to the obstacles of life. They join in the protests nowadays being made against the segregation of old people, the wrongful expropriation and medicalization of death, the conditions in certain psychiatric wards, and the like. They set against the severely Promethean vision of technological man a more realistic view of the natural limits of existence and the importance of the living environment to human equilibrium. The future will show whether this conflict will tend to become more acute. It is clear, however, that the integration of a large proportion of young people in the sector of medicosocial professions—a sector in rapid development—will not take place without harm being done if the institutions concerned continue to be regarded as 'oppressive' and if they fail to relax their structures in such a way as to favour the human and community care of the physically or mentally sick. Paradoxically it is young people who, through their aspirations and authentic relationships, remind our society that we cannot disguise what is negative in existence by individualism or by simply ignoring it!

The final demand of young people that we shall briefly examine is their aspiration towards creativity. This brings us up against the conflict of values which is probably the most irreducible of our society. For on the one hand the spheres of leisure, of affections, of sexuality, leave young people a quasi-total autonomy in which they may express their passion for what is possible, for adventure, for the project of life, and to frame for themselves a form of self-realization that does not exclude imagination or originality or creativity. On the other hand, however, the sector of production and the world of labour are dominated by the imperatives of a profitable return and by a directing will which excludes any real participation in decision making and in the definition of the objectives. This discrepancy gives rise among young people to many difficulties of integration. Our sympathy is with a socialism of auto-management, utilizing the advances of information processing to bring about a real decentralization of decision making, and to let the machine relieve man of all routine operations (Garaudy, 1972, 1975; Toffler, 1971, pp. 444–459). But we doubt whether this hope is a motivating factor that will find its realization in the politico-social conditions during the next two decades. We shall therefore provisionally have to fall back on taking stock of the sectorial mediations capable of promoting participation and creativity, progressively preparing a more global transformation of society. In this respect the role of cultural, trade union, and political associations, reorienting their members with a specific motivation (artistic activities, housing, sport, consumption, environment, etc.) might well be significant provided that these groups give evidence of imagination and do not in their turn remain a reflection of the existing social cleavages and stereotypes (Kellerhals, 1974). At present young people do not participate much in such groups, usually preferring spontaneous movements which, when the appropriate moment arrives, bring out an expression of creativity without running the risk of becoming bureaucratic. In order to confer upon them a better structured social 'visibility', the associations should seek to accept responsibility for the perspectives issuing from these uncontrolled eruptions. To do so, however, they should have the courage to break, more than they do at present, with the dominant ideology. For these young people will not allow themselves to be 're-won'. It may be possible, however, to persuade them that part of their aspirations towards creativity can be fulfilled in broader frameworks than their own groups of reference.

Conclusion: youth and spirituality

Favouring the creation of new poles of identification to allow the young to live with other views of happiness, reversing the institutional tendencies to isolate the sick or socially unadapted individual, promoting social experiments of participation and creativity; these among others are some lines of force that present themselves for action to be taken by those who remain uneasy about the conflicts of values which oppose certain aspirations of youth about the major trends of our Western development.

We will be reproached no doubt for not having given sufficient attention to deviant behaviour leading many young people to delinquency, drugs, or even to gratuitous violence. We think it is essential, however, to distinguish the conflicts of values which we have tried to indicate in the foregoing from the symptoms of conflict manifested in deviant behaviour. The latter are only the acute outward signs of profound inner problems. Their importance as such is generally magnified by the sensationalism of the mass media and should be reduced to their true proportions. It is none the less true that the prevention of delinquency and the combating of drug taking remain specific tasks that should not be underestimated.

We will also be reproached perhaps for not having adopted a directly theological point of view. But it is impossible, methodologically, without a serious analysis of historic causes and effects, to pass from the hope of a faith to the prospective evaluation of a future. The Gospel is a powerful fermentum of hope. It restores to man his faith in the possible, combats all fatalism, shows the world as for ever being reborn, relationships as life to be renewed, man as active subjectivity, an unending spring of transcendence. The Gospel awakes in every believer the faith that his social reality has never been given in advance once and for all, but that it is the work of man, historically capable of being transformed and overcome. But it also announces the reality of the Cross and affirms what the theologians have called the 'eschatological reserve': the Kingdom is not the tomorrows that will sing; it takes its place episodically, patiently, colliding sometimes painfully with the hardness of reality and made dizzy by the alienations in which men never cease to imprison themselves. That is why the Gospel is the voice of prophecy, giving birth to a creative spirituality and to a militant ethic, but it is in no way a prediction describing the scenario of future history.

This point should be underlined. For the analysis we have tried to undertake of the conflicts of values in society today and tomorrow demonstrates, it seems to us, that youth is seeking a new spirituality, if we understand this term in its etymological sense of a profound inner inspiration. The pretended secularization of our society is a catch, a lure (Luckmann, 1972). In turning away from the churches the young are only rejecting their institutional mode; in reality their disaffection conceals an intense search for the absolute. If they succeed in dropping their role of the traditional agent of socialization which they have all too easily taken upon themselves in the past, the churches may find in the young a new audience. In fact they belong through their mission to this quaternary sector, distinct from the laws of the market. They have the possibility of financing and encouraging new experiences of community life. They have sprung from a long tradition of constant work on behalf of the poor, of the sick and of those on the fringe of society. The content of the evangelical message they preach is a call to creativity. Let the churches in all conditions reunite to play a leading role in the guidance of youth. It will suffice if they find the zeal for a fundamental institutional reform.

There *is* a life before death. It *has* a meaning. It is a meaning that runs like a rumour through the quest of so many young people and is the rumour of God.

References

Arnold, P., Bassand, M., Crettaz, B. and Kellerhals, J. 1971. *Jeunesse et société*, Lausanne: Payot. (Work carried out at the request of the 'Youth' section of the Swiss Commission of UNESCO.)

Duvignaud, J. 1975. *La planète des jeunes*. Paris: Stock.

Garaudy, R. 1972. *L'alternative*. Paris: Laffont. 1975. *Parole d'homme*. Paris: Laffont.

Kellerhals, J. 1974. *Les associations dans l'enjeu democratique*. Lausanne: Payot.

Luckmann, T. 1972. La secularisation d'un mythe contemporain. *Bulletin du CPE*, Genève.

Roszak, T. 1971. *Vers une contre-culture*. Paris: Stock. 1970. La contre-culture, *Reforme*. Paris.

Servan-Schreiber, J. J. 1967. *Le défi Americain*. Paris: Denoel.

Toffler, A. 1971. *Le choc du futur*. Paris: Denoel.

8 Genetics and adolescent development: perspectives for the future

Marco Milani-Comparetti

A few general considerations may serve to frame our subject. Our discussion will focus upon the average European adolescent, the coming young generation in the Western civilization of our subcontinent. Adolescence in other or less developed cultures is expected to be quite different, but it concerns us in the present context only to the extent of its possible interactions with European youth. Our young generations are undergoing great changes, both social and biological. While the latter are partly genetic and partly environmental, it is not often recognized that social change in itself comes to acquire biological significance. For instance, today there are important changes in the depth and scope of young people's awareness of a number of genetic concepts that were formerly known only within the scientific community: genetic diversity between races and populations; variations in the quality of life as a result of the individual's genetic make-up; the genetic responsibility of individual parents to their children and, even if less immediate, of one generation to the next.

Many problems that were and largely still are so important for older generations are becoming less relevant; one of these is racial differences. Migration, school and social integration, economic interdependence and supranational ties will continue to add to young people's tendency toward mutual acceptance. The most important consequence may be the furthering of what geneticists term the 'breakdown of isolates'. In order to appreciate the nature and implications of this phenomenon, we should recall a few (necessarily simplified) fundamental genetic concepts.

We may describe the body and mind as the sum of a great number of individual traits (stature, skin colour, learning ability, weight, taste, fingerprints, voice, and countless others). Each such trait, in turn, is more or less directly controlled by genetic information carried in the DNA (DeoxyriboNucleic Acid) molecules which are repeated in the nucleus of each of the billions of cells in our body. Half of this information comes from each of our parents, through the respective gametes (the sperm and the egg). Thus the genetic information (the 'gene') for any trait comes in two versions: one paternal and the other maternal. If both versions are identical, we are 'homozygotes' for that trait; if they differ, we are 'heterozygotes'. If we are homozygous for a 'good', or healthy gene, all is well. If we are heterozygous, with one good and one 'bad' gene, we may be quite normal by simply using the 'good' version (unless the 'bad' one is 'dominant', a relatively less frequent but obviously much more damaging case). If we are homozygous for a 'bad' gene, we are in trouble; we become ill, or malformed, or mentally retarded, or we may not live at all.

Now if two parents carry the same 'bad' gene, they may be quite normal as heterozygotes, but their children run a high risk of getting it from both; if so, they will be homozygotes and thus defective. The probability of two parents carrying the same gene is obviously much higher when they come from common parents or ancestors. For example, in mountain villages or in city ghettoes most people (geographical and social 'isolates' respectively) are either close or distant relatives, with increased risk of homozygous, defective progeny. With increased exogamy (outside marriages) isolates are broken down, and the probability of homozygosity drops steeply. (It should be pointed out that homozygotes for genetic disease generally have less or no reproductive fitness, thus tending to eliminate defective genes from the population's genetic load, while heterozygotes transmit their bad genes.) Thus, since only homozygotes for *recessive* (non-dominant) genetic conditions are affected, the breakdown of isolates tends to limit the incidence of genetic disease, but in the long run it tends to spread recessive genes in the population.

The dissociation between genetic load and clinical impact in the current generations is further increased by progress in the treatment of genetic diseases. Two of the best examples concern diabetes (a metabolic defect) and Down's syndrome (mongolism, a chromosomal aberration). In both conditions fertility used to be seriously limited or prevented, thus tending to limit the propagation of the genetic defect. Current improvements in medical care are now making survival into fertile age the norm, thus tending to increase the genetic load. This means immediate advantage for the affected individuals but increased danger for the coming generations. The breakdown of isolates affects current and coming generations in other ways, with special emphasis on adolescent development.

Scientists use the term 'secular trend' in referring to the well known 'acceleration', or earlier age of onset, of height and biological maturation. This is a generalized finding in highly industrialized countries. The main markers of acceleration are variations in the mean stature of army recruits in different decades; comparative longitudinal studies of adolescent development; and comparative studies on pubertal maturation, especially in girls.

The mean stature of Swedish recruits in the period 1840–1938 increased by 8.5 cm to 174.4 (Lundman, 1939). In Italy, in the period 1880–1950, the mean conscript stature increased by nearly 5 cm to 167.5 (Gedda and Sodani, 1960). Similar data are available for other countries. The increase in mean stature among recruits reflects partly an increase in final adult stature (generally estimated at 0.5 to 1% per decade in the last century) and partly an acceleration of the growth spurt, most of which is completed at gradually earlier age. While 60 years ago final stature in Western populations was reached around the 26th year of age, it is generally reached now at 18–19 years for males and 16–17 for females. A good example of such a continuing trend is found in the graphs representing the comparative pattern of growth of girls in Sardinia in 1930 and 1965 (Aicardi, 1974) as reproduced in Figure 1. The phenomenon appears to

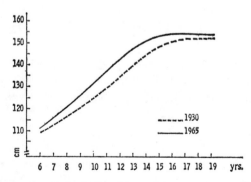

Figure 1. Absolute stature in Sardinian girls aged 6–19 as measured in 1930 and 1965. Source: Aicardi, 1974.

be generalized. School children in Sweden today are taller, and their growth spurt comes earlier; there has been an acceleration of about half a year in the last 40 years (Tanner, 1955).

Acceleration is not limited to stature. An earlier growth spurt entails earlier physical maturation, as expressed by an accelerated onset of puberty (Clements, 1953). The phenomenon of accelerated maturation is easier to observe in girls, in whom puberty is definitely dated by the first menstrual flow (menarche). On the average, girls today tend to reach puberty two years earlier than boys. Menarchal age in Scandinavian countries has shown a shift to earlier maturation of some four to six months per decade in the last century (Ljung, Bergsten and Lindgren, 1974). Earlier sexual maturation, in turn, seems to be related to earlier psychological maturation. This finding is, once more, of generalized value, and it should be carefully considered in the revision of school curricula, especially for the girls who, as we have seen, exhibit significant anticipation of biological (and psychological) maturation.

The phenomenon of acceleration in growth and biological maturation may be ascribed in part to environmental factors (such as more balanced nutrition—especially to the intake of amino acids and vitamins—or increased exposure to sunlight) and the recurring phenomenon of 'retarded acceleration' in wartime seems to indicate just this. However, growth and development are certainly controlled by genetic more than environmental factors. Studies on twins (in whom the different combinations of genetic and/or environmental superimposability afford, in well planned tests, an accurate measure of the degree of genetic conditioning for any given trait) have shown that both stature and menarchal age (Venerando and Milani-Comparetti, 1973; Gedda and Brenci, 1974) are over 90% genetically controlled.

The fact that these traits are so closely controlled by heredity leads us to search for changes in the genetic structure of the population that may explain the present trend, and the best explanation seems to be related again to the 'breakdown of isolates', which results in the well known genetic concept of *heterosis*, or 'hybrid vigour'.

This phenomenon of heterosis is especially known to plant and animal geneticists, and the best example is illustrated in Figure 2. The 'inbred' parental strains correspond to the offspring of human isolates, with extensive homozygosity and limited development; their crossing (exogamy)

Figure 2. Heterosis in corn. Representative plants from the two inbred parental strains are shown at left. A representative of their F_1 hybrid is shown third from left, and representatives of successive inbreedings (F_2 through F_8) are shown to the right. Source: Goodenough and Levine, 1974.

produces children (F_1) that are predominantly heterozygous and show markedly improved development; if they, in turn, tend to form a new mating isolate (F_2 to F_8) they revert to homozygosity and developmental limitations (Goodenough and Levine, 1974). That this phenomenon applies to human populations is shown in Figure 3, which shows how mulattoes are taller then either of the parental races at the same ages (Gedda and Brenci, 1975). Of course the total picture is much more complex, but we can safely assume that the breakdown of isolates does represent a major factor in changing the genetic structure, the pattern of adolescent development, and the health prospects of young people in the coming 25 years, with advantages currently outweighing potential risks.

Heredity and environment are the interacting forces that shape species and individuals. The relatively slow changes in the genetic factors affecting European adolescents are in sharp contrast to the rate and intensity of changes in environmental factors which, in turn, may induce genetic changes with dangerous and longlasting results. The origin of variability in all living beings (and the prerequisite for evolution from the very primitive to the present highly complex ones, including man) rests with mutations, i.e. with sudden changes in an individual's genetic information, induced by a variety of 'mutagenic agents' or 'mutagens'.

Mutagens may be either physical or chemical, some of the best known being radiation and various chemicals such as mustard gas. Their effects are often revealed only years after they have acted (genetic mutations appear only in the progeny of mutant individuals; they are generally

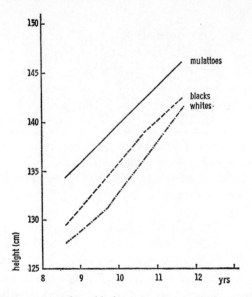

Figure 3. Absolute stature in white, black, and mulatto girls from 8½–12 years of age. Source: Gedda and Brenci, 1975.

harmful and they tend to increase the genetic load in the population). Thus mutagenic agents are often used indiscriminately before their dangers are exposed. The generalized use of diagnostic and control X-rays even during pregnancy was such an instance for many years. Many new synthetic substances (such as the omnipresent plastics, or cyclamate, or DDT) have been discovered, introduced into general use and only much later have they been found to have mutagenic or poisonous effects. The tendency to substitute nuclear for hydroelectric or thermoelectric power entails potential genetic hazards, not so much in the operation of nuclear plants (for which sufficient safety measures may be assumed) as in the disposal of radioactive waste or in cases of accident, sabotage, or even war. The sum of all present or potential new mutagenic agents may well raise the mutational load of the coming generations above the level compatible for survival of the species, unless critical control measures are enacted.

Other, more apparent changes in the environment should also be reckoned with. Any student of elementary biology remembers the change from Biston Betularia to Biston Carbonaria as one obvious example of the biological consequences of man-induced environmental changes. The current spreading of cities and industrial areas in former agricultural plains and the disappearance of large forests and woods is changing the pattern of our environment on a much larger scale. 'Ecology' prevails in the words, but hardly the deeds, of the present generation. This ratio must be reversed in the next generation in order to avoid disaster. The balance between agriculture and industry must be restored, in terms of wood farming even more urgently perhaps than food crop farming.

Another area in which genetics is bound to have ever-growing impact on adolescent development is the health prospect. Now that biomedical progress has conquered so many of the formerly prevailing causes of death (infectious diseases most of all, now prevented by improved vaccination schedules and cured by antibiotics) more and more people tend to live longer. This reflects the new pattern of morbidity in the population. Table 1 (Clow *et al.*, 1973) illustrates the changing pattern in one

Table 1 Percentage of pediatric deaths due to genetic and non-genetic illness in Great Britain[a]

	Carter (1964)[b]			Roberts *et al.* (1970)[c]
	1914	1934	1954	1960–1966
Genetic	2.0	1.5	12.0	11.0
Congenital malformations	4.0	4.0	19.0	30.5
Unknown	23.0[d]	29.5[d]	40.0[d]	9.2
Malignancy	3.0	13.5	14.5	8.8
Environmental	68.0	51.5	14.5	40.5

[a] Source: Clow *et al.*, 1973
[b] London area
[c] North of England
[d] Includes diseases termed part-genetic and multifactorial

area (pediatric age deaths) and we may assume that similar trends apply to human disease in general. The fact that genetic disease and congenital malformations (which may be generally assumed to be mostly of genetic origin) were estimated to account for 6% of all causes of pediatric age deaths in 1914, as against 41.5% in 1960–66 needs some comment. The dramatic increase in the proportion of genetic disease is certainly not entirely due to the decrease in the number of patients with acute illnesses of infectious or other environmental origin; it is largely due to the refinement in the recognition and classification of genetic disease. In other words, we are gradually becoming aware that many of the diseases that were formerly considered as being due to either 'environmental' or 'unknown' causes are really related to genetic causes or at least to genetic predisposing factors.

The increased ascertainment of genetic disease, coupled with the increased economic and social cost of the sick and the aged, tends to make individuals and society increasingly prone to accept preventive measures ranging from mass screening programmes all the way to 'therapeutic' abortion. Screening programmes may be aimed at the general population or limited to high risk populations. For instance genetic metabolic defects, such as phenylketonuria or galactosaemia, may occur with relevant frequency in the general population. Others have very low incidence in the general population but show significantly higher incidence in certain 'high risk' population groups; such is the case of Tay-Sachs disease in the Ashkenazi Jews. Chromosomal aberrations are relatively rare in the general population but they are much more frequent among the relatives of affected individuals and among the offspring of women who are approaching the end of their fertile age. Thus in both types of pathology we have both low risk and high risk populations.

Screening and diagnosis may be either pre-natal or post-natal. Pre-natal screening is generally considered for currently untreatable conditions (as is the case for chromosomal aberrations). If the unborn child is affected, abortion is the only way out for those who accept it. Post-natal screening may be applied to treatable genetic diseases (such being the case of phenyl-ketonuria, with the special low phenylalanine diet). The fact that the so-called 'therapeutic' abortion of all male foetuses is currently proposed for pregnant carriers of the haemophilia gene (although it is known that half of them are going to be perfectly healthy and the other half can now be managed) is a clear indication of how deeply the risk of suffering is currently felt in our society.

Coupled with the fear of the 'population explosion', the refusal of even the risk of a less than perfect child is bound to affect the 'genetic consciousness' component in the reproductive behaviour at the turn of the century. It should be pointed out that, unless dramatic but presently unlikely changes occur in the pattern of human reproduction (cloned individuals, genetic engineering) (Mertens, 1975), no relevant results are to be expected within the next generation as a consequence of such increased genetic consciousness.

As we have seen, improvements in the phenotypical management of genetic diseases, as in the case of diabetes, are expected to increase the survival (and reproduction) of individuals with formerly self-limiting genetic disease. On the other hand, increased panmixia and the spreading practice of genetic counselling are bound to limit the number of homozygous individuals in recessive Mendelian traits. Thus the opposing influences may tend to mask for quite some time the possible deleterious changes in the gene pool induced by therapeutic improvements. Yet this lack of apparent genetic change should not dampen the quest for increased genetic knowledge by the coming generation, already indicated by the eager interest in genetics evidenced in our schools and colleges. Much of the problem rests on how schools and universities will manage to bridge the gap between theory and practice.

A good example of how genetics interacts with the already mentioned changing attitudes of youth is genetic counselling. In recent years genetic counsellors were consulted only when hereditary diseases had already appeared in the family. A new trend is now slowly developing: people are beginning to seek genetic counselling in advance to ensure that their children will be healthy. The genetic counsellor's predicting power, and especially his intervention power, are still extremely limited. The improvement in genetic knowledge is currently enormous, but its impact is still negligible. In most cases, either we ignore the actual health prospects for each child, or, at best, offer the hard choice between contraception and abortion. This is not to say that genetic counselling is useless. However, we are still at the beginning, and some encouraging milestones, such as the treatment of phenylketonuria, are already behind us.

Generally speaking, the impact of genetics on the quality of individual life and on the behaviour of the coming generation may be viewed quite positively. Yet the current trend towards wider collective responsibilities by the social community is likely to produce some dramatic conflicts between individual and family choices on one hand and public welfare on the other. We can expect these kinds of problems to increase markedly within the next few decades and this prediction calls for increased awareness of the issues involved between and among those whose public and private decisions will affect adolescents and their progeny up to the year 2000 and beyond.

References

Aicardi, G. 1974. Carenze funzionali e accrescimento corporeo, *Acta Medica Auxologica*, suppl. 3, vol. VI.

Carter, C. 1969. *A guide to genetic prognosis in pediatrics*. London: Spastics International Medical Publications in association with Heinemann Books Ltd.

Clements, E. M. B. 1953. Changes in the mean stature and weight of British children over the past 70 years, *Brit. Med. J.*, vol. 2, p. 897.

Clow, C. L., Fraser, F. C., Laberge, C. and Scriver, C. R. On the application of knowledge to the patient with genetic disease, *Progress in Medical Genetics*, vol. 9. New York: Grune and Stratten.

Gedda, L. and Brenci, G. 1974. Fondamenti della cronogenetica e verifica a proposito della puberta femminile, *Acta Medica Auxologica*, suppl. 3, vol. VI.

Gedda, L. and Brenci, G. 1975. *Chronogénétique: l'heredité du temps biologique*. Paris: Hermann.

Gedda, L. and Sodani, F. 1960. Indagine intorno all'aumento della statura nella popolazione italiana. *Medicina Auxologica*, Roma, vol. 95.

Goodenough, U. and Levine, R. P. 1974. *Genetics*. New York: Holt, Rinehart and Winston.

Ljung B-O., Bergsten, B. and Lindgren, G. 1974. The secular trend in physical growth in Sweden, *Annals of Human Biology*, vol. I, no. 3.

Lundman, B. J. 1939. Ueber die fortgesetzte Zunahme der Körpergrösse in Schweden 1926 bis 1936, *Zeitschr. f. Rassenk. u. d. ges. Forschung am Menschen*, vol. IX, no. 3.

Mertens, T. 1975. *Human Genetics—Readings on the implications of genetic engineering*. New York: Wiley and Sons.

Roberts, K. D. and Edwards, J. M. 1971. *Pediatric intensive care*. Oxford: Blackwell Scientific Publications.

Tanner, J. M. 1955. *Growth at adolescence.* Oxford: Blackwell.

Venerando, A. and Milani-Comparetti, M. 1973. Heredity vs. environment in biomechanics, *Medicine and Sports*, vol. VIII; *Biomechanics*, vol. III, p. 151. Basel: Karger.

9 Biological aspects of development at adolescence

Marcel Hebbelinck

The physical growth patterns of a population are subject to gradual changes over extended time periods. These changes are referred to as 'secular trends' and they will be examined below in an attempt both to characterize the biodevelopmental status of the adolescent at the end of the century and to assess its implications for psychosocial development.

The following questions serve to focus the discussion:

(a) What is the secular trend for adult size and shape?
(b) What is the secular trend for patterns of child growth?
(c) What is the secular trend for the development of sexual maturity (menarche)?
(d) What is the secular trend for the end of the fertile period (menopause)?
(e) What are the social and psychological implications of this information for the youth of the future?
(f) What implications do these trends have for the physical fitness and leisure patterns of tomorrow's youth?

Adult size and shape

Secular changes in human physical growth patterns are among the most puzzling phenomena for scholars of human biology. The possibility of a shift over the years in the final stature of a given population was recognized as early as the beginning of the nineteenth century (Van Wieringen, 1972). For example, in the Netherlands in the three periods covered by the 1865–1917 drafts of conscripts, the 1917–1953 drafts, and the 1953–1970 drafts, the secular increases for mean height per decade were 1.0 cm, 1.1 cm, and 2.1 cm respectively. In other words, the positive shift for

18-year-olds continues to exist and the data contradict the belief that the end of the secular increase in final height is in sight (Freund, 1950; Bakwin and McLaughlin, 1964; Sälzler, 1967). It may well be that further upward and downward trends will occur as the result of future changes in socio-economic conditions. Such changes in the trend have occurred in the past (Oppers, 1963).

Oppers casts some doubt on the existence of a true secular trend for adult stature. He points out that most of the relevant data deal with young men conscripted for military service. Eighteen-year-old men of today have thus been compared with those of more than a century ago. While today it is accepted that almost all males of this age have stopped growing vertically, Oppers provides data to show that most young men in the nineteenth century went on growing well into their 20s. They reached a mean adult stature about 6.0 cm below today's mean values. This figure is about one-third to one-half of those reported in some studies (Van Wieringen, 1972). While making less dramatic the secular trend for final stature, the data of Oppers shed more light on the other aspect of this phenomenon, namely that today's youth are growing faster and attaining physical adulthood at an earlier age.

Child growth

It has been amply demonstrated that children and adolescents in the industrialized societies are maturing at a faster rate than their counterparts of 50 and 100 years ago. In a recent Belgian survey (Hebbelinck and Borms, 1975) it was clearly shown that a 6-year-old girl in 1971 was physically bigger than an 8-year-old in 1830 (see Table 1). Boyne *et al.* (1957) showed that British children showed significant secular gain in height and weight over a 40-year period. Among girls of 5, 8, and 12 years of age mean gains of 1 to 3.9 inches (2.5 to 10 cm) were reported. Mean weight gains for the same girls ranged from 1.25 to 18.6 lb (0.6 to 8.4 kg). For boys at the same ages mean height gains of 1.25 to 4 inches (3 to 10 cm) were reported with mean weight gains ranging from 2 to 17.3 lb (0.9 to 7.8 kg).

The possibility of a secular change in the height/weight relationship has been examined only sporadically. Broman *et al.* (1942) in Sweden and Prokopec (1961) in Czechoslovakia, both using the ponderal index

Table 1   Height (cm) and weight (kg) of 6- to 13-year-old Belgian boys and girls from 1840 until 1971[a]

Years	Sex	1840		1924		1929/30		1960		1967/68	
		Ht	Wt	Ht	Wt	Ht	Wt	Ht	Wt	Ht	Wt
6	M	104.7	17.2	109.7	18.4	110.3	19.6	114.0	20.5	116.3	20.9
	F	103.1	16.0	109.2	18.1	109.5	19.1	113.5	19.5	116.7	20.5
7	M	110.5	19.1	115.0	20.3	116.3	21.5	119.5	22.5	121.3	23.0
	F	108.6	17.5	114.7	19.9	115.3	20.8	118.8	21.5	120.9	22.2
8	M	116.2	20.8	120.5	22.4	120.9	23.2	125.5	25.0	127.0	25.6
	F	114.1	19.1	119.9	21.7	120.5	22.6	123.5	24.0	126.6	24.6
9	M	121.9	22.7	124.8	24.3	126.3	25.0	130.0	27.5	132.0	28.2
	F	119.5	21.4	124.5	23.8	126.1	24.8	129.0	27.0	131.7	27.1
10	M	127.5	24.5	129.5	26.4	130.2	27.6	135.0	30.0	136.8	31.0
	F	124.8	23.3	130.4	26.5	130.1	26.9	134.0	30.0	136.6	29.9
11	M	133.0	27.1	134.1	28.8	134.8	29.5	140.0	33.0	141.4	33.8
	F	129.9	25.7	134.8	29.0	135.3	29.7	139.5	34.0	142.7	33.9
12	M	138.5	29.8	138.2	31.2	139.4	32.9	144.5	37.0	145.5	36.6
	F	135.3	29.8	140.0	32.2	141.5	34.5	146.0	38.5	147.6	37.3
13	M	143.9	34.4	143.0	34.0	143.8	35.7	149.5	41.0	149.1	39.7
	F	140.3	32.9	145.8	36.2	147.2	38.2	151.5	43.5	150.6	41.4

[a] 1971 girls' data from Flemish sample only

(W/H[3]) as a criterion for relative weight, found that the positive secular trend in height was accompanied by a relatively smaller increase in weight, which means that there is a tendency for children to become leaner. This observation has been recently confirmed by Vajda *et al.* (1974) applying a proportionality analysis, which indicated that contemporary primary school boys and girls are taller and heavier but proportionally lighter at all age levels than their counterparts of 1920–30.

Menarche and menopause

This earlier morphological maturation is also manifest in other biological characteristics, such as the trend toward earlier age of menarche (first menstruation). In a comparative study of two national surveys of height, weight and puberty characteristics Van Wieringen *et al.* (1968) found that within one decade (1955–1965) the mean age at menarche had decreased from 13 years and 8 months to 13 years and 5 months. This implies that one-fifth of the Dutch girls reach menarche while in primary school. From the same data it is clear that 50% of the boys and girls have completed sexual maturation at 15 and 16 years respectively, and that by 17 years four-fifths of the girls and by 18 four-fifths of the boys finish maturation. Tanner's (1962) classic graph showing the secular trend for age at menarche is shown in Figure 1.

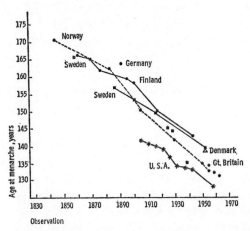

Figure 1. *Age at menarche in various countries by year at observation* (*revealing secular trend*). *Source: Tanner, 1962.*

Sälzler (1967) explored the question of whether an earlier onset of sexual maturation also entails an earlier age of menopause (the end of a woman's period of fertility), as assumed by Koch (1938). Koch believed that the earlier onset of menarche would induce an earlier start of the climacterium and an earlier ageing of the global population as well. This assumption has proved to be incorrect; on the contrary, the age of reaching menopause has been delayed by several years when compared with data from yesteryear (Backmann, 1948; Klemm *et al.*, 1963; Frommer, 1964).

The mean age at menarche in Europe is currently around 13 years: e.g. 13.5 years in Holland (Van Wieringen *et al.*, 1968); 13.2 years in Hungary (Bottyan *et al.*, 1963); 13.1 years in London (Scott, 1961); and 13.5 years in France (Aubenque, 1964). The average age of menopause is a little over 50 years: 51.4 years in the Netherlands (Jaszmann *et al.*, 1969);

50.8 years in England (McKinley *et al.*, 1972); and 50 years in the German Democratic Republic (Klemm *et al.*, 1963).

It must be pointed out that secular changes can be positive or negative. Some studies have shown correlations between secular changes in growth patterns and major changes in the lifestyles of populations (Van Wieringen, 1972; Oppers, 1963). As to the possible explanation of the described phenomena, nutritional adequacy, health status, and major changes in the political situation have been cited as effective agents. The nature of these agents has led Van Wieringen (1972) to hypothesize that positive secular changes are due largely to an elimination of growth inhibiting factors as opposed to the introduction of new growth stimulating factors.

If we accept Van Wieringen's position regarding the elimination of growth inhibiting factors and assume that their elimination will continue to occur, more and more children will come closer to fulfilling their growth potential within the limits imposed by genetic factors. One possible outcome of this combination of factors is a gradual trend toward more homogeneity in physical size and shape in the industrialized nations with fewer extremes based on unusual heredity and almost none based on negative environmental influences. This is a highly speculative statement but one which deserves attention as our societies continue to benefit from the 'good life'. By way of contrast, Himes and Malina (1975) have presented data indicating the absence of any secular trend for stature in a non-industrialized inbred section of rural Mexico.

Van Wieringen's position (1972) opposes the theory that genetic changes contribute to positive changes in growth patterns. The position of Tanner (1962); Steendijk (1966) and others (*British Medical Journal*, 1961) is that genetic factors probably play a part in the adult change if not in childhood. From this point of view, the tendency away from inbreeding in small self-contained communities, *heterosis*, produces a wider dissemination of genetic materials. Thus dominant factors for tallness may come to be present in more and more offspring.

Excellent reviews of the literature dealing with the secular trend in growth and maturation have been made by Bennholdt-Thomsen (1942, 1952); Tanner (1962, 1965); Sälzler (1967), and Van Wieringen (1972). From the extensive information available, it is evident that the secular trend has several connotations:

(a) a change at the very beginning of life as manifested, for example, by higher birth height and weight;
(b) an acceleration of the process of physical development;
(c) a change in body shape as exemplified by the changing height/weight relationship;
(d) an earlier onset of sexual maturation;
(e) an absolute increase in the final body measures; and
(f) a shift in the onset of the age at menopause.

These changes are not without importance for the youth of today and tomorrow. The trend toward earlier maturation and the reaching of greater adult dimensions sooner are reasonably well established facts and it is beyond doubt that there are many implications in several fields of the behavioural sciences as well as for legislators and policy makers in education and welfare.

Implications for social and psychological development

The question of whether the abovementioned morphological and bio-logical changes are accompanied by changes in the domains of psychological and sociological maturation is much more complicated. From studies comparing early and late maturing children we know that there are some slight positive correlations between physical and psychological characteristics. Early maturing adolescents show a higher lability of the auto-nomic nervous system (Undeutsch, 1951). Physical maturation has been shown to be positively correlated with: intelligence (Undeutsch, 1951; Tanner, 1961; Peel, 1975; Kohen-Praz, 1975); sociopsychological maturity (Grimm, 1958); interest in heterosexual contacts (Undeutsch, 1952); and sexual relationships (Kinsey *et al.*, 1948). Therefore it seems reasonable to conclude that adolescent psychological and social functioning are influenced by such characteristics as body build and time of pubertal change.

The trend toward earlier maturation accentuates the already existing gap between physical adulthood and sociocultural adulthood as conditioned by modern Western societies. In most of our societies the cultural norms require that young people wait from five to ten years after puberty before they may marry and be fully integrated into adult society. The adolescent period is also extended by the present trend toward a higher education for more young people. This has led to an enormous increase in the student population in the late 1950s and 1960s. The combined result of these forces is a slowing down of the processes of social maturation and integration (Cliquet, 1965). According to Saller (1956) this creates a conflict situation in which the individual's cultural development and maturation are hampered by the trend toward earlier physical development. He speaks of an 'asynchronism of the developmental processes', which may induce serious problems with regard to personality development.

Those in this 'adolescent limbo' are faced with a number of choices. They may *sublimate* rising sexuality by engaging in age- and sex-appropriate activities such as sports, the arts, religion, scholarship or a combination of these. A further paradox exists here, because a certain segment of society may look with suspicion on a young person who succeeds *too well* in sublimating sexual urges. Sexuality may be expressed in a variety of other ways, carrying greater or lesser degrees of social stigma. The individual may engage in heterosexual activities with similarly motivated partners. He or she may engage in homosexual activities or masturbation. Marriage at an early age may also be chosen, thereby satisfying one of society's expectations but defying another regarding the appropriate age for marriage.

The foregoing suggests that the adolescent in the year 2000 will live in a period of great social and psychological turmoil. Young people will continue to be faced with new kinds of decisions to make, frequently with no assistance in developing new decision making mechanisms. While societies are changing rapidly, the adolescent is still the victim of what Frisk (1975) calls 'social inertia' in adapting to changes in teenage needs.

Before ending this brief consideration of the biological status of youth in the year 2000, it seems appropriate to touch on the question of physical activity. The importance of exercise during childhood for maximum realization of physical growth potential has been well established (Espenschade, 1960). Further evidence is available (Rarick, 1973) that delineates the broad role played by various forms of exercise in contributing to many aspects of development during childhood and adolescence. It has become fashionable recently to deplore the predicted trend toward a sedentary society, particularly among our youth. If one accepts this gloomy prophecy it is reasonable to predict a negative secular trend in physical fitness. However, opposed to this line of reasoning, one may point to the trend toward more and more leisure time for more people. It seems possible that the next generation will more effectively use the extra hours available to them for non-work activities and that they will be more aware of the importance of regular exercise. A significant indicator is the recent upswing in the physical activity levels of women and girls in all countries. By the year 2000 exercise and physical fitness should be established as the concern of all and not confined to an élite.

Too little is known of the various interactions between socio-psychological, cultural, and human biological forces for anything scientifically definitive to be said at present. This should not, however, prevent us from making reasonable guesses and from attempting to change socio-cultural settings for the sake of facilitating the development of coming generations.

References

Aubenque, M. 1964. Note documentaire sur la puberté et la taille des filles, *Biotypol.*, vol. 25, pp. 136–146.

Backmann, G. 1948. Die beschleunigte Entwicklung der Jugend, *Acta Anat.*, vol. 4, pp. 421–480.

Backwin, H. and McLaughlin, S. M. 1964. Secular increase in height. Is the end in sight? *Lancet*, pp. 1195–1196.

Bennholdt-Thomsen, C. 1942. Die Entwicklungsbeschleunigigung der Jugend, *Ergebn. Inn. Med.*, vol. 62, pp. 1153–1337.

Bennholdt-Thomsen, C. 1952. Ueber das Akzelerationsproblem, *Z. Menschl. Vererb.-u. Konst. forsch.*, vol. 30, pp. 619–652.

Bottyan, O., Deszo, G. Y., Eiben, O., Farkas, G. Y., Rajkai, T., Thoma, A. and Veli, G. Y. 1963. Age at menarche in Hungarian girls, *Ann. Hist.-Nat. Mus. Nat. Hung. Pars Anthropol*, vol. 55, pp. 561–582.

Boyne, A. W., Aitken, F. and Leitch, I. 1957. Secular change in height and weight of British children including analysis of measurements of

English children in primary schools: 1911–1953, *Nutr. Abs. Rev.*, vol. 27, pp. 1–18.

British Medical J. 1961. Editorial, vol. 2, p. 502.

Broman, B., Dahlberg, G. and Lichtenstein, A. 1942/43. Height and weight during growth: review of the literature, *Acta Paediat.* (Uppsala), vol. 30, pp. 1–66.

Cliquet, R. 1965. Enkele tendensen en problemen op het gebied van de voortplanting in de industriële samenleving, sociaal-antropologisch beschouwd, *Tschr. Soc. Wet.*, vol. 10, pp. 3–56.

Espenschade, A. 1960. The contributions of physical activity to growth, *Res. Quart.*, vol. 31, pp. 351–364.

Freund, J. 1950. Der gegenwärtige Stand der Akzeleration bei Neugeborenen und Kleinkindern, *Z. Kinderheilk.*, vol. 67, pp. 592–609.

Frisk, M. 1975. Puberty: Emotional maturation and behaviour. In: S. R. Banenberg (Ed.), *Puberty, biological and psychosocial components*, pp. 236–247. Leiden: Stenfert Kroese.

Frommer, D. J. 1964. Changing age of the menopause, *Brit. Med. J.*, vol. 2, pp. 349–351.

Grimm, H. 1958. Stand der körperlichen Reifung und des Sexualinteresses bei der Grosstadtjugend, *Beitr. Sexual forsch.*, vol. 13, pp. 50–55.

Hebbelinck, M. and Borms, J. 1975. *Biometrische studie van een reeks lichaamsbouwkenmerken en lichamelijke prestatietests van belgische kinderen uit het lager onderwijs.* Brussel: Centrum voor Bevolking- en Gezinsstudiën, Technisch Rapport no. 5.

Himes, V. H. and Malina, R. M. 1975. Age and secular factors in the stature of adult Zatopec males, *Am. J. Phys. anthrop.*, vol. 43, pp. 367–370.

Jaszmann, L., Van Lith, N. D. and Zaat, J. C. A. 1969. The age at menopause in the Netherlands, *Internat. J. Fertility*, vol. 14, pp. 106–117.

Kinsey, A. C., Pomeroy, W. B. and Martin, C. E. 1948. *Sexual behavior in the human male.* Philadelphia: W. B. Saunders.

Klemm, P., Meglin, I. and Winter, R. 1963. Menöpausenalter und Akzeleration, *Dtsch. Gesundh. wesen*, vol. 18, pp. 192–206.

Koch, E. W. 1938. Wesen und Abschluss der Wachstumveränderungen, *Dtsch. med. Wschr.*, vol. 2, pp. 1068–1074.

Kohen-Praz, R. 1975. Problems of assessing relationships between physiological and mental development at adolescence. In: S. R. Barenberg (Ed.) *Puberty, biological and psychosocial components*, pp. 191–197. Leiden: Stenfert Kroese.

McKinlay, S., Jefferys, M. and Thompson, B. 1972. An investigation of the age at menopause, *J. Biosoc. Sci.*, vol. 4, pp. 161–173.

Oppers, V. M. 1963. *Acceleratie analyse*. Amsterdam: Thesis.

Peel, E. A. 1975. Development of intelligence and education. In: S. R. Barenberg (Ed.), *Puberty, biological and psychosocial components*, pp. 167–185. Leiden: Stenfert Kroese.

Prokopec, M. 1961. Nektere zavery z antropometrickych vyzkymu m ladeze z let 1947 as 1957, *Acta Fac. R.N. Univ. Comen.*, vol. 6, pp. 1 and 81.

Rarick, G. L. 1973. *Physical activity, human growth & development*. New York: Academic Press.

Saller, K. 1956. *Zivilisation und Sexualität*. Stuttgart: Enke Verlag.

Sälzler, A. 1967. *Ursachen und Erscheinungsformen der Akzeleration*. Berlin: Volk u. Gesundheit.

Scott, J. A. 1961. *Report on the heights and weights (and other measurements) of school pupils in the county of London in 1959*. London County Council Report.

Steendijk, R. Y. 1966. The secular trend in growth: maturation, *Tijdschrift voor Sociale Geneeskunde*, vol. 44, no. 14, pp. 518–523.

Tanner, J. M. 1961. *Education et croissance*. Genève: Delachaux et Nieslé.

Tanner, J. M. 1962. *Growth at adolescence*. Oxford: Blackwell.

Tanner, J. M. 1965. The trend towards earlier physical maturation. In: J. E. Meade and A. S. Parker (Eds), *Biological aspects of social problems*. London: Oliver and Boyd.

Undeutsch, U. 1951. Psychologische Beobachtungen über die Akzeleration der Jugendentwicklung, *Homo*, vol. 2, pp. 24–42.

Undeutsch, U. 1952. Somatische Akzeleration und psychische Entwicklung der Jugend der Gegenwart, *Stud. gener.*, vol. 5, pp. 286–298.

Vajda, A., Hebbelinck, M. and Ross, W. D. 1974. Size and proportional weight characteristics of Belgian children since 1840. Paper presented at the VI *Internat. Symposium on Pediatric Work Physiology*, Seč, Czechoslovakia. To be published.

Van Wieringen, J. C., Wafelbakker, F., Verbrugge, H. P. and de Haas, J. H. 1968. *Groeidiegrammen 1965 Nederland. Tweede landelijke survey 0–24 jaar.* Groningen: Wolters-Noordhoff.

Van Wieringen, J. C. 1972. *Seculaire groeiverschuiving.* Leiden: Thesis.

10 Family and adolescents in the near future

Jerzy Piotrowski

The object of this paper is twofold. First, an attempt will be made to characterize the changes which may be expected in the structure and functions of the family and in personal patterns of youth up to the year 2000 and, second, possible changes in the attitudes of youth towards the family will be set against the background of changing social values.

The task would appear rather easy since the year 2000 falls within the near future. Those who will be founding families at the turn of the millennium have already been born or will be born shortly. Their personality, as far as it is shaped by the family, will be shaped in conditions basically not different from those of today. If what sociologists and anthropologists say about the influence of socialization in the family on the shaping of the basic personality of the child is true, it can be assumed that no important changes in the relationship of the youth and the family are to be expected over the next decades as compared with the existing situation. Systems of values and patterns of behaviour remain rather constant from generation to generation, particularly if they are transmitted in a covert manner. Value systems thus transmitted influence the attitudes and behaviour of generations, ideological models of attitudes and patterns of action. New social phenomena, as cultural phenomena, can develop from pre-existing systems only through people who have experienced those pre-existing systems themselves. So if there are no wars of catastrophes or other specially revolutionary events, the expected future can be deduced from the existing situation.

At this point we come across an important difficulty arising from the shortage of scientific information on the existing situation regarding the family and the youth, and especially on the changes taking place in this respect. Little is known about the patterns of changes and their specific determinants. Thus, there are no scientific bases for inference as to the direction of future changes. Even if we know which elements existing so far (let us call them 'traditional elements') have been or will be undergoing social erosion or have been becoming dysfunctional we can only assume that there will be some kind of adaptation. In general it is difficult to determine which of the possible solutions will be adopted. Sometimes it is possible to determine the criteria demanded of the new solutions, and to determine the general direction if specific requirements are to be kept. The preservation of the functioning family unit is one example.

In these circumstances my reflections can have not so much a scientific and prognostic character as a more loose and intuitive one, that of free futurologist reflections. Their starting point will be mainly my knowledge of the contemporary Polish urban family, of the processes of changes occurring in that family and in the position or status of its members, with special attention paid to the position of the youth. My reflections will be directed to the transformations of the contemporary family now and in the future; then to the matters of youth, to problems concerned with its relationship with its family of orientation against the background of its general social relations; and, finally, to the attitudes of the youth towards the institutions of marriage and family. As far as possible I should like to consider the differentiation that may be observed in the status, attitudes, and behaviours of boys and girls from different social walks of life or environments.

Marriage and the family

Traditionally marriage was the prerequisite for founding a family in each and every society. Contracted in a manner adopted by custom or law, marriage acquired social sanction and was equivalent to founding a family. This pointed to procreation as the basic function of marriage and family. The relation between marriage and family, once so tight, is being gradually transformed into a looser arrangement. The institution of marriage has been getting more autonomous. Nowadays the bride and groom often do not give a thought to children on getting married. Even those who take into account the arrival of children imagine that it will occur in some indefinite future. Frequently union is not seen as a procreative one and everything possible is done to avoid having a child.

Cohabitation as a non-procreative union is rather frequent now, although still mainly among student and worker youth. As a rule the institution is purely matrimonial or paramatrimonial and does not carry the implication of founding a family.

In addition to such special and experimental forms, the increasing differentiation of marriage from the family manifests itself by the importance attached to a specific emotional union, to love and attractiveness, mutual attachment and devotion, cooperation and understanding ('marital happiness'). A substantial violation of mutual love may become a legal cause for the breach of the marital union and, to some extent, of the family as well. This pattern bears witness to the fact that the old priority of procreative union in matrimony has been taken over by a hedonistic–consumptive union, one aiming at individual satisfaction. It is one of the more important manifestations of a change in values which has been developing for quite a time. Traditionally the individual interests of members of the family were subordinated to the good of the family as a whole (or of an even larger community). Nowadays it has been more and more emphasized that the family's existence makes sense as far as it serves the good of its individual members. The family is for the individual and not the other way round. This corresponds to a major extent to social consciousness. The family has been losing much of its institutional character. It is less often considered, and, what is more, does not consider itself an organ of the larger society, the state, the church, or the local community. Individual happiness of the member of the family as the supreme criterion is accompanied by a closing up, a characteristic egoism of the family group.

A marriage generates a family when a child arrives. By its birth, but also through adoption, the child creates a family. Functionally, for and because of the child, the family is necessary. Child producing used to be demanded from marriage. Nowadays, left to the free decision of the spouses, it is stimulated by more subtle ideological and social sanctions. Many women think that they prove themselves only through motherhood as 'genuine' women; others feel that child bearing is a duty; some integrate both attitudes. Generally however they are satisfied with one or two children. The movement to free women from the constraint of child bearing is more and more effective as evinced for example in the increasingly widespread use of contraceptives and in the increasing assertion of a right to terminate unwanted pregnancies. The populations of a few highly developed countries will continue to diminish.

It is just this possibility of planning and regulating reproductiveness that, joined with the autonomy of marriage, will make it easier to dissolve marriage in the future. In turn, this makes for a greater popularity of marriage: witness the high percentages of men and women in wedlock in Europe and in America today. There are also other factors involved, which make it possible for the young to decide on their own to get married, e.g. early economic independence and a resultant social independence.

In most cases, however, in Poland and certainly in many other countries, the arrival of a child, intended or not, often brings financial problems, those of nursing and care, as well as the stresses involved in now having to add parenting to existing roles. And these problems tend to instigate renewed cooperative relationships with the family of orientation, usually between the new mother and her mother. This may infringe upon the isolation, or seclusion, of the nuclear family.

The pluralism of socially accepted patterns, structure, functions and roles of the members of a family living together is characteristic of contemporary society. Even though other patterns are by no means infrequent, the dominant pattern is the nuclear family. In general, the nuclear family is considered the 'standard' type. Basically it consists of legally wed parents and their children. As a biologically complete procreative system, the nuclear family can be identified in a large number of societies, both widespread geographically and at various levels of social development. In our time, the nuclear family has acquired not only great importance but considerable internal autonomy and isolation from both the more extended family and the larger society. However, there are also households which include grandparents or other relatives (brothers and sisters, brothers-in-law, for example) in addition to parents and children. And many nuclear household groups maintain closer or looser relations with grandparents, less often with brothers or sisters, etc.

Not every family includes both parents among its members. Every tenth family with children below 16 years of age in Poland is a one-parent family. No longer is this one of the consequences of war. The great majority are families of divorced or separated women, a smaller subset those of widows, and more rarely of single women. One-parent families headed by a man are infrequent (about 5% of all one-parent families).

If we classify the families under discussion by nuclearity and by whether they include a married couple or one parent only, we obtain the picture shown in Table 1. Results more or less similar to those of Table 1 could certainly be obtained from many other countries. The table does not reflect the variety of types of family groups in common households. In particular there are various patterns of relations between parents and grandparents. Other types of families consist of childless legalized married couples and non-legalized ones (cohabitants). The latter are rather marginal and still relatively infrequent.

Table 1

| | Parents present | | |
	Both[a]	One	Total
Other relatives			
Absent	75.5	6.5	82
Present	15.5	2.5	18
	91.0	9.0	100

Note: This table is based on research conducted under the guidance of the author in Polish towns in the years 1967 and 1968 on a sample of families with children where wives were 20 to 50 years old.
[a] Married couples only

In itself the differentiation of various structures is certainly nothing new in the history of the family. Custom used to determine rather strictly 'proper' forms of family existence and other forms were more or less tolerated as negative deviations. Now, however, there is a growing tolerance of changes in family structure and the changes are regarded not so much as deviations but as modifications. A case in point is the change in attitudes toward the one-parent family. This has been caused by a steady and ever more complete emancipation of women and in a way, too, by the gradual relaxation of prejudice against unmarried mothers and against children born 'out of wedlock'. It appears that one-parent families will become more frequent. Their number will continue to grow over the next decades owing not only to increases in the divorce rate, but also to the continued development of other forms of coexistence and to pressures for the independence of women. Various types of families are socially accepted on equal terms with the 'classical' nuclear family or its extended modification provided they are not seen as undermining values.

Other new 'experimental' forms of marriage and family which intentionally infringe on basic values in one way or another have been gaining acceptance with greater difficulty. And even here, as may be seen from the Scandinavian experience, sanctions vary. Cohabitation has already acquired certain rights in the way of legal protection and official accommodation, but it is also subjected to control and sanction by societies which assume the relative stability of such a union. Group marriages or, more properly, group families, attract not only a lesser degree of acceptance and social cooperation but also are of less interest to society as a whole. They constitute cooperating groups of families which themselves adhere to traditional canons. Communes get the least acceptance. In general it can be said that with the exceptional, generally tolerant, attitude of Swedish society towards all kinds of innovations, acceptance diminishes and distrust or dislike increases as the principles and slogans of the 'experiments' diverge from traditional values and, indeed, counter them. Mistrust of novelty also is rationalized on the basis of the child's interests. These are assumed to be endangered by the instability of an unsanctioned parental union, one functioning more for personal satisfaction than for procreation.

Nevertheless, procreation creates the family and the family is the institution of procreation. A lining of functions has grown around the family which is necessary to its very existence. These are educational, social, and economic (or better, acquisitive, in the sense of acquiring the means of living), protective and preventive, and last but certainly not least, affective. These functions constitute a relatively stable syndrome even though the ways of performing them, their content, importance, and hierarchy have continued to vary from culture to culture and down through time.

In spite of the familiar assertion that the various functions of the family have been assumed by other elements of industrial societies, the family continues to perform all of them. In the complex modern world, however, the family can perform them satisfactorily only in collaboration with other institutions. A few examples follow. An expanded public health service and various hospitals and dispensaries have taken over the care and treatment of the sick when specialized knowledge is required. Nevertheless, studies of work and time expenditure show that the family's share in caring for its members in sickness and in prevention is larger than that of the total of public services. Education is also often cited as an example of a function taken over from the family by society. But it continues to claim the attention of the family not only in the pre-school period of the child's life, but up to its maturity, and sometimes even longer. The role of the family in primary socialization, in influencing attitudes toward life and work; toward marriage and family; and toward learning and the forming of personality is no less absorbing than it was before. Schooling, youth clubs, youth organizations and other educational institutions do not facilitate the tasks of the family; they do not substitute for the family; but they do add new problems to the old ones. Another aspect of the division of duties between the family and public services is the necessity of serving as intermediary between family members and external institutions. For example a sick member of the family and the services of public health must be brought together. Or, in another area, the necessity of having its young member go through the complex system of educational institution requires assisting him in the process of learning in various ways ranging from financial to emotional support.

It has been growing more difficult for the family to exercise its functions because it is less bound by the rules and conventions which used to determine its values and standards of conduct. Now it has the possibility, and also the compulsion, to form relations within its own sphere in an individual way, to stimulate spontaneous cooperation. All this requires greater personal and moral maturity, the more so when the main bonds are attractiveness and personal satisfaction.

The family always performs its functions for the benefit of society (i.e. various extended social groups, such as the state, the nation, the local community), for the benefit of its members, and for the benefit of its desired development as an entity. It does so irrespective of its consciousness of the functions—that is, whether it wants to or not. Procreation used to be treated first and foremost as a social obligation. It is becoming a private affair but nevertheless it does not stop being for the benefit of society. Here the evolution can be seen in the shifting of priorities, from the old family which had to be above all an institution of the extended society, to the contemporary (particularly middle-class) family which wants to function for the benefit of its own common interest and later on for the future family, where the interest of the family as an entity as well as its duties towards society will be fully subordinate to the welfare and full development of each of its members. These models are not as much opposite to each other as it would seem. The highest well-being of each and every one requires a good performance of the entity. Moreover individuals as well as families are elements of a more extended social system with its material elements, values and standards, which impose not only certain limits and necessities on human endeavours and activities, but also influence substantially the formation of desires and needs and of favoured ways of gaining satisfaction on material, affective, and intellectual levels.

Transformations of roles within the family are important and perhaps the most directly felt of the changes being considered. In the traditional institutional family the roles of each individual were specialized, differentiated, complementary, and hierarchical. The wife and children were subordinate to the authority of the husband and father. The husband was the breadwinner and the wife was the home maker. The biological reasons for this degree of psychological and physical differentiation are uncertain, except for the woman being child bearer. But even this cause for differentiation of roles has been seriously undermined since scientific and technical progress has given the woman the possibility of controlling her motherhood.

The differentiation of husband and wife roles is diminishing and along with substantial flexibility in role definition in the family has come a repudiation of differential prestige and importance of the occupations of men and women. Equality does not necessarily mean identity; there must be an equal freedom of options, of creating one's own lifestyle in the family in the same way as in society.

Important progress in this respect must be stated. Equal rights of men and women in every domain of social life have been guaranteed by constitutions of many countries and if they are not entirely obtained yet, there is acceptance of them as something absolutely justified. In Poland, as in other socialist countries of Eastern Europe, propaganda has been developed in favour of the professional activity of married women, thus popularizing Marx and Engels' position that economic independence acquired owing to 'the participation of the woman in social production' is a necessary condition of their equality of rights. In our country, for example, where 75% of married women between 20 and 50 years of age hold jobs, the working career of the woman has now become as much an integral part of the social role of the woman as that of mother. The comparable numbers of working women in Czechoslovakia, the Soviet Union, Hungary, or the German Democratic Republic are similar or even higher. A great majority of women treat their working career as their life role. They have been working full time and with great continuity. There are representatives of women in every occupation; there are large numbers of them in the professions. The independence gained through a working career is highly appreciated but this independence is not oriented away from the family. It rather strengthens the prestige of the woman as a co-support of the family, strengthens her integrating role, and augments her authority at home, in the eyes of both husband and children. It is thus of help in strengthening equality in family relations.

We have noted in empirical studies that the longer and the steadier the work of the married woman, the more egalitarian are the opinions in her family on sex roles and the greater is the degree of cooperation of the husband at home. The principle of the domination of the husband at home and the subordination of the interests of other household members to his own interests is being denied in favour of equality and community. The right of the woman to decide matters on her own, as for example taking up a job or entertaining social contacts with people who are unknown to the husband, has been recognized. In general more modern and egalitarian opinions are held by working than non-working married women, by husbands of working than of non-working wives, and by women more than by men.

Work held by women is an important democratizing factor in internal family relations but it is not sufficient on its own. In Poland as much as in other European countries, married women who have been working have kept the main responsibility for running the house and for the care and education of children, a responsibility which by very common opinion reflects negatively on their working career. And thus it can be said that even though women have made great progress towards equal rights, there are still important obstacles standing in the way to achieving that goal completely. Their removal demands time. It is a matter of shedding traditional ideas and behaviours and creating new styles of life, organizations, and institutions. Whenever the processes of change are experienced consciously, understood and accepted, a conscious adaptation can be accelerated. And thus change does not follow the same course in every milieu. The higher the level of education, the higher on the average is the share of women in working careers; the larger the range of their independence and equality, the better the adaptation to new roles at home and elsewhere.

The general level of education among the young has been growing fast. Education is seen as preparation for work. Girls share in this on equal terms with boys, with the difference that they give preference to humanities, including medical science and law, while boys give preference to technical subjects. It has been an accepted practice to recognize the right of the woman to work and to be paid on equal terms with men. There is less eagerness to adapt conditions of life outside work in such equalitarian directions, especially in the way of running the home and the distribution of roles at home.

Roles of the adolescent in the family

The duties of adolescent girls or boys in the family are basically the same. The stereotypical answers to questionnaires about this topic are: 'children should be nice and good', and thus well adapted to the current life of the family, whatever it may be. They also should 'learn well', that is, prepare for their future work. In a majority of homes they are not explicitly taught about or prepared for family life; girls to a much greater extent than boys are asked to help in house chores in spite of declarations that boys and girls should help at home in an equal way. The young thus acquire a low evaluation of home chores which is reflected in repugnance towards those chores. They are seen as marginal, as standing in the way of more important, more personal matters. Thus conflicts and frustrations sometimes arise when in their own home the young must face in turn the necessity of getting those chores done.

The role of the adolescent in the family is complicated and ambiguous. Against the background of egalitarian trends, the adolescent is treated at home on an equal footing as a comrade and at the same time as a child who demands care and requires surveillance. Outside the family adolescents feel grown up and, in many a matter, are more knowledgeable than their parents. Materially protected for the duration of their schooling, young people are relatively free of any duties towards their family except for the duty of learning. But as far as the actual learning is concerned they are totally on their own, and their parents have very limited possibilities for control. However, over this period there is also a natural socialization: the young internalize the patterns which exist in their own family or their mutations.

The critic of the society of adults in general is concerned not so much with basic principles as with the observed discrepancy between actual conduct and the principles held up to the young. Criticism against one's own family, greatest in the last period of secondary schooling, the period therefore of detachment from family dependence, diminishes little by little and attitudes are less negative. The attitudes of young adults toward their family are basically positive. This is reflected in declared life aspirations of the young, among which pride of place is held by the creation of a happy family and work. This is confirmed in practice: more than ever young men and women get married and they do it earlier than before. And more than ever they want happiness in marriage, living in community, friendship and love, and a great majority do it in a traditional form. This can be explained by the family's being a natural system. It seems that the scope of its possible modifications without the essence of the system getting lost is rather narrow.

New experimental lifestyles, such as group marriages or communes, carry more importance as means of propagating the principles of marital and familial communities than as specific solutions. Such principles as love and friendship, candour, sincerity and friendliness, respect of the needs of personality development of each member of the community are not new as such. Instead, through the process of their radical reformulation they have been freed of their coating of conventional compromises and shown in their fresh, real colours.

Summary and concluding hypotheses

In summing up, the following hypotheses may be put forward:

1 It seems that marriage and family patterns similar to those of today will subsist up to the year 2000. There will be development in the direction of:

(a) a small nuclear family closed in the framework of its own living quarters (which does not mean isolation from intergeneration contacts but a pluralism of solutions to the problem);
(b) a further privatization and de-institutionalization, which will extend the possibilities of individual formation of family structure, internal family relationships, family functions and roles; and
(c) a growing importance of personal bonds—bonds of real community—over objective, material, or procreative ones.

2 These changes will loosen conventions and standards in general, including a greater independence and freedom of the youth within the family during a period of adolescence acquired earlier and lasting longer. The evolution is toward individualism in the sense of respect for individual personality and the conditions of its development. This includes harmony with the family, based on more liberal mutual attitudes.

3 I believe that the basic aspirations of adolescents are positive and creative. Much will depend on the opportunities for development, advancement, and creativity facing young people. A threat to the relation between the family and adolescents may come from the outside, from the relations predominant in its social environment.

References

Gottlieb, D. (Ed.). 1973. *Youth in contemporary society*. Beverly Hills and London: Sage.

Piotrowski, J. 1970. *Old people in Poland and their vital capacity*. Warsaw: IGS.

Piotrowski, J. 1971. The employment of married women and changing sex-roles in Poland. In: A. Michel, *Family issues of employed women in Europe and America*. Leiden: Brill.

11 Adolescent peer relations: a look to the future

Willard W. Hartup

Experience with peers is a universal component of adolescent development. Even so, the psychological significance of this experience is not well understood. For this reason, the first portion of the present paper contains an evaluation of the assertion that peer interactions are necessities, rather than luxuries, in human ontogeny.

Subsequent sections of the paper are devoted to predictions about the future of adolescent peer relations. Unfortunately, formulation of such predictions is extremely difficult. The existing literature is largely ahistorical, and most conceptualizations of peer relations do not facilitate historical analysis. A new conceptualization is attempted.

The significance of peer relations in childhood and adolescence

The significance of early peer relations is most clearly revealed in studies of non-human primates. This research shows that juvenile peer interactions are determinants of adult aggressive and sexual behaviour (Harlow, 1969), as well as patterns of parenting behaviour and altruism (Trivers, 1971). In some instances, these interactions involve agemates i.e. individuals who are similar to each other in terms of chronological age or developmental status. In other instances, socialization requires interaction with members of the species who are somewhat older or somewhat younger than the individual himself.

Primate ecologies usually provide opportunities for both same age and cross age interaction, although tremendous variation occurs in the type of interaction which predominates. Among species that live in small, scattered enclaves, peer interaction occurs within groups that include infants and children, as well as adolescents. Thus, cross age interaction is common among vervet monkeys, certain species of baboon, and chimpanzees, all of whom live in small social units. On the other hand, among species which live in large colonies, such as the langur monkey, same age interaction tends to predominate. The psychological significance of these variations is not well understood, so that contemporary primatologists are attempting to obtain improved field data concerning the peer relations of the various species (Dolhinow and Bishop, 1970). For the moment, however, the consequences of same age peer interaction as contrasted with cross age interaction cannot be fully specified.

Peer interaction is as common in human social development as in the development of the non-human primates. Archaeological studies confirm that, since prehistoric times, the conditions under which man has lived have always provided an opportunity for juveniles to interact with each other. During man's early history, such experiences occurred largely within small groups composed of infants, children, and adolescents—that is, within groups composed of individuals who varied considerably in age. Mixed age peer cultures can still be observed in a few parts of the world (e.g. among the !Ko-Bushmen), although child–child contacts are age graded in most contemporary cultures. In twentieth century Europe, for example, a large number of children's contacts with other children involve individuals who differ in chronological age by one calendar year or less. But some form of peer interaction, either same age or cross age, has been a universal dimension of social experience since the origin of the species. Only in rare and isolated circumstances have individual families been known to rear their young without providing for interaction with peers.

Because peer interaction is a universal characteristic of human socialization, its adaptive significance needs to be carefully studied. Here, it is asserted that 'normal' social development cannot be achieved in the absence of such interaction. Although the mature personality derives from myriad events, including experiences within the family and within the school, it is necessary for the young members of our species to interact occasionally with individuals whose capacities and social status are similar to their own. Children derive much from interacting with individuals who are older, larger, and wiser than themselves, but there are some human capacities that emanate only from interaction with equals.

Consider, as an example, the socialization of aggression. No society has ever existed in which adults have assumed exclusive responsibility for this task. On the contrary, nature has created a situation which necessitates aggressive peer interaction while, at the same time, necessitating the inhibition of hostile activity in adult–child interaction. Anthropological studies show that these constraints are most inflexible during late childhood and adolescence. One of the most dramatic changes between younger and older children found by the investigators who conducted the 'Six Culture Study' (Lambert, 1974) was a marked decrease in the use of family members as targets of aggression and an increase in the probability of targeting onto non-siblings. Among older children, the social context in which most of the aggression occurred was play; some $2\frac{2}{3}$ times more aggression occurred during play than during casual social interaction. So, it is not difficult to conclude that older children and adolescents have learned that the 'safe' situation in which to be aggressive involves equals and that situations involving adults, particularly family members, are 'not safe'. Such data are especially impressive when it is understood that interpersonal aggression is not a rare event. On the contrary, the children in these cultures were involved in some nine instances of aggression every hour.

Consider, now, how beautifully adaptive these circumstances are. First, rough and tumble activity, which seems to be necessary for the effective socialization of aggression, is not compatible with the constraints built into most adult–child relationships. The family, for example, is largely devoted to protecting the child from danger, ensuring an adequate food supply, and providing the child with an opportunity to learn certain skills. To further these accomplishments, the family encompasses a set of relationships known as specific attachments (Bowley, 1969). These attachments, which persist throughout childhood and adolescence, cannot be maintained within a social system in which uninhibited aggression is allowed to occur. Parents cannot carry out their functions as parents when children cannot restrain their rage and, at the same time, children cannot withstand unbridled parental abuse. In fact, unconstrained aggression between individuals leads to detachment. Thus, aggression within the family weakens those selfsame bonds which make it possible for the family to fulfil its most basic adaptive functions.

Is peer interaction, then, a substitute for family interaction? Not quite. Children seek the 'safety' of the play group because it is uniquely adapted to the socialization of aggression, not solely because it provides escape from parental sanction. Effective aggressive socialization requires a certain number of *equalitarian* experiences—that is, semi-aggressive and aggressive encounters which are sometimes successful and sometimes not. Only in rough and tumble interaction with peers are such opportunities maximized (Harlow, 1969). What chance, after all, does the child have in either a fist fight or a shouting match with a fully mature adult? No, adult–child interaction does not provide the range of aggressive experiences that are needed for the maintenance of mature social relations and mental health. Our knowledge concerning the origins of aggression strongly suggests that experience with peers has no effective substitute.

Sex can be cited as another aspect of development to which the contributions of the parent–child relationship are severely constrained. Gender typing (i.e. the child's appreciation of his or her sexual identity) occurs very early (Maccoby and Jacklin, 1974) with parents contributing more to this process than peers. But there is little doubt that the sexual attitudes and practices of the mature individual are shaped, in large part, by contacts with agemates. Today, and throughout man's history, the most frequent agents for the transmission of sexual mores have been older children and adolescents (Kinsey, Pomeroy and Martin, 1948).

Sexual socialization, like aggressive socialization, may occur within the peer culture for sound reasons. The experimentation necessary to the establishment of adult sexual behaviour is no more compatible with the parent–child relationship than the experimentation necessary to the socialization of aggression. Sexual practice within the context of parent–child relations would create vastly different gene pools from those which have evolved and, owing to its non-equalitarian basis, would create styles of sexual behaviour that would lead to minimal success in procreation. No, human development seems to be programmed so that the contributions of parents and peers to the individual's sexual socialization are not interchangeable.

Other arguments could be mounted to support the thesis that socialization requires commerce with both adult and sub-adult members of the species. For example, it is doubtful that a fully generative ethical system can be developed entirely within the context of adult–child relations. Many writers, including Piaget (1932), have emphasized the unique contributions of peer interactions to moral development, and there is every reason to believe that the effects of experience with peers extend to other behavioural domains as well (Hartup, in press). Enough has been said, however, to conclude that peer relations are essential components of normal human development.

Peer relations I and II

Peer relations among children and adolescents can be discussed on two levels. First, there are basic, universal dimensions of the peer experience—necessities and processes which underlie overt normative behaviour. Second, there are surface structures in peer interaction—patterns of overt behaviour and normative regulations which characterize particular individuals and/or groups at particular times. These levels in peer interaction can be called peer relations I and II, respectively.

Peer relations I are the underlying structures which lead to individual differences in social behaviour. They are internal substrates that determine the child's special sensitivity, in certain behaviour domains, to agemate interaction. These structures are not the particular behaviour patterns or lifestyles that emerge from the peer experience. Whether one throws eggs at passing cars, steals hubcaps, or engages in mutual masturbation are surface aspects of peer-determined behaviour.

The structures which constitute peer relations I derive from both biological and social sources and, to some extent, are developmentally labile. The child's extraordinary sensitivity to aggressive stimulation from agemates has a long evolutionary history. But the processes which determine the individual's overt behaviour also include the vicissitudes of social learning (witness the considerable influence of peers as models—Hartup and Lougee, 1975) and cultural experience.

The surface elements in peer relations (peer relations II) correspond in some ways to the phenotypic aspects of social behaviour since they include those behavioural modes which characterize particular individuals in a particular culture at a particular time. These dimensions of peer interaction are enormously varied across cultures and sometimes change very rapidly over time. For example, the normative aspects of adolescent grooming vary on a semi-annual timetable in many Western cultures.

Those normative constellations, called 'lifestyles', are good illustrations of peer relations II. Such elements provide a nomenclature for adolescent identity formation and also reveal the structure of the adolescent social system. Thus, *sporties* are adolescents of both sexes who engage in sports, who attend sports activities, and who drink beer; *workers* are those students who have jobs, who are highly motivated to accumulate money, who own cars, and whose social life revolves mostly around the automobile; *crispies* are students who use drugs on other than a one-time basis, who are the best football players, and who do not work very hard at school; *musicians* are students who spend much time in the music room, who participate in performances of one type or other, who attend or assist with performance activities, and who drink alcoholic beverages; and *debaters* are those who read a lot, get good grades, participate in clubs focused on intellectual activities, and who drink Pepsi-Cola at their parties. Each of these lifestyles contains provisions that relate to the deeper structures of peer relations I but the particular normative regulators which the peer culture espouses exemplify peer relations II.

Although peer relations II may be situation-specific, one should not assume that these elements derive solely from experience. Agonistic interaction among young children, for example, contains motivating elements that show very little variation from culture to culture (McGrew, 1972) and which may be more or less direct products of genetic encoding. There can be little doubt, however, that most surface structures in peer relations are enormously malleable, being sensitive in many ways to environmental vicissitudes. Evolution may prescribe the existence of adolescent enclaves and their importance to the development of the individual, but it does not prescribe the use of drugs or the automobile as normative regulators that mark off one peer culture from another.

Levels in peer relations and an historical perspective

Few social scientists have concerned themselves with historical factors in peer relations (a deplorable condition) and most popular discussion of the matter is marred by a lack of differentiation between peer relations I and II. The simple caveat is sometimes stated that our research data are era-specific but, at the same time, the literature is replete with simplistic generalizations: 'Everything about adolescent peer relations is constantly changing'; or 'Little about adolescence is new under the sun'. However, neither of these generalizations is warranted. Change is ubiquitous at some levels in peer interaction but not others (Douvan and Adelson, 1966). The remainder of this paper is devoted to support for the hypothesis that historical trends (both continuities and discontinuities) can be elucidated most clearly by separate consideration of peer relations I and II.

The future and peer relations I

Inasmuch as peer relations I are determined in large part by the tedious processes of evolution, one would expect little change in these dimensions of the adolescent peer experience by the year 2000. Ready access to age-mates will continue to be provided within most cultures, and spontaneously formed peer groups will continue to serve as the principal locus for socialization in many domains, especially affiliation, aggression, sex, and moral behaviour. Those structures in personality and social behaviour to which peer interaction is a primary contributor in the year 1975 will also be determined by peer relations in the year 2000.

Aggression and sex

The centrality of the peer culture in the socialization of aggression is certain to continue. While changes may occur in the surface (normative) aspects of aggressive socialization, there is every reason to believe that children and adolescents in the year 2000 will require commerce with equals in order to achieve a mature adjustment with respect to aggressive motivation in the same degree as their 1975 counterparts. In reverse, it can be expected that unsatisfactory experiences with peers will continue to contribute to individual maladjustment—to 'acting out' disturbances, to manifestation of bizarre or unusual modes of aggressive attack, and to unusual timidity and lack of effectiveness in coping with the aggressive attacks of others. Similarly, the continued centrality of the peer culture in the socialization of sex would seem to be assured.

Affiliation

The adolescent peer group also functions importantly in the socialization of affiliation. The ontogenetic basis for affiliative behaviour develops within the family, but the peer group furnishes attitudes and expectations necessary to the establishment of interpersonal relations with agemates—both of the same and the opposite sex (Erikson, 1950). Research reveals, for example, that 'social reservedness with peers' among adolescents is associated with an inward looking orientation, high anxiety, and low social activity (Bronson, 1966). Poor peer relations in early adolescence also predicts neurotic disturbance, psychosis, and adult character disorders of a variety of types (Roff, 1963). This evidence, of course, is not easy to interpret. Do unsatisfactory experiences with peers lead to anxiety, lowered self-esteem, and hostility which, in turn, lead to further rejection? Or, do behaviours and attitudes deriving from intra-individual sources induce breakdowns in the individual's peer relations? Whatever the direction of causal influence, the existing literature furnishes no evidence that contradicts the basic hypothesis—peer experiences are of pivotal importance in the development of effective interpersonal relations (Roff, Sells and Golden, 1972).

Given this state of affairs, certain data are disturbing. D. H. Heath (1969), who has interviewed American high school seniors for more than 20 years, reported that the following changes occurred between 1949 and 1969: the proportion of subjects indicating that they did not care to be a member of a crowd or a gang increased from 33% to 47%; the proportion who viewed friends as a means for relieving tension and worry declined from 71% to 55%; and the proportion indicating that trouble within the peer group should be shared rather than assumed by oneself declined from 63% to 45%. (These proportions may be somewhat higher among European adolescents—Kandel and Lesser, 1972.) Meanwhile, the results of studies conducted in several American universities during the 1960s showed that the number of individuals who reported themselves never to have had a best friend or who reported frequent loneliness exceeded one-third of the population. These data have received considerable attention in both the popular and scientific literature because they seem to indicate that the capacity of the peer culture to assist in affiliative development is declining. Since intimate social relations are basic to much human accomplishment, one worries about such a change if, in fact, it is true. At the moment, it is not known whether this change characterizes adolescents other than middle-class students or whether a reversal in this trend is now occurring. But these structures in adolescent peer relations bear close watching by every individual interested in youth 2000.

Moral development

Also deserving close observation during the next quarter century are the processes underlying moral and ethical development. Keasey (1971) found that children who belonged to relatively many clubs and social organizations had higher moral judgement scores than children belonging to fewer organizations. Leadership and popularity were also positively related to level of moral judgement. Other investigators (see Hartup, 1970) have demonstrated that leaders in adolescent peer groups tend to be well socialized individuals, whether the norms endorsed by the peer group are approved by the core culture or disapproved by it. But these data, too, are difficult to interpret. Does experience with peers facilitate moral development (Piaget, 1932) or do well socialized individuals simply find it easier to gain access to leadership positions? There are no definitive answers to these questions.

Whatever the case, there is little doubt that interaction with one's agemates exerts a powerful influence over the attitudes, aspirations, and values of the adolescent. If an adolescent's best friend uses marijuana, the chances that he will be a user are greater than when the best friend is a non-user (Kandel, 1973). But such facts obscure one of the most important characteristics of peer contributions to moral and ethical development. *Peer relations contribute to moral development in a manner which is synergistic with the contributions of adults.* Thus, adolescents whose best friends use marijuana and whose parents use psychotropic drugs are more likely to become users of marijuana than youngsters whose peers are users but whose parents are not (Kandel, 1973). In other cases, normative behaviour sometimes comes under the control of the peer group or, alternatively, remains under the control of the adult culture, depending on the nature of the norm (Brittain, 1963). But clearly, adolescent values are not shaped exclusively by either the adult culture or the peer culture.

Will the manner in which parent and peer influences combine to determine adolescent moral behaviour change during the next quarter century? Those scientists (e.g. Bronfenbrenner, 1975) who predict dissolution in the nuclear family in Western culture would respond affirmatively to this question. Since this writer does not predict such dissolution, however, it is expected that youth 2000 will continue to experience moral socialization as a process in which both parents and peers participate—although there may be some readjustments in these experiences.

Summary

Peer relations I will change relatively little during the next 25 years. Cataclysms of world war or economic upheaval might alter the deeper dimensions of the peer experience, either to lessen the importance of peer interaction to the individual and his development or to increase it (cf., Freud and Dann, 1951). Drastic changes in family organization could also cause readjustments. But, in our view, the kinds of cultural change now foreseeable are not likely to disturb the current balance in peer and parent participation in adolescent socialization.

On numerous occasions, policy makers have argued that the peer culture should be more formally utilized in the upbringing of children and adolescents. Perhaps, but one should be wary of any intervention which transforms the peer culture from an equalitarian to an authoritarian agency. The evils of the Hitler youth did not lie solely in the corrupt morality which that peer system transmitted. To the contrary, such authoritarian peer systems intrinsically deny the individual adolescent an essential proving ground for the socialization of individual responsibility—namely, peer relations which are based on reciprocity and give and take.

Educators and social workers have been experimenting, lately, with new schemes whereby older children and adolescents are employed as teachers or mentors for younger children (Allen, in press). Commonly, such programmes are designed to assist children who are having difficulty in learning to read or who may not be 'turned on' to school. While these interventions resemble the informal, give and take conditions which have long prevailed in multi-age peer groups, the use of such systems would be ill advised if access to informal interaction with agemates is devalued. Excessive formalization of the peer experience or over-zealous placement of adolescents in adult roles *vis-à-vis* their peers are not warranted in terms of current knowledge.

The future and peer relations II

Because peer relations II are relatively ephemeral, it is easy to assume that they are unimportant. Nothing could be further from the truth. Members of adolescent cliques spend most of their waking hours worrying about this level in their peer relations, and no peer culture can be described without reference to the normative regulators which govern it. Thus, Sherif and Sherif (1964) described one group of peer cultures:

> Members of groups in middle and high rank areas would share cigarettes from a package, but not the same cigarette, nor a drink from the same bottle. [One group] lived in a mixed ethnic neighborhood, somewhat more prosperous than several other low rank neighborhoods, and its members all attended school. They once discussed their disdain for sharing a cigarette. The leader told of his great embarrassment on being stopped when on a date by a schoolmate who asked him for his cigarette butt. In other low rank areas, where money and possessions are scarcer, a cigarette was routinely shared by passing it around, as were drinks and other consumables. In planning a party, every member was expected to contribute what he had, but was not usually excluded if he had nothing. On the contrary, the member who had more, especially if he were leader, contributed more (p. 172).

The salience of these structures cannot be overstated. Adolescents themselves are preoccupied with them, parents obsess overtly about them, and they furnish endless amounts of copy for editorial writers and television broadcasters. Indeed, peer relations II generate considerable tension in adolescent socialization.

Most authorities insist that this tension is not severe, and that adolescence is a period of relative concordance between parents and their offspring (Douvan and Adelson, 1966; Kandel and Lesser, 1972). In historical perspective, though, is this concordance diminishing? Has the so-called generation gap widened significantly during the past quarter century so that the concordance–discordance balance in parent–child relations has shifted? The evidence is scanty, but this does not seem to be the case. Disagreements between parents and their children have occurred since man's prehistory; these discordances will continue to be a hallmark of adolescent development. There is no basis, however, for predicting increased parent–child discordance in peer relations II by the year 2000.

More likely, concordant parent–child relations will continue, assuming that families are no more pressured by external forces in the year 2000 than in the year 1975.

One significant change in peer relations II has occurred since World War II. There has been an increase in the degree to which 'far out' normative regulators are accepted by the peer culture. A much broader range of lifestyles is exemplified in adolescent societies than 25 years ago, and this has occurred at every level of socio-economic status and in every Western culture. Currently, one may choose to be gay or straight, to live singly or plurally, high or low fashion, university educated or technically trained, and the peer culture will support such diversity.

What social conditions have precipitated this increased diversity in the normative regulation of behaviour, particularly the rapidity with which it has developed during the past decade? These questions are most properly answered by the social historians, but one hypothesis can be hazarded here. Recent decades have fostered increased diversity because they have been marked by two conditions: social tension, and the absence of social disaster. When there is tension within the system, but no grave threat to survival, the individual has both the incentive and the permission to experiment with alternative designs for living. The absence of tension, on the other hand, breeds stagnation rather than social experimentation. Social catastrophe also prevents diversification in normative behaviour but for very different reasons. During catastrophic times, conformity is necessary for collective survival.

Tense, but non-catastrophic conditions have prevailed during most of the past 25 years and seem likely to prevail for the remainder of the century. The outer limits of diversity have not been reached, nor have the capacities of adolescents to live under increased diversity been fully tested. Thus, the time seems right for the generation of greater and greater diversity at the surface levels of adolescent peer relations.

What does this mean in terms of social planning? First, it should be understood that diversity in peer relations II is not always well adapted. The forces that generate increased diversity in adolescent lifestyles generate both benign and malignant social norms. At the moment, many Western nations are experiencing an explosion in the occurrence of youthful violence and crime. Half of all arrests in the USA are of teenagers and young adults; in fact, the modal age for violent crime is

15 years. According to data reported recently in *Time Magazine*, 44% of the nation's murderers are 25 or younger and, of those arrested for street crimes (excluding murder), 75% are under the age of 25 and 45% are under the age of 18. Other trends are equally alarming: while many young terrorists may belong to old-style gangs much of today's crime is solitary. Gang wars are less common than they once were, but the lone criminal is an increasingly common phenomenon. Females participate in violent crimes more frequently than in earlier days, and the quality of some of this violence is unbelievably gruesome. This rise in teenage crime does not seem to be an artifact derived from either the increased number of teenagers in the general population or the greater effectiveness of law enforcement agencies in apprehending the teenage criminal as compared to the adult criminal. Rather, the increase in adolescent violence seems to derive from the freedom to experiment with alternative lifestyles (especially in more pluralistic societies) and tensions produced by co-existing conditions of extreme poverty and extreme affluence.

Overall, the surface elements of adolescent peer relations have changed rapidly during recent years and continued change is likely. Increased diversity in adolescent designs for living reduces social dissonance in some instances but not others. Since peer relations II are common sources of tension between the peer culture and the larger social system, such changes merit continuous observation.

Conclusion

One prediction about the future of adolescent peer relations can be made with certainty: there will be fewer peer groups in the year 2000 than in the year 1975. Demographers are not predicting a reversal in the declining birth rate (at least in the West), so that a decline in the size of the adolescent population relative to the size of the adult population should characterize the next 25 years. This trend, however, is not very interesting. Classrooms in our secondary schools and universities can be converted easily to other purposes, and jobs can be found for those persons (including professors) who will no longer be needed to care for and feed large numbers of adolescents in schools and other social institutions.

But both peer relations I and II need close observation. Youth 2000 must continue to have numerous opportunities to socialize under equalitarian conditions. Formalization of adolescent peer relations should not be attempted on a massive scale, although certain problems (e.g. the matter of violence) must be solved. By and large, there is no reason to expect adolescent doomsday by the turn of the century. On the contrary, those elements in present peer relations which are 'right', as well as those elements which are 'wrong', will continue to characterize human development for many decades after the year 2000.

References

Allen, V. L. (Ed.). In press. *Children as teachers: Theory and research on tutoring.* Madison: University of Wisconsin Press.

Bowlby, J. 1969. *Attachment and loss*, vol. 1. New York: Basic Books.

Brittain C. V. 1963. Adolescent choices and parent-peer cross-pressures, *Am. Sociol. Rev.*, vol. 28, pp. 385–391.

Bronfenbrenner, U. 1975. Ecological factors in human development in retrospect and prospect. Paper presented at biennial meeting of the International Society for the Study of Behavioural Development, Guildford, UK.

Bronson, W. C. 1966. Central orientations: A study of behavior organization from childhood to adolescence, *Child Develop.*, vol. 37, pp. 125–155.

Dolhinow, P. J. and Bishop, N. 1970. The development of motor skills and social relationships among primates through play. In: J. P. Hill (Ed.), *Minnesota symposia on child psychology*, vol. 4. Minneapolis: University of Minnesota Press.

Douvan, E. and Adelson, J. 1966. *The adolescent experience.* New York: Wiley.

Erikson, E. H. 1950. *Childhood and society.* New York: Norton.

Freud, A. and Dann, S. 1951. An experiment in group upbringing. In: E. K. Eisler (Ed.), *The psychoanalytic study of the child*, vol. 6. New York: International Universities Press.

Harlow, H. F. 1969. Age-mate or peer affectional system. In: D. Lehrman, R. Hinde and K. Shaw (Ed.), *Advances in the study of behavior*, vol. 2. New York: Academic Press.

Hartup, W. W. 1970. Peer interaction and social organization. In: Mussen's Carmichael, *Manual of child psychology*, vol. 2. New York: Wiley.

Hartup, W. W. In press. Peer interaction and the behavioral development of the individual child. In: Schopler, *Child development, deviations, and treatment: Proceedings of the first international Leo Kanner colloquium.* New York: Plenum.

Hartup, W. W. and Lougee, M. D. 1975. Peers as models, *Sch. Psychol. Digest.*, vol. 4, pp. 11–21.

Heath, D. H. 1969. The education of young children: At the crossroads? *Young Children*, vol. 25, pp. 73–84.

Kandel, D. 1973. Adolescent marijuana use: Role of parents and peers, *Science*, vol. 181, pp. 1067–1070.

Kandel, D. B. and Lesser, G. S. 1972. *Youth in two worlds.* San Francisco: Jossey-Bass.

Keasey, C. B. 1971. Social participation as a factor in the moral development of preadolescents, *Develop. Psychol.*, vol. 5, pp. 216–220.

Kinsey, A. C., Pomeroy, W. B. and Martin, C. E. 1943. *Sexual behavior in the human male.* Philadelphia: Saunders.

Lambert, W. W. 1974. Promise and problems of cross-cultural exploration of children's aggressive strategies. In: J. DeWit and W. W. Hartup (Eds.), *Determinants and origins of aggressive behavior.* The Hague: Mouton.

Maccoby, E. E. and Jacklin, C. N. 1974. *The psychology of sex differences.* Stanford: Stanford University Press.

McGrew, W. C. 1972. *An ethological study of children's behavior.* New York: Academic Press.

Piaget, J. 1932. *The moral judgment of the child.* Glencoe: Free Press.

Roff, M. 1963. Childhood social interaction and young adult psychosis, *J. Clin. Psychol.*, vol. 19, pp. 152–157.

Roff, M., Sells, S. B. and Golden, M. M. 1972. *Social adjustment and personality development in children.* Minneapolis: University of Minnesota Press.

Sherif, M. and Sherif, C. W. 1964. *Reference groups.* New York: Harper and Row.

Trivers, R. L. 1971. The evolution of reciprocal altruism, *Q. Rev. Biol.*, vol. 45, pp. 35–57.

7

12 The adolescent and the school in Europe

Torsten Husén

The present paper attempts to convey three major points. In the first place, formal education today covers a much longer period of a person's lifespan. The overwhelming majority of adolescents in the industrialized countries are to be found in schools and not at workplaces with adults. Second, the school of today is not able to shoulder the task of socializing young people, mainly because most of its activities by nature lack both functional relevance and meaningful participation. Third, in order to cope with the present crisis in the secondary school the latter has to be 'de-institutionalized' in certain respects and brought in closer contact with the adult world and working life.

The changing role of the adolescent

The social role of the European adolescent has during the last few decades undergone a change so rapid, profound, and revolutionary that many of us have not been able to catch up with what actually has happened. It would therefore seem appropriate to point out some basic facts which justify the introductory sweeping statement.

The most striking change is that the overwhelming majority of adolescents today are found to be in schools and not at the workplaces. Before World War II only a small social and intellectual élite in Europe proceeded in full time schooling beyond mandatory school age at 13 or 14. Until very recently the major educational functions took place in the family. The school's two major functions were auxiliary and supplementary. The small élite, many of them with destinations in the professions, early entered special schools (grammar schools, *gymnasia*, *lycées*) in order to obtain the proper grounding for more elevated occupations. The great majority, following the passage of legislation on compulsory elementary education, had to enter schools where they were taught the three R's and sometimes also the scriptures. The two systems of schools fitted an ascriptive society where education and social background were almost perfectly correlated.

The years after World War II witnessed a breakthrough for the notion nurtured by the liberal philosophy of equal opportunity according to which educational status, as well as subsequent career, should be achieved, that is to say reflect 'genuine' capacity of aptitude (*freie Bahn dem Tüchtigen*, Husén, 1975). Universal secondary education began to be introduced in the more affluent and/or industrialized European countries after the war. Here we need only point to the Education Act in England in 1944, the decree issued by the French government in 1959, and the Swedish comprehensive education acts of 1950 and 1962. Thanks to statistics collected by OECD and the Council of Europe we are able to follow in detail the enrolment explosion which has hit one stage of education after the other (OECD, 1971 and 1974). The exponential increase first occurred at the lower secondary level; then, with a time lag of a few years, at the upper secondary level; and finally it reached the university level. The inflow of students broke forecasts which were notorious for their conservatism. Owing to legislation raising the mandatory school leaving age and to the increased number of young people who proceeded to upper secondary school, some European countries are now rapidly approaching the point when the great majority of adolescents are found in school instead of at the work places (this is already the case in the USA and Japan).

The following personal example suggests the rapidity of the change. When I completed the six-year elementary school in 1928, the great majority, in fact almost 90% of the 13-year-olds, left in order to join the ranks of the adult world. Only one out of ten went on to the lower secondary school. Less than one out of 20 in the age group reached upper secondary school. Only one out of 50 entered university. Today the mandatory leaving age is 16; there are provisions in the upper secondary school for some 90% of the age group; and, at least as late as 1971, one out of four entered institutions of higher education.

Concomitant with expanded enrolment, the school as an institution has been assigned functions which were previously discharged either by the home or the work place. The school is taking on socializing tasks which previously were not its business. Instead of entering the adult world

7*

to learn adult roles, adolescents find themselves in institutions where (for reasons that shall be spelled out later) they have little contact with adult society. We are in fact witnessing a large scale age segregation which has been reinforced by the phenomenon we used to call urbanization and at the core of which is a huge restructurization of the economy from agriculture to manufacturing industry and from manufacturing industry to service industry.

In earlier days the home was a place of togetherness in work and leisure. But first the fathers and then the mothers moved out of the home to work in a shop or an office. This radically changed the process of being initiated or 'socialized' into the adult world. Various legislative steps were taken to keep adolescents away from the workplaces. Indeed, many young people who grow up in urban centres today take a rather dim view of the world of work.

The changing role of the school

It is striking to note that together with the increased number of years of formal schooling goes a tendency to keep students away from adult roles and to create conditions for an enlarged student role. Schools have become bigger and the typical adolescent in Europe today is 'processed' in a school plant that accommodates about 1000 young people. The enlargement of the organization means fewer personal contacts and more bureaucratic formality. The school day is chopped up into uniform periods and breaks between them according to the clock. What goes on in the classroom is prepared in detail. Methods of instruction are dominated by a classical 'frontal instruction' that assumes passive absorption on the part of the student. Systematically shielded from responsibility, he often learns to become irresponsible. More than 20 years ago when I was conducting a research project on school discipline in the city of Stockholm, I coined the phrase 'functional participation' to indicate work practices conducive to the development of initiative and responsibility among students. My observations confirmed the absence of functional participation. In the report submitted on the outcomes of the study I pointed out that we cannot expect young people who leave school to be capable of more responsibility than the school has given them an opportunity to acquire.

The first point we have tried to convey is that the school not only covers a longer period in a person's life, but it has also taken over socializing functions which were previously handled in adult settings, such as the workplace, where adolescents were more often treated as adults. The second point is that the school has not been able to shoulder its new responsibilities. Hence, symptoms of our current crisis are legion: the secondary school of today is on a collision course with society. We must try to take our bearings in order to be able to make corrections before the collision occurs.

The problems indicated above began to be investigated some 20 years ago. Pioneering studies of the 'adolescent society' were conducted by the Chicago sociologist James S. Coleman, who set out to investigate the value climate in secondary schools and to disentangle the relative influence of the home, the school, and the peer group on that climate. Coleman came to the conclusion that adolescents in a way were segregated from the rest of the society, that the peer group exerted the strongest socializing influence and that the school (as represented by the teachers) could not compete at all when it came to influencing young people. The generation gap in value orientation implied by such a conception has been challenged by Andersson (1969) among others.

Recently Professor Coleman has chaired a panel on youth problems in the President's Office of Science and Technology. The panelists were drawn from a wide range of scientific disciplines, such as history, psychology, sociology and anthropology. The mandate was simply to explore what kind of environments in present day society could best contribute to making young people mature, helping them to become adults.

The report of the panel (Coleman *et al.*, 1974) points out that in an agrarian society young people learned what they needed to know in order to fulfil their adult role in the home and at the workplace. The school served only as a supplement. But in modern society, where young people increasingly end up in occupations other than those of their parents (in some 80–95% of the cases), a long period of specialized preparation is necessary in order to make them function satisfactorily as adults. Separate institutions had to be set up in order to accomplish these tasks. The task of maturing a child today has become almost entirely a monopoly of the school, whereas the home tends to be closed down during the day. The report points out:

Our basic premise is that the school system, as now constituted, offers an incomplete context for the accomplishment of many important facets of maturation. The school has been well designed to provide some kinds of training but, by virtue of that fact, is inherently ill-suited to fulfil other tasks essential to the creation of adults (Coleman *et al.*, 1974, p. 2).

To cast the problem in terms of a single formula: the school is 'information-rich' but 'action-poor'. It is a place where conceptual and verbal tools are taught but where little 'learning by doing' can take place. The realities of the outer world are dealt with via abstract verbal media. On the one hand this is the real strength of the school. Abstract concepts and verbal tools are necessary in order to teach young people to cope intellectually and technically with the surrounding world. On the other hand, this is also a weakness, particularly because of the tendency to make verbal and abstract exercise an end in itself. One who successfully masters the exercise is rewarded, while one who is able to apply what he has learnt is not. B. F. Skinner once sarcastically remarked that the American student who in impeccable French could say, 'Please pass me the salt', gets an A, whereas his French counterpart who utters the same words gets the salt!

The school of today no longer possesses a monopoly of information. Other agents, such as mass media, libraries, and voluntary associations, are competing. Furthermore, the real 'action' is outside the school, not least at the workplaces. Dealing with things outside the school in an abstract and verbalized way during instruction is easily conducive to passivity on the part of the adolescent student. The school cannot substitute richness of action for richness of information and this is the core of the problem of motivating young people who are 'institutionalized' for most of their teens.

The conception of why young people in our society are having difficulties in maturing into adulthood has been challenged by a group of Stanford economists specialized in the economics of education (Behn *et al.*, 1974). The Coleman panel published its report under the title 'Youth: Transition to Adulthood'. Under the title, 'The Transformation of Adulthood: Its Implications for Youth', the Stanford group turns the matter around. They neither accept the proposition that the school in our present society is 'not a complete environment giving all the necessary opportunities for becoming adult', nor do they endorse the proposition that 'opportunities for responsible action' provided outside the school would be a solution. The critics' main point is that the various socializing agencies, primarily the school and the workplace, are not at odds with each other to the extent that the Coleman panel maintains. They refer to the socialization literature and submit that the various agencies correspond fairly well and that there is a direct relationship between the demands of the work organization and the various agencies of socialization, not least the school. It is maintained that 'a major role of the school is to reproduce the social relations of production', furthermore that the socialization works differently depending on the social class of the children. Work traits that vary between social strata are moulded 'according to social class in order to fill out the highly unequal work hierarchy inherent in capitalist production'. Thus the dissatisfaction with both school and work that we find among so many young people 'is directly related to the alienating environments of both work organizations and schools than by inadequate socialization for meeting demands of work'.

The view presented by Behn *et al.* is by and large the same as that advanced and empirically tested by two other economists (Bowles, 1971; Bowles and Gintis, 1973). To be sure, whether the dissatisfaction among teenagers with the school and its shortcomings in preparing for adult life in the type of society we now have, and possibly could conceive of having in the foreseeable future, should be put on the school or on society is a matter of political ideology. Neither the extent to which the school serves only as a sorting and selecting agency for industry and business, nor the extent to which cognitive competence provided matters for adult success is as simple as conceived by Bowles and others (Husén, 1974b). There are instances where school and working life obviously are not at odds with each other (OECD, 1975). As will be spelled out later, the need for independence and responsibility required in working life is not met by the scope for self-initiated activities and the preparation provided in the school. In other respects, however, the school is a reflection of the type of society we have. Thus the competitiveness and the strong emphasis on cognitive excellence is in the last analysis an anticipation of a society where cognitive competence increasingly becomes an instrument of social mobility and individual success (Bell, 1973).

There is ample evidence to show that in highly industrialized countries, such as the USA, the Netherlands, and the Federal Republic of Germany, the attitude towards school becomes increasingly negative as the students progress through the grades constituting compulsory schooling. Even among those who opt to proceed through the upper secondary school the general attitude tends toward the negative side. In surveys conducted by the International Association for the Evaluation of Educational Achievement (IEA), representative samples of 10-year-olds, 14-year-olds, and students in the last grade of the pre-university school were given an inventory of statements, such as 'I should like to have as much education as I can possibly get'. On the basis of a number of such statements that could be either endorsed or rejected, we constructed a 'Like School' Scale (Husén *et al.*, 1973). In the first place, we found a consistent deterioration from the 10- to the 14-year-old level in liking for school over all the industrialized countries. In countries where 15- and 16-year-olds were tested as national policy, such as Sweden, comparisons could be made throughout the last three grades of compulsory schooling. Low-performing students and students with underprivileged home background tended to show the most marked, progressively negative, attitudes. Among them, the additional benefits in terms of increased knowledge gained by staying on some extra years in school turned out to be very small—if not non-existent.

As can be seen from Figures 1 and 2, the most pronounced negativism is found in affluent, industrialized countries, such as Sweden, the Federal Republic of Germany and the Netherlands, whereas students in developing countries with miserable school resources showed a highly positive attitude towards schooling. In the absence of further analyses of these data, the best explanation that can be advanced at present is simply that in the affluent countries there are many other agents that compete in attracting young people, the mass media, various leisuretime social activities, sports, etc. A Marxist explanation (as we saw above) would be that the school reflects the adverse qualities of the working life and therefore, in spite of all its resources and amenities in the rich countries, it is conceived of as repressive and irrelevant.

In spite of the negative feeling towards schooling, an increasing proportion of the age group chooses to proceed with further schooling after the completion of the mandatory period. In the IEA survey there was also a School Motivation Scale based on items such as 'Do you consider

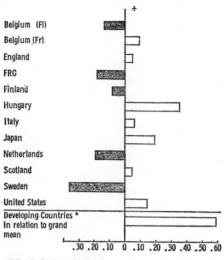

Figure 1. Mean standard scores for 10-year-olds in various countries on the 'Like School' scale in the survey conducted by the International Association for the Evaluation of Educational Achievement (IEA). The scores are given on a standard international scale with a grand mean across countries of O. Source: Husén et al., 1973.

it important that you perform well in school?'. It might on the surface seem strange that the motivation score tended to go up as the student progressed through the grades. But the explanation is a rather obvious one. The amount of formal schooling is increasingly becoming a criterion of selection on the job market. Jobs for which there were earlier no particular requirements in terms of level of education attainment tend to become upgraded in that respect. Employers increasingly tend to look for formal credentials in recruiting labour. This so-called 'credentialism' has as a consequence that those who are without credentials tend to lose out to those who made it to a higher level on the educational ladder. Young people are keenly aware of the tendency towards credentialism and feel a strong push to stay on in school as long as they can stand it in order to find a place on the market when they leave school. More education is taken simply in order to defend one's place in the line of applicants or one's present status on the labour market. The climate of credentialism tends to create competitiveness and a scrambling for marks, since these

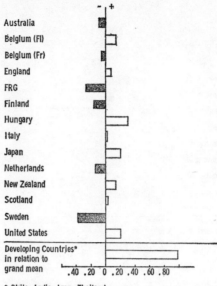

Figure 2. Mean standard scores for 14-year-olds in various countries on the 'Like School' scale in the survey conducted by IEA. The scores are on a standard international scale with a grand mean of 0. Source: Husén et al., 1973.

often are used as main criteria in the selection from one level to the next within the educational system itself.

De-institutionalizing the school

Given the background which we have sketched above, it is no wonder that during the last few years people have begun to question the worth-whileness of keeping all young people in full time schooling until the end of their teens. The most radical critics have called for complete 'de-schooling', whereas more constructive critics have come up with alterna-tives that can be combined with schooling, such as revised content and methods of instruction that could counteract the 'action-poor' approach. The common denominators here are constituted by classroom practices conducive to activity, initiative, and taking of responsibility and the establishment of connections between school education and adult life, particularly working life.

But before describing alternatives, we shall review the kind of competences and skills that are required of those who are going to live in the rapidly changing society of today and tomorrow. There are basically two types of skills: the cognitive skills which are imparted by the school at its best on the one hand; and, on the other, social skills which psychologically are based in the affective domain, such as skills in the care of dependent persons, decision making skills, and bureaucratic and organizational skills which become more and more important in a complex society with which one has to cope as an employee, customer, entrepreneur, and manager. Evidently, the school as an institution can play only a limited role in achieving such goals. Other resources, such as the family, community groups, and the workplace, would have to provide environments effective for maturation, not least as socializing agents.

Traditionally, and as long as it is not institutionally reshaped in a radical way, the school limits itself to the role of providing intellectual skills. But in a changing society the school cannot provide an intellectual fare consisting of specific items of knowledge for lifelong use. The shift that has to take place in the content of teaching is the one from specific items of knowledge, which in many cases might soon become obsolete, to intellectual skills that could be applied on a wide—and largely unforeseen—variety of tasks and situations. Therefore priority has to be given to developing the ability to learn new things, to learning skills which are prerequisites for later independent study. The particular skills I have in mind are the ones that are instrumental in building up communication. Those who lack the ability to communicate adequately in their mother tongue tend in the long run to fall below the poverty line. The decision making power in complex situations and the ability to deal with the bureaucratic organizations of today depends not only upon the mastering of the know-how about society, for instance where and how to obtain information, but also on the ability to master the verbal and conceptual instruments which carry meaningful messages.

The school for adolescents of today ought ideally to convey to its students an awareness that what they learn during many school years does not suffice for the rest of their active life. A school preparing for tomorrow would have to instil in its students the feeling that education in our time is not something that one is taking and completing in childhood and adolescence but is a lifelong process. The dilemma, however, is that instead of having a taste for more, a quite sizeable number of students dislike school. This is one reason, among several, that new possibilities opened up by programmes of adult education have not appealed to the majority of those who are socially deprived and who could have gained most from these programmes.

In the wake of the enrolment explosion and the rising costs of education (not least rising unit costs), there has been a growing realization of lack of connections between schooling and working life. This was one of the reasons why the OECD Council asked the Secretary-General of OECD to set up an *ad hoc* committee of experts to prepare a policy paper (OECD, 1975) where the major problems are brought into focus and recommendations are made to achieve a better integration between education and the job world. The lack of such connections is, as has been spelled out above, due to changes that have taken place in the role of the family, school, and the workplace. There has been a strong tendency to relegate more and more to the schools, which have become increasingly institutionalized, with a tendency to become isolated from society at large. In my view, the solution is not to 'de-school' but to 'de-institutionalize' the school and in the process bring it into closer contact with society at large, including other competence-producing agents.

The lack of connection between school and working life is, however, not primarily due to a failure of the school to provide 'saleable skills' but lack of real work orientation altogether. This was referred to above as lack of 'functional participation'. There is nothing that makes it necessary for adolescents to spend the whole day being instructed by teachers who also spend the full day on the same premises. What is the purpose of abruptly throwing young people out into the labour market after they have completed a full package of education as defined by some set curriculum, often a uniform state curriculum? One could consider a more gradual transition which step by step introduces young people into adult responsibilities. One alternative that has been suggested is a kind of sandwiching between classroom instruction and part time work. In Sweden we have for a long time had a system of so-called practical vocational guidance, which in fact is a work experience programme for a few weeks which has to be taken by *all* students before completion of the nine-year comprehensive schooling. It is part of a systematic vocational guidance with the purpose of offering the young people at least a taste of the conditions and the demands imposed by the job world. It has often been noticed that after the work experience weeks the students have returned to school with improved motivation. It is as if the school work had gained enhanced relevance. These are experiences which apply to adolescents still of compulsory school age. In countries where the majority enter upper secondary school, one could seriously consider the possibility of letting those who are in school from 16 to 18 or 19 have an opportunity to acquire work experiences over a continuous period or to spend part of the day in school and part of it at workplaces.

Efforts to get young people temporarily or permanently into the job world are running up against the stumbling block of a highly rationalized market economy. Youngsters directly from school—as well as workers close to retirement—are not considered profitable prospects by employers. Furthermore, as pointed out in the OECD report on education and working life, legislation about pay and social responsibilities can act as barriers to the hiring of young people. Instead, certain legislative incentives to employ young workers should be provided. For example, employers in Sweden who hire young people are under certain conditions eligible for subsidies from the Labour Market Board for the wages paid to the young workers.

Our society is in many respects an age-segregated one. Young people have little contact with adults in their role of incumbents of occupations. The extended family does not exist any more. Since retired people are taken care of in separate institutions or are provided with separate housing, the young have few, if any, contacts with the aged. But in order to mature, one must have opportunities to meet the adult world in its various facets. In order to make such an encounter a maturing experience one should provide the young people with an opportunity to work with adults in real-life situations. We should let adolescents practise for certain periods in occupations in the rapidly expanding, labour-intensive service sector, such as in child care, in pre-school institutions, sick care in hospitals, and care of the aged. Even if their contributions are rather modest, they are highly meaningful. It would give them experiences of persons from other generations, social backgrounds, and subcultures. And, not least, it would promote that aspect of social maturation which in our society tends to be so underdeveloped, namely the experience of having others dependent on one's actions. Young people until the end of their teens are almost systematically indoctrinated into the role of being clients, into dependency upon parents and teachers. We could consider in this context the possibility of letting older students teach their younger schoolmates. This is by no means utopian, and experimental evidence is indeed encouraging in terms both of the benefits gained by those who are taught, for instance remedial reading, but also for those who teach.

Work experience also means working with other people and this implies involvement in interdependent activities directed towards common goals. This is also something that the school, with its emphasis on individualistic competition and scrambling for marks, almost systematically prevents students from experiencing.

Finally, we have, without considering its perversity, accepted the fact that a person, called a teacher, spends his whole life in an institution, called a school, where he tells students about things and circumstances outside the classroom. The wealth of information that exists in public institutions and agencies is not properly utilized. Of course, teachers are needed to assist in systematizing and presenting the information that is considered important. But the school should take systematic advantage of the competence and expertise that is found in abundance outside the school which, as has been pointed out above, is not any longer the only 'information-rich' agency. For example, journalists, writers, and politicians in local government represent an enormous untapped reservoir of competence and talent that could be put to use both intermittently and for sustained periods. In a way, every experienced incumbent of an occupation is a potential teacher.

There is a radical view that adolescence, the constantly prolonged period between physical maturity (puberty) and the entry into adult roles and responsibilities, is an 'invention' in order to justify keeping young people in full time schooling until the end of their teens or even longer, until they leave university with a basic degree or diploma. There is something in the allegation that the youth culture or 'adolescent society' has emerged concomitantly with holding young people in school longer than in previous days. G. Stanley Hall (1904) published his monumental two-volume work on adolescence, which was to a large extent based on questionnaires administered to high school youngsters. Charlotte Buhler

(1921) published the first edition of her *Das Seelenleben des Jugendlichen,* which was based on diaries written by students from upper middle-class intellectual homes. Both conceived of adolescence as a stage in the bio-logical development of the individual. Stanley Hall, who perceived developmental theory and the conception of consecutive stages of develop-ment as 'music' to his ears, regarded adolescence as a universal stage independent of social and cultural influences. Since then, sociology and developmental psychology have given us a more faceted and sophisticated conception of how young people mature psychologically and socially. We also know that physical maturity now occurs one to two years earlier than at the turn of the century, which further accentuates a dilemma we are facing, namely that in spite of the fact that young people physically become adults earlier we tend to treat them as dependent and immature children longer than before. As pointed out above, an institution that does not see its principal role as the one of preparing young people to become independent and of providing social skills that will facilitate working with other people by permitting young people to take an active role in moulding their own fate is heading for trouble. The claim for reshaping of structure, content, and methods of instruction in the universal secondary school has to be conceived of in this context.

References

Andersson, B.-E. 1969. *Studies in adolescent behaviour: Project YG.* Stock-holm: Almqvist and Wiksell.

Behn, W. H. *et al.* 1974. The transformation of adulthood: its implications for youth. *The School Review,* vol. 83, no. 1. Chicago: University of Chicago Press.

Bell, D. 1973. *The coming of post-industrial society.* New York: Basic Books.

Bowles, S. 1971. Unequal education and the reproduction of the social division of labor. In: M. Conroy (Ed.), *Schooling in a corporate society.* New York: David McKay Co.

Bowles, S. and Gintis, H. 1973. IQ in the U.S. class structure, *Social Policy,* vol. 3, nos 4–5, pp. 65–96.

Buhler, C. 1921. *Das Seelenleben des Jugendlichen.* Jena: Gustav Fischer.

Coleman, J. S. 1971. How do the young become adults? *Review of Educational Research*, vol. 42, no. 4, pp. 431–439.

Coleman, J. S. *et al.* 1974. *Youth: transition to adulthood.* Report of the Panel on Youth of the President's Science Advisory Committee. Chicago and London: The University of Chicago Press.

Comber, L. C. and Keeves, J. 1973. *Science education in nineteen countries.* Stockholm: Almqvist and Wiksell and New York: John Wiley–Halsted Press.

Hall, G. S. 1904. *Adolescence.* New York: Appleton.

Husén, T. 1944. *Adolescensen: Undersokningar rorande manlig svensk ungdom i aldern 17–20 ar.* Stockholm: Almqvist and Wiksell.

Husén, T. 1971. Present Trends and Future Developments in Education: A European Perspective. Peter Sandiford Memorial Lectures. Occasional Papers no. 8. Toronto: Ontario Institute for Studies in Education.

Husén, T. *et al.* 1973. *Svensk skola i internationell belysning.* Stockholm:Almqvist and Wiksell International.

Husén, T. 1974a. *The learning society.* London: Methuen.

Husén, T. 1974b. *Talent, equality and meritocracy.* The Hague: Martinus Nijhoff.

Husén, T. 1975. *Social influences on educational attainment.* Paris: OECD/CERI. (Also available in French.)

OECD. 1975. *Education and working life in modern society.* Report of the Secretary-General's Ad Hoc Group on the Relations between Education and Employment. Paris: OECD.

13 The attitudes of adolescents to education and work*

Jacques Delors

Adolescence is not a simple parenthesis between childhood and adulthood, definable by the arbitrary criterion of age: 15–20 or 16–24. It is better defined as a complex process of transition from a choiceless social status to one which is personally acquired. The child is held within a web of family relationships, is obliged to go to school, and is tempted by the mass media (which take advantage of his relatively responsive nature). The adult gradually acquires financial independence through his work and reaches an autonomous social status by breaking his links with the school and leaving his family home. This transitional period, whose nature and duration vary considerably with each individual, is one of instability and anxiety. Each adolescent has to build his social personality through an amalgam of experiences which are still dominated by the educational system and work.

But even when the question is framed in this way, there remains a further difficulty which must be faced: Can adolescents be considered as a homogeneous social group with their own cultural values, or are they to be seen as a composite group made up of individuals from different social and cultural origins? The first hypothesis tends to emphasize the generation gap; the second accentuates economic, sociological, and political criteria in addition. From our point of view these two approaches must be combined in order to understand adolescents' attitudes toward education and work. Young people share, to a great extent, a certain number of identical behavioural patterns, to be seen for example in some of their attitudes to the traditional means of socialization (family, school) or to dominant values systems (authority, work, happiness, and so forth).

* Originally prepared in French. English translation by Philip Cockle.

Yet these new patterns do not seem to eliminate either political divisions or social differences. This means that if our prospective analysis is to be satisfying from a mesostructural point of view it must embrace three extraneous factors: the family and social milieu or origin, the school, and work. Young people are influenced by these three 'institutions' but at the same time they exert their own influences and, to a certain extent, mould them. It is with these dialectical relationships between adolescence and youth on the one hand and education and work on the other that the following remarks are mainly concerned.

Adolescence and the educational system

In order to select a few questions relevant to the future we must first grasp the trends currently affecting the educational system, deduce what is likely to happen, and then confront what we find with the principal expectations of young people, such at least as we can discern within a complex reality in full transformation.

The present trends of the system

The education system is giving rise to more and more dissatisfaction and this feeling is common to parents and employers, industrial associations and trade unions. In one sense the expansion of education has created as many problems as it has solved. This is probably because the enthusiastic supporters of such expansion expected too much of it in the struggle for equal opportunity and cultural advancement and overestimated what education could do in the preparation for working life. It would be useful to glance here at the present consequences of three characteristic phenomena: the growing duration of studies, the rigidity of structures, and the disjointed relationship between study and work.

In the first place, whether because of legislation prolonging compulsory education or because of spontaneous social demand, adolescents are staying at school longer. The result is a higher level of knowledge and greater aspirations and one consequence of this seems to be the dissatisfaction of many young people with the working conditions they are offered later.

In the second place school structures react slowly to evolutions in the social system and in the system of production. The school system seems to be responding less and less well to what young people expect of it: they want to be trained properly for a job but also want their creative aspirations and potentialities to be recognized. The technological evolution of Europe since the last war, for example, has taken a very long time to be reflected in the subject matter of technical training courses.

Third, it is still vitally important to improve the relationship between the training provided and the jobs available, but no system appears able to control the factors on which a wholly satisfactory relationship depends. Some particularly striking observations can be made here. Social origin very largely explains the kind of training chosen by young people; the choice of profession depends to a great extent on stereotyped impressions, and jobs are still, in real life, categorized as being for men or for women. Moreover, career guidance at school is often haphazard and does not allow for the possibilities of the labour market: it works badly and is often introduced too early. The result is that a large proportion of young people do not want to practise the profession they have learned, while others are obliged to do jobs which have little relation to their qualifications.

This means that changes in attitude and behaviour have not put an end to the traditional social divisions which govern to a great extent what children study at school and how they take their place in active life (Université Paris, IX-Dauphine, 1975).

Prospects for the educational system

In considering the place for young people in the year 2000, certain questions mainly to do with the level of training, the value of certificates and diplomas, and school counselling and guidance deserve priority. Will the school system in European countries provide an adequate training for the entire age group, or will it abandon a certain proportion on the way, some because they are disadvantaged by their social and cultural origins and others because they choose to refuse the system? It is the former case which explains why nearly 25% of those born in any given year leave the school system at some point without any certificate or qualification. The second alternative partly explains the existence of drop-outs. Furthermore, will there be a tendency to extend the period of compulsory schooling within unchanged school structures, or will it be insisted that the level of what is taught must be improved? The latter case implies that the goals of the educational system as a whole must be re-examined for, failing this, the school might once again come to grief in its attempt to achieve equality of opportunity through education. Such a re-examination concerns both the status of work and the hierarchy of prestige in our societies. A meritocratic society, as we can readily observe, reproduces itself by constantly discovering mechanisms which tend to slow down political reform and hinder the evolution towards a community which would be more warm-hearted and more respectful of individual talents. This explains the evident link between the educational system and the labour system. So long as the labour system is based on a strict hierarchy with very few opportunities to rise or share in a variety of advantages, it is all but impossible to imagine a reform of the educational system which would succeed in achieving more equality. Here there would be much food for thought on the role of diplomas and privileged channels, for both have a somewhat ambiguous role. They perpetuate the meritocratic system yet offer the individual guarantees on the labour market.

The large scale diffusion of lifelong education will doubtless disturb this rigid situation. It is too soon to measure how it will live up to its promise of giving a second or third chance to those who have been unable to take full advantage of their formal education; of helping to develop the individual's personality and independence, and so forth. Thanks to its flexibility and its ability to respond immediately to certain needs for reconversion or reorientation, lifelong education has already enabled many adolescents and adults to adjust themselves to the labour market. Does this mean that it can furnish a satisfactory global answer to the problems posed in all countries by the need to adapt training to the jobs available? There can be no doubt that the training/job complex of problems is being shifted from basic education to a system of 'recurrent education', the combination of periods of training and periods of work extending throughout life from the age of 16. But will such transformations provide an adequate response to the expectations and aspirations of young people?

The new attitudes of young people towards the school

An analysis of the behaviour patterns of adolescents which can serve to explain current trends is an important prerequisite for the definition of the new reforms for the school system. The school no longer shares a monopoly of information with the family. It competes with the media and with other features of urban life. Thus there have arisen more independent patterns of socialization, in which the adolescent no longer builds his personality through his relationship with family and teachers alone; he is also confronted with the world around him, a source of both temptation and opportunities. Moreover, adolescents are increasingly aware of the gap between what they are taught in school, which seems irrelevant to their problems, and their own experience of life. They regard the traditional teacher–pupil relationship as based on an outdated and unsatisfactory model. When the school does not respond to their new aspirations, they react by becoming passive and detached, bored, and indifferent. Some adolescents, often those from less privileged backgrounds and enrolled in less 'noble' courses of study, express their loathing for school more vigorously. They become determined to leave school at the first opportunity in order to begin work and learn about life for themselves. Most young people appear to choose their direction without adequate information about the various professions. They want more autonomy in this respect whether their choice is based on personal preferences or on the prestige of the profession concerned. In addition, their option is often the result of rejection or failure rather than positive choice. But the lack of adequate information plays an important part for there is nothing to correct the false impressions with regard to career outlets which many young people have.

To sum up, we are faced with two opposing situations. Some adolescents are determined to leave the school system because they have not found it adequate and because they want to be independent, especially as regards money. Others, on the contrary, prolong their studies because they are afraid of the 'new life' for which they feel badly prepared. In some cases, we can discern a more general challenge to both the training provided and the kind of work available.

Three vital questions

The problem is of great importance for it raises many general issues about the kind of relationships which will exist between education and society in 20 or so years' time. We will however limit ourselves to three questions.

1   What will be the place of the school in relation to other forms of socialization during childhood? Should not the school be modified so as to integrate this new distribution of tasks, or, on the contrary, should we try to maintain the school's predominance? Both cases would necessitate re-examination of school courses, the subjects taught, teaching relationships, and the school's openness towards the world outside. Opportunities for individuals to try out different professions for themselves and gain different kinds of social experience should also have their rightful place so that young people can learn to make their own choices. This is what is suggested for the 16-21 age group in the report presented to OECD by a group of experts working for the Secretary-General (1975).

2   Will the new attitudes of the young towards the school have an influence on the reforms needed? If the answer is yes, it would be helpful to have more knowledge of these attitudes, even when they are of a marginal nature. It is possible that the young would not be given enough autonomy to reconcile youth with the school, or at least that part of youth which challenges it. It is equally vital to pursue study and action to find ways of countering the powerful resistance to equal opportunity on the part of the social system as a whole.

3   Taking into account the new demands of young people for professional training and the unavoidable need for professional mobility, how will vocational training be distributed between formal and lifelong education, and between the school and workplace?

Young people and working life

In our societies work is still the most important means of acquiring social status. But the work itself is less important for a person's place in society than its various byproducts. Technical development, by dividing up work tasks, has undermined the role of work as a means to achieve personal fulfilment and reinforced the hierarchical tendencies of social status, which are also encouraged by the individualism of a meritocratic society. In advanced countries, rapid urbanization and the geographic mobility which goes with it have greatly decreased the role of the family in introducing young people into social life. The initiation rites of the past, by which societies could reproduce their own specific character and thus enable every young person to gain a social status accepted by all, have virtually disappeared. They are replaced only by the moment of first starting work and of gaining financial independence. How can we pick out 'future facts' concealed in the reality of today? The great variety of situations discourages analysis, for aspects of the old society are so intermingled and the first signs of the new one have hardly made their appearance.

Young people within the production system

The situation of young people within the production system is characterized by a gap between the level of their training and the work they do. If we leave aside the small, highly favoured proportion of the population, we find that young people, fewer of whom work in large companies than their elders, hold less qualified jobs, especially in the secondary sector. They earn much less than adults at the same job or with the same training. For them the unemployment rate in all industrialized countries is much higher than it is for the active population as a whole. The present economic crisis has made it difficult to absorb those leaving school, thus accentuating structural trends which began to emerge a few years ago. Finally, an analysis of how they are distributed throughout the socio-professional categories discloses that in OECD member countries their promotion prospects are becoming weaker and promotion itself later. Beyond the current economic recession, then, the structural upheavals in the economy are likely to cause young people great difficulty in employing the talents and tastes developed by the educational system on the basis of the present day division of labour; nor will they be able to satisfy through their work the needs and desires created by the image of adolescence and youth presented by the mass media. In our view this is one of the most important problems raised by post-industrial society. If it is not correctly understood and solved it could engender more inequities, at great social cost, and even give rise to new forms of revolt against the dominant sociopolitical system.

The two main structural problems revealed by the current situation of young people in the economic system concern therefore the idea of full employment and the compatibility between the evolution of productive work and a higher level of education. Full employment, defined according to the standards of the 1960s, can only be achieved in our present economic structures by a high rate of growth. If this rate of growth is to decrease in coming years, it will become very difficult for the labour market to absorb the cohorts of youth which arrive each year, especially in countries also having to face the consequences of recent population growth. These difficulties are therefore in danger of becoming structural. The present ways young people get their jobs, often through personal contacts, could become a new factor of inequality in the labour market if society does not take heed. The second question is whether or not our society can accept a growing gap between the educational level of young people and the kind of work they are offered. Here the case of France is revealing. In 1972 one-third of those with the CAP (the basic professional qualification) did not manage to obtain qualified jobs; 10 years before only a quarter had been so affected. The intensely capitalistic style of growth in our societies and its tendency to make jobs simpler does not seem compatible with the increasing level of education. The relations between education and employment will have to be analyzed in a less functional and less mechanical way so that a new equilibrium can be found. This could come from changes in job content, but it could also be obtained by a lower level of education. Such a trend, which is already affecting higher education in the USA, is very disquieting.

The new attitudes of young people towards work

The refusal to work is still a marginal attitude but young people are more and more opposed to authoritarian supervision and try to avoid industrial work or repetitive work tasks in the service sector. There is still only a small minority which refuses to work, even in Great Britain and the USA. Moreover such an attitude only very rarely affects young people from the working classes for whom a professional career is one of the essential aspects of their lives. It is more widespread amongst those with a higher level of education, with less compelling financial pressures, and for whom society finds it harder to offer jobs with the sort of fulfilment they seem to desire. In spite of its marginal nature, this attitude, which challenges one of the foundations of industrial societies, could have a great social impact both on the general attitudes of youth as a whole and on the kind of job offered by the production system. The extent of its influence now and in the future will depend on how far marginal patterns of behaviour, mainly involving the young, will affect society.

Opposition to the traditional forms of authority is, however, much more widespread, both at school and at work. The coercive organization of work which leaves no place for individual initiative or responsibility is refused, and so too are the demeaning human relationships which often characterize the industrial milieu and, more generally, working life in large industrial or administrative complexes. In particular, there is a powerful demand for justice, authenticity, and sincerity in social relationships. Furthermore, their higher level of training and the general improvement in living conditions outside work lead young people to reject split up work tasks and to criticize the broader lack of interest in the jobs they do. Labour turnover and absenteeism among young workers and office staff illustrate the development of this attitude. We find, in short, apart from the reluctance to work in industry, that young people tend to aim for the tertiary sector and highly qualified jobs in the secondary sector. In the last few years new kinds of work, which some see as belonging to a 'quaternary' sector, have become the most in demand despite their low salaries and limited outlets. These jobs, which offer autonomy, flexible working hours, the opportunity to establish human relationships, the feeling of doing something useful to society and so on, should serve as a guide for changing the nature of work so that young people can be positively attracted to productive labour, and not negatively as is often the case today.

The place of work in society

There are three main areas to be examined: the place occupied by work in the social status accorded by our societies; the place of young people in the system of production and consumption; and the impact that new attitudes on the part of the young might have on the kind of work offered within the production system.

1   At present, our societies accord special importance to the profession in defining the social status of individuals. As young women, for example, come to desire more equality they tend increasingly to seek jobs. But at the same time certain marginal kinds of behaviour are tending to spread

the idea that social status no longer depends on the job itself but on life outside work. Recently two French sociologists have developed this viewpoint. Duvignaud (1975) used an extensive survey to confirm that the profession had become less important for young people in their hierarchy of social activities and that its place had been taken by personal relationships. They no longer centred their lives around where they worked but around small 'islands' built up from their non-work activities. Rousselet (1974) foresees the development of 'refuge' activities, compatible with the present system of split up work tasks, in which young people could fulfil themselves. Their work would then become simply a means to an end, and the phenomenon described by Goldthorpe (1969) would spread to society as a whole. In this way a new model of society would emerge. For the majority of people, work would lose most of its importance and take up a much smaller proportion of their time throughout their lives, and a new scale of values would give preference to an individual's personal life, his leisure, his friendliness. There can be no question that this would imply very great changes; in fact, the mutation would be such that the 'ruling classes' and the 'technostructures' might well try to uphold the former model for themselves as a foundation for their prestige and leadership.

2   The role of adolescents in the economic chain has lost its stability. Parallel to the market for goods and services directed to adolescents and accelerated and exaggerated by mass media publicity, a specific labour market for young people is developing which is far below their level of education. Apart from the graduates of higher education, who can still refuse jobs of little prestige, the great majority of young people are obliged to accept unskilled work offering but very remote prospects of a professional career. Here again society could attempt to redress this lack of balance by removing all possibilities of enrichment and fulfilment through work and by making work a straightforward bargain between time and money. This would mean an upheaval in the value system of Western societies.

3   There is another possibility: the new attitudes of young people could exert their influence on the nature of work. If their demands lead them to refuse certain kinds of work indispensable to production, the production system would quickly develop content for certain professions. Either they

would speed up the substitution of capital for labour and introduce automation for repetitive tasks. This could lead to unemployment and affect the profitability of capital. Or, alternatively, they would improve and develop on a large scale the experiments being made in all industrialized countries to broaden and enrich jobs. The problem would then be whether such measures—very fruitful where adult workers are concerned—would satisfy the demands for autonomy, responsibility, and human warmth expressed by the young. This is the path of industrial democracy and we can see its beginning in all countries. Norway and Sweden, in particular, are following a coherent and integrated policy which at the workshop or office level is aimed to develop each worker's capacity for autonomy and initiative, and at the company level, to create the conditions for a more just distribution of power between the holders of capital, the managers, and the employees. It is very difficult to form an opinion today on the impact these experiments will have on the behaviour of young workers. Prudence and intellectual rigour tell us not to count on a single miraculous solution to the malaise which besets our societies.

So many transformations are under way, so many questions remain un-answered that we must avoid the easy intellectual way out of saying, like the old proverb, that 'youth has its day', and that consequently we are faced with nothing more than conflicts between generations or short-lived crises of adjustment. It is not possible to hold that the changes which have taken place, rightly or wrongly, in the private lives of individuals or in their spiritual or religious behaviour will have no effect on social life and in particular on two of its pillars: education and work. We must therefore take up the challenge that adolescence and youth have presented. Young people are looking closely at our crisis-ridden society from the standpoint of their own experience, and are concerned about their self-expression and their personality. This brief report has shown that the present period of transition poses many problems which will require innovation and experimentation to make the educational system more flexible, more open to dialogue, but also to diversify working life so that those involved will be able to enjoy greater participation.

But these measures would be partial, albeit indispensable. Beyond them the goals of society, the meaning of collective activity, and the relation between the community and the individual are called in question. The only way out of the present crisis lies in a sustained philosophic and political effort to fit education and work into a new vision of man and society, to reconcile lived values with values which should be encouraged. Only then could we hope to triumph over the risks of disintegration represented by the persistence of inequalities, the growth of boredom and indifference, and the ever-broadening hold of goods bought for money.

References

Duvignaud, J. 1975. *La planète des jeunes*. Paris: Stock.

Goldthorpe, J. H. 1969. *The affluent worker*. Cambridge: Cambridge University Press.

OECD. 1975 (May). *Education et vie active dans la société moderne*. Paris: Rapport de l'OCDE.

Rousselet, J. 1974. *L'allergie au travail*. Paris: La Seuil.

Université Paris, IX-Dauphine. 1975. *Les problèmes d'insertion professionelle des adolescents de 16 à 18 ans sur les modalités d'insertion professionnelle des diplomes de l'enseignement superieur*. Paris: Etudes du Centre de Recherche Travail et Société.

Appendix 1

Brief biographies of participants

Kersten Anér has written several books of essays on political, theological, and popular scientific subjects. Her latest is a book on data power in industrialized societies. Her doctoral degree is in literature and she has worked as a journalist and radio journalist. Since 1969, she has been a member of the Swedish Parliament.

Jacques Delors has recently published on change, on social indicators, and on social planning. He is Professor at the University of Paris-Dauphine and Director there of the Centre for Research on Work and Society. In addition, he serves in a variety of consultative roles relating to economic and social policy.

Samuel N. Eisenstadt is the Rose Isaacs Professor of Sociology at the Hebrew University in Jerusalem. Author of *From Generation to Generation*, 'Archetypal Patterns of Youth', 'Generational Conflict and Intellectual Antimonianism', and *Tradition, Change, and Modernity*, many of his interests cluster about the intersection of modernization and the sociology of youth.

Marc Faessler is a theologian who presently serves as Director of the Protestant Research Centre in Geneva, Switzerland. In addition to his interest in young people, he is a Teilhard de Chardin scholar and has published on a variety of topics having to do with religion and modern man.

Willard W. Hartup is Professor and Director of the Institute of Child Development at the University of Minnesota in the USA. His research has touched on a number of areas of social and personality development, including imitation learning, attachment in infancy, aggression, and peer relations. At present he is studying social interaction between children of differing ages.

Marcel Hebbelinck has published widely on the physiology of effort, on human biometry, and on the analysis of movement. At the Free University of Brussels, he is Professor and Director of the Laboratory for Human Biometry and Movement Analysis. He serves, in addition, as Chairman of the University's Commission on Social Affairs.

John P. Hill is Professor and Chairman of the Department of Human Development and Family Studies at Cornell University in the USA. His present research has to do with the impact of cognitive change at adolescence on relations with parents and peers. He served for five years as Editor of the *Minnesota Symposia on Child Psychology* and for a term as Associate Editor of *Developmental Psychology*.

Torsten Husén holds the University Chair in International Education at the University of Stockholm. Since 1971, he has also served as Director at the University's Institute for the Study of International Problems in Education. Recent publications include *The Learning Society*, *Talent, Equality, and Meritocracy*, and *Social Influences on Educational Attainments*.

Fred Mahler is Deputy Director of the Centre for Research on Youth, Bucharest, Roumania. His principal interests have to do with the sociology of youth, the family, ethics, futurology, and methodology and epistemology of the social sciences. His latest book is *La Génèse et la Dynamique de l'Idéal de Vie des Adolescents*.

Marco Milani-Comparetti is Professor of Biology and Director of the Institute of Biology and Genetics at the Medical School of the University of Ancona in Italy. He is the author of articles and books on basic biology and biology and sports.

Franz J. Mönks is Professor and Chairman of the Department of Developmental Psychology at the University of Nijmegen, the Netherlands. At present he also serves as the Dean of the Psychological Laboratory. A major interest, personality development in adolescence, has been reflected in studies of the future time perspective of young people. He will serve as Coordinating Editor of the new journal of the International Society for the Study of Behavioral Development: *The International Journal of Behavioral Development.*

Jerzy Piotrowski is Professor of familial sociology at the Instytut Filozofii I Socjologii Polskiej Akademii Nauk in Warsaw. He has written several essays on the roles of women, changing sex roles and about old people in Poland.

Leopold Rosenmayr is Professor in the Institute for Sociology of the University of Vienna. He has published extensively on adolescence, some recent examples being 'New Theoretical Approaches to the Sociological Study of Young People' and 'The Pluridimensionality of Work Commitment: A Study of Young Married Women in Different Social Contexts of Occupational and Family Life'. Professor Rosenmayr also maintains an active scholarly interest in the ageing.

Hilde Rosenmayr is a research associate of the Institute for Sociology of the University of Vienna. She has published on the development of American sociology and on modern society.

William Wall has conducted research and written on many subjects related to adolescents in school and society and has been particularly concerned with the relations between education and mental health. He is Professor of Educational Psychology and Director of the Department of Child Development and Educational Psychology of the University of London Institute of Education.

Willem Welling is Executive Director of the Bernard van Leer Foundation of the Netherlands to which he came after working in UNESCO in a series of assignments having to do with international education. He is author or editor of several publications dealing with problems of higher education in various parts of the world. He has been or is active in a variety of national and international professional organizations.

Appendix 2

Selected background reading

Aries, P. *Centuries of childhood: A social history of family life.* New York: Vintage Books, 1962.

Coleman, J. S. *The adolescent society.* New York: Free Press, 1961.

Debesse, M. *La crise de l'originalité juvenile.* Paris: Press Universitaire de France, 1941.

Douvan, E. and Adelson, J. *The adolescent experience.* New York: Wiley, 1966.

Erikson, E. H. *Identity: Youth and crisis.* New York: Norton, 1968.

Flacks, R. *Youth and social change.* Chicago: Markham, 1971.

Furter, P. *La vie morale de l'adolescent: bases d'une pédagogie.* Neuchatel: Delachaux et Niestlé, 1965.

Gagnon, J. H. and Simon, W. *Sexual conduct: The social sources of human sexuality.* Chicago: Aldine, 1973.

Hollingshead, A. B. *Elmtown's youth.* New York: Wiley, 1949.

Kandel, D. B. and Lesser, G. S. *Youth in two worlds.* San Francisco: Jossey-Bass, 1972.

Kohlberg, L. and Kramer, R. Continuities and discontinuities in childhood and adult moral development, *Human Development*, vol. 12, pp. 93–120, 1969.

Kossakowski, A. *Über die psychologischen Veränderungen in der Pubertät.* Berlin: Volk und Wissen, 1966.

Lutte, G. *Le moi idéal de l'adolescent.* Bruxelles: Dessart, 1971.

Lutte, G., Mönks, F. J., Sarti, S. and Preun, H. *Leitbilder und Ideale der europäischen Jugend.* Wuppertal-Elberfeld: Henn, 1970.

Mollenhauer, K. *Erziehung und Emanzipation.* München: Juventa, 1973.

Musgrove, F. *Youth and the social order.* Bloomington: Indiana University Press, 1964.

Neidhardt, P., Bergius, R., Brocher, T., Eckensberger, D., Hornstein, W., Rosenmayr, L. and Loch, W. *Jugend im Spektrum der Wissenschaften.* München: Juventa, 1970.

Peel, E. A. *The nature of adolescent judgment.* London: Crosby Lockwood Staples, 1973.

Piaget, J. Intellectual evolution from adolescence to adulthood. *Human Development*, vol. 15, pp. 1–12, 1972.

Spranger, E. *Psychologie des Jugendalters.* Heidelberg: Quelle and Meyer, 1955.

Tanner, J. M. *Education and physical growth.* London: University of London Press, 1961.

Thomae, H. *Vorbilder und Leitbilder der Jugend.* München: Juventa, 1965.

Welten, V. J., van Bergen, J. M. S., van der Linden, F. J. and Stoop, W. *Jeugd en emancipatie.* Bilthoven: Ambo, 1973.